Lord Knows, At Least I Was There:
Working with Stephen Sondheim

Available from Moreclacke Publishing

Books by Robert Armin

The Used and Abused

The Flash of Midnight

Sheva, the Benevolent (A Play)

Harlan Ellison's Mortal Dreads (A Play)

Books by Sherman Yellen

Spotless: Memories of a New York Childhood

Cousin Bella — The Whore of Minsk

December Fools and Other Plays

Book by Paul Ford

Lord Knows, At Least I Was There:
Working with Stephen Sondheim

Rediscovery Series

Mabel Wynne and Other Tales of the Romantic Age
by Nathaniel Parker Willis (Robert Armin, Editor)

Why They Married
by James Montgomery Flagg

Lord Knows, At Least I Was There

Working with Stephen Sondheim

Paul Ford

MORECLACKE PUBLISHING
New York City

Audiobook available from Audible.com and Apple Books

For information, contact Moreclacke Publishing at

info@moreclacke.com or

325 West 45th Street, Suite 609, New York, NY 10036

First Paperback Edition

Moreclacke Publishing, New York, New York

ISBN-10: 0-9960169-9-5

ISBN-13: 978-0-9960169-9-5

Published in the United States of America

When I attended the 2011 Broadway revival of Stephen Sondheim's 1971 musical *Follies* at the Marquis Theatre, I went backstage to say hello to a couple of people. Bernadette Peters seemed happy to see me. After talking about the show a bit, she asked if I had seen other productions. I told her I had seen the original 1971 production twice when I was 18 years old and worked on the 1985 Lincoln Center concert version, not to mention catching several other productions since. She said, "Well, *you* should write a book."

I said, "I'm thinking about it."

Someone standing near us said, "Uh-oh!" and I said, "No. It wouldn't *all* be just gossip and resentments."

Bernadette laughed and said, "Oh no, it'll be the *truth*."

Paul Ford
New York City

Contents

Foreword

What does one say about a human being who has the gift of being able to listen to you better than we know how to listen to ourselves? Who is so in tune with you musically that he knows where you're going before *you* do. Who breathes with you as one, and has the humility and modesty in performance to be able to almost disappear, making it seem like the music is coming out of the ethos surrounding you.

Other than my wife and my children, Paul Ford gave me the greatest gift imaginable—his encyclopedic knowledge of the genre referred to as musical theatre, which includes film music, as well. He took the time and had the grace and patience to help me explore everything he would bring into the studio. When we found a song we liked, he would turn my verbal descriptions of the feelings I was after into simple, gorgeous accompaniment that would highlight the lyrics and illustrate the story as best as we could. I might say that "I want it to sound like a Carousel in Limbo, spinning faster and faster, then lifting off into the heavens, as if the camera were pulling away from our musical image to disappear into space." To find someone who didn't find those descriptions strange, who understood my emotional language... well, that is what is called *beshert*—meant to be. I would give him time to interpret my desires, listen to him tickle those ivories, and in very short order I'd be saying, "That's it! It's perfect! You got it! You're amazing!!!"

And that's how we mined and arranged hours and hours of music that became our repertoire, and which we performed for nearly 30 years. And without a doubt, it was the best part of my professional life. After every concert, the lights went to black, and as I walked in the dark to the back bare wall of every theater we played in, I thanked whatever greater power in our universe that had helped me get through this night, and just before the lights came up, I would ask the same greater power—whatever you want to call it—to bless this man at the piano, and watch over him, and please take care of him. Paul Ford was the musical heartbeat of my soul.

I have always referred to Paul as the Library of Congress of the Musical Theatre Genre. He has a photographic memory for every note sung or played. Just ask Sondheim. Paul writes almost nothing down because it's all in his astounding brain. Oh, sure, he writes it down eventually, just to make sure we

i

maintain a record of the endless hours of music we've made together, but he is a musical genius, and as with most geniuses, he is fierce in the defense of the craft and art he loves so dearly.

Now, I believe in a Jewish tradition called *loshon horo*, which means not to speak ill of others. I admit there is a very big difference between serious criticism (some may call it feedback) and speaking ill of others, but most performers can't tell the difference, myself included. But there is something profoundly refreshing about reading a book written by someone who has such a passion for an art form he reveres, for the enormous craft and history of it, who loves the people who honor it, and is not afraid of sharing his disfavor of people who do not. So, if you're someone who is allergic to strong opinions, stop reading right this second and never turn another page. But if you have a sense of humor and wonder, and if you can open up your heart and mind to hear the musings of this musical and obsessed savant, you will enjoy being educated, shocked, surprised, appalled, and offended. You will also find yourself laughing hysterically and, if you are like me, overwhelmed with emotion and not being able to stop the tears fighting for oxygen.

Paul Ford shared his work ethic and passion with me and gave me my musical life. I promise you, my friends, these are Paul Ford's deepest, purest, funniest, most thoughtful, caring, loving, and furious truths. It is a window into a world so many of us love, have loved, and will continue to love for as long as we live. It is the very private voice of a man named Paul Ford, who comes alive like no other when he is listening, playing, and making music. Teaching himself and the rest of us how to make the day a little better, a little happier, and to not waste your precious time and start being alive! Listen to the musical soul of Paul Ford in his own words.

I guarantee at the end of a sometimes challenging read, you'll have had fun, and having fun through the music of this genre is Paul Ford's wish. He made it come true for himself, for me and, as you'll read, for pretty much anyone involved in this singularly American art form for the last five decades.

As we say in our family to anyone we love when their birthdays roll around every year, "WE ARE SOOO FUCKING HAPPY YOU WERE BORN!" For me, every day is Paul Ford's birthday.

Mandy Patinkin
January 9, 2022

Lord Knows, At Least
I Was There

1. A Hundred Million Miracles

In 1962, at the age of nine, I marched with a purpose into our living room in Atlanta, Georgia, where sat an old Wurlitzer spinet piano that had belonged to my grandmother. She passed away before I was born and willed the piano to my older brother, Tommy. I found on the keyboard, as my mother showed me, "Middle C." I played it. I played it nine times in a row in the pattern of what I would later learn was one eighth note followed by six sixteenth notes followed by two eighth notes. This was the second phrase of music in the refrain of a song I had just sung and (clad in a kimono) paraded around to in my fourth grade "Oriental" themed pageant titled *The Land of the Rising Sun*.

I went from that first set of notes to find the notes that came in the phrase before them. Seven eighth notes and one quarter note—the notes that matched what I heard in my nine-year-old head. They were the following: C above Middle C, B right below, G# below (one of those black keys), back up to A, an F# below (another one of those black keys) and three Gs (above Middle C). Then I played the sequence of Middle Cs that I had just played before. This process went on until I had learned the entire four-minute song we had sung in the pageant. I knew it in my head and now I wanted to match it to the piano keys. The song was by Richard Rodgers and Oscar Hammerstein II from their 1958 Broadway musical *Flower Drum Song*. A sweet simple song called "A Hundred Million Miracles." This song and this musical were the "Jonestown Kool-Aid" I drank, and it was fatal. Or almost.

I said yes to my mother's suggestion that I start piano lessons at age ten. She found a teacher around the corner from us—a young wife and mother, Jeanette Lang. Jeanette was right out of the University of Georgia music department. I played my "A Hundred Million Miracles" tune for her and told her that we had just seen *Flower Drum Song* at Atlanta's Theatre Under the Stars (TUTS), a summer stock company in nearby Chastain Park. She countered with the fact that a college friend of hers, Paul Eichel, played the leading man, Wang Ta. I was starry-eyed and ready to go into this piano-playing thing. I took lessons from her for seven years, played tons of legit music and show music at her recitals, and we are still in touch today. I began practicing (and/or listening to) music two to six hours a day when I should have been participating in real life. I was obsessed.

In high school, when a rotten, musically-deprived rock 'n' roll band (they're called garage bands and that's where they belong) from two neighborhoods away was disturbing our peace, I opened our front door, pushed my new Story & Clark piano up to it, and started pounding out Richard Rodgers's "Slaughter on Tenth Avenue Ballet," Jule Styne's *Funny Girl* Overture, and Leonard Bernstein's *West Side Story* mambo in (hopeless) defiance of the noise pollution from that stinkin' rock 'n' roll band. I had already taken a stand and made my choice. Only "good" music for me—not that rock 'n' roll shit!

In 1970, at age 17, I received my first paycheck in exchange for playing the piano. The job search was over. Once I figured out that "music equals paycheck," I didn't want to waste another second on "How am I going to support myself?" or "What kind of vocation did I want?" I dusted my hands off and said, "That's it, done, finished! There is no need to look any further. No need to explore or try other interests." I dove head first into the fantasy world of the Broadway (and film) musical world with which I was obsessed— not just "any old music" mind you, but the Broadway (and film) musical world. There would be nothing else... ever.

2. Opening Doors

I was born in Atlanta, Georgia in 1953. In 1958, my mother took me to see the film version of *South Pacific* at the Fabulous Fox Theatre. I walked out of the movie theatre starry-eyed, and not just from Joshua Logan's cornea-burning Technicolor experiments (which, to this day, I completely defend because they took me away that day—FAR, FAR AWAY—and I was happy to go!), but from the Ken Darby heavenly backup choir singing of "Bali Ha'i." While I was being chased by bullies on the playground at school, I kept hearing this music and wished to be "taken away" to that mystical island.

My mother bought the 45-rpm record set of the original Broadway cast album with Mary Martin. Why didn't she buy the movie soundtrack, you ask? "The original casts are better and have more music!" she opined. However, there were no Ken Darby heavenly choirs! It took me awhile to figure out the difference between Broadway cast albums and soundtracks from movies.

In 1961, I saw my very first musical stage show, Cole Porter's *Can-Can*, at Theatre Under the Stars. I remember a tall, statuesque, blonde woman in a shocking pink gown. It was the one and only Dolores Gray singing "I Love

Paris." A vivid childhood memory. *Gypsy*, starring Jane Morgan, came next, and, finally, *Flower Drum Song*.

In fourth grade we did our "Oriental" themed pageant and I heard my first long-playing (LP) original Broadway cast album, *Flower Drum Song*, with its fantastic cover art. The teacher played it for us every day for two weeks. At 10, I started piano lessons, and within a year I bought (or I should say, I pleaded for my parents to buy) my first Broadway musical vocal score, *Oklahoma!* I had begun to explore other Rodgers and Hammerstein musicals. They had generously bought me several new recordings of shows and films— the soundtracks from *Oklahoma!* and *The King and I*, the cast album of *Kiss Me, Kate*, and Mary Martin singing selections from the scores of *Anything Goes* and *The Bandwagon*. I was entranced. Inspiration hit me to put on a production of *Oklahoma!* in our carport, so one rainy night, with an audience of ten little hooligans from the neighborhood, four girl friends and I lip-synched to the movie soundtrack of *Oklahoma!* Since I was the only boy, I played Gordon MacRae's Curly, and the four girls played Laurey, Ado Annie, Aunt Eller, and, in one gender-bending role, Will Parker. A sudden last-minute rewrite came about when I decided a character needed to be *added* to our show. It was a character only mentioned in the lyrics of one of the songs, but I thought it would spice things up to include her. And who should play the role but me? So while my friend was lip-synching her way through the lyric "One of the gals was fat and pink and pretty..." from the song "Kansas City," I made a spectacular entrance on the carport steps as the girl from the "Burlycue" show, referred to in the lyrics, complete with blonde curly wig (my mother's), my T-shirt tied in a knot and stuffed to give myself giant bazooms, a big floppy skirt, and a Chinese fan dangling from my brassiere, which I would open and close to tease the neighborhood boys. Plus, lots of jewelry and a pound-and-a-half of make-up on my face. I belly-danced for the rest of the number and, yes, I was a hit! This was my first and last performance in drag.

Our next carport production was much more ambitious. I would play the King in *The King and I*, leading a cast of eight twelve-year-olds, lip-synching our way through the movie soundtrack. My mother painted a backdrop with golden pagodas and the title of the show in "Oriental" lettering, and we covered the carport with anything that reeked of luxury—pillows, satin quilts, sheer curtains, a candelabrum. Mother made a special Yul Brynner costume for me—a pair of oversized bloomers and an open vest in one of her two favorite colors, turquoise, with gold lacy paper doilies adorning the vest. I had a cardboard crown with gold doilies glued on it, a stocking cap to make me bald, lots of jewelry, and a pound-and-a-half of make-up on my face.

The rest of the cast was adequately costumed by their mothers and our Anna Leonowens had a luxurious hot-pink satin Antebellum dress. Our neighborhood 12-year-old "Carol Burnett," always willing and enthusiastic, had a large stuffed toy boa constrictor, so we featured her in a "snake dance" to a reprise of "The March of the Siamese Children." At the end of the dance, the boa constrictor choked her to death and she was dragged off stage. Finally, my big moment came. Anna and I would lip-synch and dance the famous polka to "Shall We Dance." This was some of the most exciting music I had ever heard — much more exciting than, say, "I Wanna Hold Your Hand," which had just started to poison the airwaves, yelled by four punks with weird haircuts. We lip-synched our way through the song and I was getting very excited as the dance approached. But, as we mouthed our last lyric ("Shall we dance, shall we dance, shall we dance?"), ending with our feet poised for the big polka to follow, our sound lady, a neighborhood mom, thought that our vocal was the end of the song and picked the needle up off the record. She had been so good at dropping and lifting the needle accurately up to this point, but there we were with... silence... no polka! I was sweating, glancing offstage through the kitchen door to where our big Hi-Fi was positioned. More silence. I ran offstage and hissed in true diva style, "WHAT HAPPENED TO THE MUSIC!!!????"

Scared for her life, she whimpered, "I'm sorry. I thought that was the end." "NO-NO-NO-NO! YOU HAVE RUINED EVERYTHING!!!"

I recovered and went back "onstage" for my death scene. It was a devastating, crushing show business disaster. A once in a lifetime performance ruined by an amateur sound mother.

The audience sitting on the driveway, on the lawn, and in chairs, loved the show anyway and we made $3.60 — a dime a head. Then we struck the set and returned the costumes. I, however, continued to lounge in my gold and turquoise bloomers for a few days. And thanks to the wonder of Eastman Kodak, there are eight color production stills surviving to this day to prove that it actually happened.

Two years of piano lessons later, I made my public coming out debut as a "sissy" piano player in seventh grade. An enormous mistake, as I was immediately shunned.

My piano playing was quickly getting better and my (great guy) father started to notice. He came home from work one day and walked me to the piano in the living room. From under his coat he pulled out a brown paper bag. In the bag was a slim book of music called *30 Years 30 Hits*. He put it in front of me and said, "Can you play this one?" pointing to "Toot, Toot, Tootsie (Goo'bye)."

"I guess," I said, and I played through it. He started to sing! Not just sing but PERFORM—a whole routine! I was horrified.

"Stop it!" I wanted to shout. But he insisted on another.

"This one!" pointing to "Sleepy Time Gal," verse and all. This was ghastly. What are these songs, and what the hell was he doing with his arms and feet?

"Now this one! 'Doodle-Doo-Doo.'"

Ohmigod, this was torture, but nothing prepared me for the spectacle he made of himself on (gulp) "Hard-Hearted Hannah!" And he knew all the lyrics!

He said, "Tonight when our bridge club comes over, we'll take a little break, and you come out and we're gonna do five or six of these songs."

No way! No way! I would not be exploited in this manner. That night I locked my door and put a pillow over my head, but he got a screwdriver out and unlocked the door. I shuffled to the piano, whining, and started to play. He tore the house apart, and my parents' friends ate him up. I got out of there as fast as I could and barricaded myself in my bedroom. For the next three years, we did this routine every couple of weeks.

Twenty years later, I was sitting with Mandy Patinkin at his apartment playing a song that I thought would be right up his alley, Maltby and Shire's "I Don't Remember Christmas (and I Don't Remember You)." You know, that hateful "list song" about how much I hate you and "your sheepskin rug?" After a few minutes, he said, "I don't want to sing angry, sad songs like this. I wanna sing happy songs!" So, I brought him happy songs, including the book *30 Years 30 Hits*. For the next 23 years, our most successful opening number would be... "Doodle-Doo-Doo," followed by other tunes—"Over the Rainbow," "On the Atchison, Topeka and the Santa Fe," and "When the Red-Red-Robin Comes Bob-Bob-Bobbin' Along,"—all from the book *30 Years 30 Hits*. God bless my dad! We got a lot of mileage out of that book. My dad was the greatest. And so was my mom, but that's another story.

My parents continued to take me to TUTS summer stock shows and by the eleventh grade, I was doing my first high school musical, Bob Merrill's *Carnival*. I thought the show was lame—not nearly as good as *Lili*, the film upon which it was based. High school was extremely traumatic, and I stayed home from school for weeks at a time. But in the fall of my senior year, I put my best foot forward and went back to school to play for our senior musical, *On a Clear Day You Can See Forever*.

Almost immediately, I received a mysterious phone call from a neighboring high school that was also doing *On a Clear Day* and needed an all-purpose piano player. I was offered a whopping $75 for three weeks of work. What? Money? A paycheck?!?! I migrated to that school and stayed on their staff for the next five years, doing many shows, and traveling to New York City numerous times to see many of the great Broadway productions of the early and mid-1970s. I was one of two staff members and the only pianist of a fledgling performing arts school, the Northside School of Performing Arts. There were 350 students enrolled! My own high school could barely scrape together 25 students for its choir/drama department. At the new school, I played the piano.

I played the piano a LOT!

Reluctantly (because I never really wanted to grow up or leave my parents' home), I registered at Georgia State University in the fall of 1971, and after much waffling, auditioned for the music department. I stayed at GSU off and on for five years, changing majors twice—from music to math, then back to music—but never finishing a degree. I participated in five college musicals and plays at the university while continuing my High School of Performing Arts duties. How I did this, I don't know! Like I said, I played the piano a LOT!

After reaching a "burnout" point at age 21 and deciding to leave the world of "children" to start earning an "adult" living, I left the high school and auditioned for a local musical group, The Workshop Theatre. We did a production of the new Broadway musicals *Pippin* and *Over Here*, condensed into one evening called *Broadway Times Two*, and became a local hit. I was also living away from home for the first time. Along with classes at GSU and The Workshop, I did several other community theatre productions and started a nice association with The Atlanta Children's Theatre, playing three long-running musicals in the wee hours of the morning.

My college work was suffering, so I made a choice. I chose to go the "professional" musical theatre and night life (cabaret/lounge/drinking) route and left college. At GSU, I was in "music education" and had done two field trips to elementary schools in preparation for becoming a schoolteacher. No... thank... you. Plus, I was not going to then, now or ever play a "senior recital" on a stage by myself. I was through with schools of all kinds. I was a local professional and a Union member. And a heavy drinker...

The Workshop Theatre morphed into the Manhattan Yellow Pages Cabaret—a troop of 15 singer/dancers that performed for three years, inspiring other such local groups to start up. During the mid-1970s, there was a lot of work and a lot of Broadway-style singin' and dancin' in Atlanta. I was the musical director of the shows and pianist for our trio. I arranged six shows, including a *History of The American Musical Theatre Chorus*, a revue incorporating songs from the new show, *A Chorus Line*, and briefly featuring Atlanta-born Barbara Hancock, who had played Susan the Silent in the movie version of *Finian's Rainbow* opposite Tommy Steele and Fred Astaire. The other shows were revues dedicated to the songs of George Gershwin, Cole Porter and Irving Berlin, a "contemporary" collection of show tunes, and a 1950s tribute called *A Rose and a Baby Ruth* (less rock and roll, more Marilyn Monroe). We were a success.

So, what does one do with success? One fucks it up! Our producer moved our troop from the cozy, wealthy Buckhead area to the new (and quickly flopping) Omni Center in downtown Atlanta—a place where no one in their right mind would go. I did my last revue in Atlanta there. *The Crazy Horse Saloon Revue* was a knockoff of a Las Vegas show, complete with topless girls. It was atrocious, but I fell in (gay) love with one of our New York dancers.

Suddenly, Atlanta was shutting all of its musical theatre doors and opportunities were few. Cabarets and dinner theatres were folding, and our Vegas revue was simply awful! I did one more children's show and a production of *Side By Side By Sondheim* at the Alliance Theatre and then moved to New York. No, not to follow my dream, but to follow that New York dancer I was in love with!

As luck would have it, I was able to move easily into the city with a little breathing time to adjust and check things out. The year was 1978 and I was 25 years old (much younger than I was actually feeling thanks to five years of boozing it up every night in the cabaret world). I got jobs in dinner theatres in Connecticut, a wonderful job doing a production of *The Golden Apple* at the York Theatre in Manhattan and played many auditions. At the end of my first year, I got the call for my first Broadway show, *I Remember Mama*, through music contractor John Monaco. (More on this story later.) He moved me from that short job to playing rehearsal piano on Bob Fosse's *Dancin'* (including subbing in the pit, my Broadway debut). I never held a baton in my hand in my life, but I chose to audition for the job of assistant conductor for the third national tour of *Annie* and got the job! My first big job. And I stayed on the road for a year, conducting two weeks of performances during that time. Returning to New York, I took over a duo-pianist job on Tommy Tune's *A Day in Hollywood/A Night in the Ukraine*, which was my first Broadway run, followed by another year on the road with that show.

Near the end of the tour, my father suddenly passed away, so I went home to Atlanta for a bit. It was now 1982 and I went back to New York determined to settle down, take a good look at my drinking, and not travel for a while. My next job was a revue called *Upstairs at O'Neals'* which ran for nine months, while playing rehearsals for various revivals and tours going out. Summer came around and stock was happening, so I was hired for my one and only seven-week summer stock tour—a show I love dearly, *Irma La Douce*, starring Juliet Prowse (a terrific lady). Unhappy with the conditions of that tour, I stuck to my guns about staying put in New York City. John Monaco, the contractor, called again with a new job—second rehearsal pianist for a workshop of a new Kander & Ebb show starring Liza Minnelli and Chita Rivera, conducted by Paul Gemignani, called *The Rink*. Wow! WOW! This was IT!

The first day of the workshop, I had every feeling possible—excitement, terror, awe, anticipation, delirium, disappointment, confusion, and horror. The horror was that after the initial read-through, to my utter astonishment and in my (never) humble opinion—*The Rink* turned out to be a terrible show. (More on that later!) After a few weeks, I was given the choice to stay with *The Rink* or go directly to the Broadway production of Stephen Sondheim and James Lapine's *Sunday in the Park with George* starring Mandy Patinkin and Bernadette Peters, both shows conducted by Paul Gemignani. I requested to sleep on it, but then blinked my eyes and said yes to the Sondheim IMMEDIATELY. 1984-85 was the golden year of my life. I was 30 years old, 165 pounds, in a new relationship, working with fantastic people, but most of all, free of alcohol for the first time in 12 years! Words can't describe what a wonderful time that was. Not perfect—never perfect—but wonderful!

Following that golden year, I encountered my first traumatic, lollapalooza flop, Charles Strouse and Stephen Schwartz's *Rags*. I didn't drink over it, but I did gain 100 pounds. After it closed, I was rescued by a job on Sondheim and Lapine's next musical, *Into the Woods*, a two-and-a-half-year adventure and my longest run on Broadway. Ha! None of this 25-year run thing for me! One-and-one-half-years was all I ever got. I should say at this point that after my tentative conducting experience on the *Annie* tour, I decided to put the baton down and put my talents elsewhere. I wanted to play the piano—pure and simple.

During the run of *Into the Woods*, I was put together with Mandy Patinkin to help him prepare his first solo album. When it was completed, Mandy wanted to sing publicly and with just piano! After working with a large assortment of high school divas/divos and local "stars" in Atlanta, I wasn't sure if I wanted to ever enter a relationship with a REAL STAR—something that might be an all-consuming, change-of-life experience. After a brief consultation with Mandy's wife, Kathryn, who told me simply to express my fears and concerns to the "right person" (Mandy), I approached him at rehearsal one day.

"I am terrified to work with you and to make such a big commitment. I'm terrified of playing solo piano for you on stage. I'm just terrified, period!"

He said, "So am I! I'm vomiting just thinking about it! *You're* afraid of making mistakes? Tell you what we're gonna do. If I make a mistake, or if you make a mistake, we'll stop the show and TALK ABOUT IT!" I said okay. It would be a 25-year working relationship!

During this new period of "solo" piano accompaniment in front of thousands of people in concert halls and on television, not only was I experiencing enormous performance phobias, but I was also suffering from physical problems brought on by my having gained 100 pounds and the fact that I was drinking heavily again. On top of that, my companion of six years, Charlie, was diagnosed HIV positive. The next six years were a hellish mix of terrific opportunities, uncomfortable performing conditions, back problems, weight problems, devastating hangovers, and personal tragedy. Mandy and I performed all over the country and in London and Canada, and I managed to squeeze in participation in several more Broadway shows. During the 1994 Broadway production of Sondheim and Lapine's *Passion*, my friend and partner Charlie died, and I found myself sitting in a bar, 300 pounds and counting, physically in torment, mentally anguished and feeling very much alone. I had drifted from my family—no one except my mother knew about Charlie for 12 years! I wasn't closeted, I just chose not to include anyone in my relationship. My life had become extremely compartmentalized.

My then-current therapist (in a long line of therapists) suggested *strongly* that perhaps I was drinking myself to death and needed to go to Alcoholics Anonymous. I said "yes" to him instead of my usual "ABSOLUTELY NOT!" and started a whole new life. It was 1995 and I was 42 years old.

Mandy and I kept our concerts going and I continued what I called the "other part" of my career by working on interestingly mediocre shows and absolute catastrophes. Among the "interesting" shows were Kander and Ebb's *Steel Pier* and *The Adventures of Tom Sawyer*, featuring the delightful and talented Linda Purl as Aunt Polly. Less compelling were many revivals of shows I had once loved, but after we "revised" and "improved" and "fixed" them, they became not-so-fond experiences (and miserable flops). The exception was the Tony Award-winning revival of Stephen Sondheim's

Assassins, for which I had played the original Playwrights Horizons production in 1990. This production is scorched in my memory as one of the most thrilling and delightful, not to mention hilarious (thank you, Mario Cantone) times of the final part of my career. I musically assisted Paul Gemignani on many Ravinia (Chicago) Music Festival musicals, most notably *Gypsy* with Patti LuPone, several PBS televised Broadway Specials, multiple Sondheim birthday tributes, several shows for the City Center Encores! series, and many "one-nighters" at Carnegie Hall, such as *Anyone Can Whistle* with Madeline Kahn and Bernadette Peters, and *Show Boat* with Nathan Gunn, Gregg Edelman and Carolee Carmello.

Mandy and I developed several touring shows that have included "friends" along the way. After a warmup at Joe Papp's Public Theatre, we debuted at the Helen Hayes Theatre in 1989 with our concert, *Mandy Patinkin: Dress Casual*, followed by the performance pieces *Mamaloshen, Experiment, Celebrating Sondheim, An Evening with Patti LuPone and Mandy Patinkin*, and *Mandy Patinkin and Nathan Gunn in Concert*.

Mostly due to the influence of sobriety and age, I have mercifully been free of stage fright and performance anxiety for more than fifteen years, which is certainly a gift beyond my wildest expectations. One night during a 2002 performance of *Celebrating Sondheim* at the Henry Miller Theatre in New York City, I said my prayer asking to "be of service" before walking on the stage and proceeded to have a highly joyful experience from the very first note to the last. "What was that!?!" I thought. Never had I experienced that! And the next night it happened again! As they say, "don't quit before the miracle happens."

For fifteen years, I participated every June in a Professional Musical Theatre Workshop at the Manhattan School of Music. I coached sixteen students in a four-week intensive program started by Paul Gemignani. Other staff members over the years have included Carolann Page, Joanna Merlin, Ginger Thatcher, Austin Pendleton, with many other guest speakers and teachers. This was my summer job and it was a nice addition to my income until it came to an unceremonious end. We were all fired! I was playing, as mentioned before, several revivals of shows at the Roundabout Theatre—*Pacific Overtures, Assassins, 110 in the Shade, Pal Joey*. Many of these were not faithful to the original writing and musical arrangements, much to this *purist's* dismay. There was a lot of "fiddling" with classic musicals, accompanied by much negative, disparaging talk about the original creators' work, which made the working atmosphere, for me, an unpleasant (if not poisonous) situation. And the evil that is "political correctness" was rearing its ugly head, causing everyone to question every aspect of every old musical. The downsizing of most of these shows in terms of the number of actors, musicians, sets, costumes, the general lack of historical knowledge, and rock-bottom production values, was contributing to a far less fulfilling experience for me, both in *working* in theatre and *seeing* theatre. Several incidences involving job loss, personality conflicts, and a general lack of enthusiasm on the part of most of the participants, led me to start thinking about how much longer I wanted to do this work.

Playing concerts for Mandy and Patti LuPone and some of the Sondheim celebrations was, for me, *making music,* and the pay for these was appropriate, considering my experience, where I was working, and with whom I was working. In March 2011, I left a rehearsal of a dead-on-arrival musical, *The People in the Picture* (one of five jobs I was trying unsuccessfully to juggle), and wrote a short, respectful letter of resignation for *all* of the jobs, ending a 30-year relationship with conductor Paul Gemignani. I would never work on another Broadway musical again.

At present, I feel relief from the negative, hostile pressure, the too many hours, the gross mishandling of cherished old shows, and the dwindling money. I made it financially through the next four years on Mandy concerts alone and was pleased about our schedule ahead. At 58, I was now pension-eligible (many pianist friends had begun to take theirs), but I had to hang on for a few more years.

After becoming sober, music and theatre (once a source of pleasure, if a shaky validation for living and a false ego-booster) became what it really boils down to—a service commitment, a job along the lines of dishwashing, catering, or bus driving. It became much more manageable for me when approached this way, but it lost all of its magic. I've been tickling the ivories on a daily basis since I was 10 years old. What I feel about my work six decades later, is that being a pianist, accompanist and arranger is a lonely job. You might be one of only one, two, or three pianists, depending on the size of the show. The job can be very manageable if the composer composes, the copyists copy, the musical director reads music, and the actors are musically literate. But often I've found myself walking actors through the tiny steps of learning music, playing their parts over and over and over, never using the musical knowledge I acquired for anything but creating an elementary language to communicate. (I might as well have been teaching elementary school!) I can't remember the last time I suggested to an actor that they follow the music because most of them can't read music!

My duties have, on occasion, involved actually *composing* everything in the score (except for the melody and basic harmony), as was the case with *Tom Sawyer*. When you consider the underscoring and dance arrangements for that show, David Krane literally composed the equivalent of a complete film score, while I transcribed melodies and harmonies from tape recordings of the composer's voice and guitar performances. Often, I arranged the songs on the spot with the whole cast scribbling away on their sketchy, photocopied lead sheets, which I had stayed up at night to computerize. I was frequently told to "play it for the cast" when there was simply no *it* to play! It could be challenging and exciting, or a huge waste of rehearsal time, especially since months had gone by during which time this work could have been prepared well in advance. My job has been frustrating or methodical or fast, furious fun, but very rarely is it acknowledged. To this day, I ask actors I meet who the musical director or pianists are on the show they are doing or about to do and the answer is always... "Oh, I don't know."

We pianists (I hate the term "keyboard player") are the "aural motor" of every day of rehearsal work, but our names can be forgotten in introductions, souvenir programs, polite conversation, paychecks, opening night invitations, and scheduling. My job has always been to listen, remember absolutely everything I hear, and get it *right*. But of course, no one ever told me this information. I have witnessed many auditions, creative meetings, discussions, and personal conversations where absolutely no one was listening to anyone else, and the assumption is that "someone is taking notes" on all the non-decisions not being made. That person (on the musical front) has often been me, and not necessarily the musical director or even the composer.

But then, there were the Stephen Sondheim musicals... a much different experience.

3. You Gotta Get A Gimmick

THEATRE UNDER THE STARS, ATLANTA, GA
GYPSY

When I was nine, my mother took me to the 1962 Atlanta Theatre Under the Stars (TUTS) summer stock production of *Gypsy* starring Jane Morgan, with music by "Jewel" Styne and "words" by Stephen Sondheim. My only memory is of a woman playing the character of a stripper named "Tessie Tura." She was singing something about "bumping" and "gimmicks." Her costume had fringe hanging down from her crotch, and every time she "bumped," the fringe flew up and slapped her on her belly. It tore the audience apart. Her personality and the song carried all the way back to row ZZ in the Chastain Park outdoor amphitheater where we were sitting.

In 1978, I was rehearsing a hilarious 1920s musical, *Mary*, at the Equity Library Theatre in New York City with an actress of a certain age, Fiona Hale, who played the role of the matron in the show. She was quite a character who worked in Hollywood under a different name and appeared in one of Joan Crawford's later melodramas from Columbia Pictures, *Harriet Craig*. Fiona told me stories about Crawford and her "damn dogs," and how every time she (Fiona) came on the set, Crawford would say, "Are you really going to wear THAT?" Fiona told me she currently had a roommate, another actress who had an unusual name. I asked for her last name and, sure enough, her roommate was the "Tessie Tura" from *Gypsy* in 1962. I sent my regards and praise to her.

In 1997, I was sitting in a morning meeting of Alcoholics Anonymous on the Upper West Side. An elderly woman raised her hand to say, "My name is _____ and I'm an alcoholic." Thirty-six years later, I was sitting facing "Tessie Tura!" I did something I shouldn't have done. After the meeting, I introduced myself as politely as I could and told her how much I enjoyed her performance from 35 years earlier. Her eyes widened. She muttered "Thank you," and scurried away. I never saw her again. I shouldn't have done that, but I just had to tell her!

ROXY THEATRE, ATLANTA, GA
GYPSY - THE MOVIE

Shortly after seeing the stage version, my mother took me to the Roxy Theatre in downtown Atlanta to see the movie version of *Gypsy* starring Rosalind Russell, Natalie Wood and Karl Malden, with music by "Julee" Styne (I was learning) and "lyrics" by Stephen Sondheim. I particularly enjoyed the last hour, and my mother laughed out loud during Russell's "Rose's Turn." She thought it was the funniest thing she'd ever seen! She also told me that she and my dad had seen the real Gypsy Rose Lee perform years earlier at the Fox Theatre. On New Year's Eve, my mom let me stay up late to watch Rosalind Russell in *Auntie Mame* on TV. A couple of years later, they took me to the premiere (at the Roxy) of Russell's latest comedy, *Rosie*. Before the movie began, there was a fashion show of her costumes, and she actually made a personal appearance. I just remember how old her hands looked.

I became obsessed with the soundtrack LP of *Gypsy* and played it endlessly on my little three-piece stereo. I was especially impressed with how funny the lyrics were but was a little shocked that Mr. Sondheim would use such vulgar language as "Some people sit on their butts, got the dream, yeah, but not the guts" for such a refined lady as "Madame Rose."

I was also obsessed with Natalie Wood. I was a good sketcher and constantly drew Natalie Wood in her strip costumes on my schoolbooks. This resulted in some nasty girl's prank phone calls making fun of me. Nevertheless, I remained obsessed with Ms Wood and fantasized about actually being her. Well, I haven't *stopped* fantasizing about being her... *just being her.* I WANTED TO BE NATALIE WOOD!

In 1981, on the first night in Toronto of my tour of *A Day in Hollywood/A Night in the Ukraine,* as we were checking into our hotel rooms, I turned the TV on to the news that Wood had drowned off the Island of Catalina. I insisted everyone drop their luggage, come into my room, and have a moment of silence for my beautiful Natalie. Six weeks later, we were in Los Angeles with the tour, and I was standing at Grauman's Chinese Theatre looking down at her footprints. They were full of water! (I know, I know, the courtyard had just been hosed down, but I liked my fantasy better—that her ghost was standing before me, dripping wet!)

And in 1978, on my first day in New York City, I had the thrill of playing a dance call audition for a choreographer named Bert Michaels, who just happened to be the original "Yonkers" in the movie of *Gypsy.* (More later!)

THEATRE UNDER THE STARS, ATLANTA, GA
A FUNNY THING HAPPENED ON THE WAY TO THE FORUM

In the summer of 1965, my mother took me to see Stephen Sondheim's *A Funny Thing Happened on the Way to the Forum* at TUTS. Not expecting anything, we absolutely screamed at this show. Danny Dayton played a tall, skinny Pseudolus. Afterwards, I was let loose backstage to get autographs. Miles Gloriosus was played by an impressive actor, Erik Silyu. Why do I remember him? I knocked on his dressing room door (where were the stage managers? I was being allowed to just wander around!) and the door opened. I gasped at the muscle man standing before me in a towel right out of the shower.

"(*Gulp*) Oh, Mr. Silyu. You were grrrrrrrrrreat! Could I have your chest... uh... autograph, please?"

"No problem, kid!"

In 1972, I played the piano for the Georgia State University Players production of *Forum*. I was coming out of the closet in full force and having a great time doing this show. The first of our twelve performances was divine. The audience loved us. The next eleven nights, nothing... crickets... Obviously, the first night was friends and family. The rest of our audiences consisted of the burnt-out students/hippies who were taking over the whole world. I have never really enjoyed this show since then, but I do believe that when it's properly produced, the cast *must* be old, fat, ugly, Jewish and, most importantly, *heterosexual*. I'm waiting to see that production. I was mortally offended by the Jerry Zaks Broadway revival starring the super gay Nathan Lane, and even worse, his replacement, Whoopi Goldberg. An awful experience.

WEST SIDE STORY - THE SOUNDTRACK

In 1965, I took a chance and bought (or my mom did) a somber-looking, bright-red soundtrack LP with bold black lettering. By this time, I was drawn to jazzy, brassy songs like "Grant Avenue" from *Flower Drum Song* and "Let Me Entertain You" from *Gypsy*, more than "People Will Say We're in Love" from *Oklahoma!* The first track on this new LP, the "Prologue," looked very promising. I loved overtures and instrumentals, and this looked like a major one. It was long, it was developed, it was fierce. But I wasn't completely sold until the jazz section of "Dance at the Gym." That really blew me away. Lyric-wise, I found "The Jet Song" incredibly sexy, and I really loved "krup-you" at the end of "Gee, Officer Krupke." Hot! (Even at the age of 12, I knew it meant "Fuck you!") Rumor now has it that Leonard Bernstein wrote "krup-you."

And that Leonard Bernstein! That incredible music... I desired to hear more!

With *Gypsy* and *South Pacific*, I discovered the differences between Broadway original cast recordings and the film soundtrack recordings. The Broadway cast albums usually had more music crammed on them, but a faraway echo-y sound, while the soundtrack versions had fewer songs but a more upfront immediate sound, with gigantic orchestras and heavenly choirs. The *West Side Story* original cast LP did not have the jazz dance music I loved so much, but did include the "Mambo," which became one of my all-time favorite pieces of music to hear or play on the piano. And the "Cha-Cha" music made me laugh the first time I heard it because I had been hearing it for some time on a local Atlanta TV program as the intro music for *Cinema 65*. At the end of the TV intro, before the movie began, the local announcer would say "presented to you in crystal... clear... color" as the *West Side Story* "Cha-Cha" music buttoned.

LINCOLN CENTER REVIVAL
WEST SIDE STORY

My first trip to New York City in 1962 included the Rockettes. I was nine years old and really too young to take it all in. My second trip six years later included a fight with my parents' friend, Virginia Stringer, who was traveling with us. The fight was over who was the greater singer—Eydie Gormé or Barbra Streisand? She kept bragging about having seen *Golden Rainbow* and that Eydie had it "way over" Babs. I never got to tell her how much I grew to love the recording of the musical *Golden Rainbow* over the next 20 years, and how much I came to appreciate old Eydie.

I was excited about our trip. We had tickets to see *Mame* at the Winter Garden Theatre. Unfortunately, this was the replacement cast with Janis Paige, but Helen Gallagher as Agnes Gooch was terrific. And Vera Charles was played by Audrey Christie who was Natalie Wood's mother in the film *Splendor in the Grass*. I found *Mame* disappointing and always have, especially compared to the straight play and film *Auntie Mame*. The first act is so bumpy, and the second act has all the laughs. So much great stuff had to be cut out to make room for songs. This was going to be my first Broadway show in a Broadway theatre.

But... earlier in the week we went up to Lincoln Center to check out the Metropolitan Opera House and the New York State Theatre and, lo and behold, were able to purchase fifth row center seats for the 1968 revival of *West Side Story*. This was a literal revival, not a *revisal*, or *revusical*, or a *revisalobotomy*, or a *"they didn't know what they were doing the first time so we're gonna fix that"* full-out rewrite. We were met with a full orchestra and the original set and costume designs, not to mention choreography and direction. As is published in the vocal score, I was expecting the opening strains of the "Prologue" as the curtain went up. But instead, the orchestra played a full-out exciting Overture. My mother and Virginia Stringer were sobbing at the end of the curtain call. I was completely overwhelmed. The cast was Kurt Peterson, Victoria Mallory, Barbara Luna, Avind Harum (a 6' 3" Riff!), and Patti LuPone's brother, Robert, all of whom I've met over the years and have personally thanked for making my first Broadway show so powerful.

So, what of this Stephen Sondheim guy? Well, two thrilling shows, at least on record, in revival, and on film—*Gypsy* and *West Side Story*. With tough, sharp, incisive lyrics. But the Forum score... well, the songs did not make much of an impression on me. So, for Sondheim, the score was lyrics: 10, music: 3. *West Side Story* was my third purchased piano/vocal score, and I feverishly plowed my way through the "Prologue," "The Dance at the Gym," "Cool," and the "Somewhere Ballet."

So far, I had spent $27.00 on sheet music. (I'm sorry... my *parents* had spent $27.00 on sheet music, God bless 'em!) And God bless Jule Styne, Rodgers & Hammerstein, and Leonard Bernstein. Oh yeah, and that Sondheim guy... he was okay, too. But he really should stick to lyric writing!

ETHEL MERMAN IN PERSON

The second vocal score of a Broadway musical bought so generously by my parents for my budding library of music was *Gypsy*. In 1969, we were in New York visiting my sister, who was living in Ridgewood, New Jersey. I was now a huge fan of Ethel Merman from the original cast recording of *Gypsy*. I read her new autobiography and had her sign it at a book signing in a mall in Atlanta. In the book she mentioned doing volunteer work at Roosevelt Hospital. My mother and I stopped by the front desk of the main entrance to Roosevelt Hospital, then on Ninth Avenue, to inquire if it was true that Ethel Merman occasionally volunteered in the gift shop. The man behind the desk looked both ways and whispered, "Come back tomorrow at noon."

Off we went. Next day, a Thursday, we arrived at 11:30 and sat in the large lobby between the entrance and the gift shop. At noon on the dot, an old lady clomped down the steps and across the lobby. My mother started laughing uncontrollably. We waited a few minutes to let this "old lady" get settled and we entered the gift shop. There were three ladies in orange smocks standing behind the counter yacking. They all had name tags. One of them said "ETHEL." I politely approached Ms Merman and introduced my mom and myself. We told her how much we enjoyed her, and could she possibly sign my *Gypsy* score and original cast album. She looked at the score which was already ragged from use and said "Oh, look at this!" (She must not have seen the published score before.) She signed her name, we bought a pack of Certs, thanked her graciously, and left her to her business.

On the way out, I hissed at my mother, "What were you laughing at?"

She said, "I was expecting a YOUNG Ethel Merman! Did you see those skinny bird legs?" I loved my mother.

In 2009, I matted the autographed cover of the score and gave it to Patti LuPone for her 60th birthday. She had won a Tony Award the preceding year for her revival of *Gypsy*.

4. I'm So Glad I Came

When I was gearing up for my senior year in high school, I dropped 75 pounds thanks to a therapist who gave me speed for three months. He told me that if I really believed I was a homosexual, I was going to have to get rid of all the fat. "Homosexuals hate fat people," he told me. He was, and is, completely correct!

That mysterious phone call offering me my first paying job at the neighboring Northside High School of the Performing Arts (for *On a Clear Day You Can See Forever*) threw me into a whole new world. The director of the 350+ student performing arts program at the very wealthy (and thoroughly integrated) high school was a man named Billy G. Densmore. He was just the type of person to singlehandedly head this kind of operation—crazy, eccentric, driven, egomaniacal, a real character, and a completely obsessive taskmaster. I was the only other musical person on his staff from 1970 through 1975. Under his regime, I rehearsed and played full high school productions of *On a Clear Day You Can See Forever*, *Hello, Dolly!*, *Fiddler on the Roof*, *Cabaret*, *Applause*, *Purlie*, *The Me Nobody Knows*, and *Company*, plus accompanied a group of 30 that toured all over the city performing in other schools. We were "star babies" (and we knew it). This man kept my fingers wiggling for hours every day, seven days a week, and paid me my first legitimate salary for music. He also opened up a whole world to me that I'd never dreamed of. After four depressing, lonely, soul-deadening years at my own high school, overnight I had 350 new friends. Yes, I felt like an overnight sensation. A star had been born. It was a lot more than I could handle and my feelings of insecurity were now battling with my huge emerging ego. I was in my "I'll show *them*" mode, full throttle. Who was *them* you ask? Why, everyone I had ever met in my eighteen years, of course! My teenage life finally took off like a rocket, but I was not ready for the onslaught of people, work, responsibility, excitement, and show business madness ahead. Alcohol was the ticket.

Twice a year, I helped chaperone two busloads of students on a New York trip for a week of Broadway shows, dinner at Mama Leone's, subway rides, and gawking at the Times Square weirdos. On our first trip, the female chaperone took the girls shopping and Densmore took me and the boys, most of whom were 18, to a 42nd Street porno theatre to sit through twenty minutes of a subtitled, black-and-white, Spanish titty movie. Believe you me, we all *knew* what he was up to... and he got nowhere. Also on that trip, several of us piled into a taxi. I was looking around the interior of the cab and my eyes settled on the taxi driver's ID card and photo. I couldn't believe my eyes! I leaned over the front seat and asked, "Did you go to the University of Georgia with Jeanette Lang and did you play Wang Ta in *Flower Drum Song* in Atlanta in 1963?" He almost ran us off the road! It was him! It was Paul Eichel!

Thanks to the school, here is a list of the original Broadway shows and revivals I saw from 1970 to 1977, along with my observations. (I was already quite the one with critical opinions.)

PROMISES, PROMISES. Absolutely the greatest. Burt Bacharach was "good" pop music—theatrical, dramatic, funny. And what was that "Turkey Lurkey Time" number??? Ohmigod... who was that woman dancing (Donna McKechnie)??? Ohmigod... I also got an earful of Sondheim's foremost orchestrator, Jonathan Tunick. Dazzling!

THE BOY FRIEND (REVIVAL). Sandy Duncan (along with Broadway baby and Sondheim veteran Harvey Evans) stole the show right out from under *Laugh In*'s Judy Carne in the Julie Andrews role.

APPLAUSE. Fun trash, the worst songs, the worst sets, the worst costumes, and I loved every second of it. This was a prime example of a great songwriting team trying to "get with it" by writing hideous rock/pop songs, but the story was unbeatable and the performances knocked it out of the ballpark.

COMPANY. Life changing, hilarious, and also good pop music (very Bacharach-like). Way to go, Stephen Sondheim (and Jonathan Tunick, orchestrator)!

TWO BY TWO. The first musical where I discovered that even a master (Richard Rodgers) could write a bad show.

THE ME NOBODY KNOWS. Trashy songs about trashy poor kids, not moving, not interesting, not compelling (probably my first and, unfortunately, not my last rock musical).

EARTHLIGHT. My first off-Broadway hippie musical with nudity. Wow, a penis... but the guy that came with the penis looked like Charles Manson. No thanks!

TOUCH. Another horrible hippie communal musical. Oy, make it stop!

HAIR. And yet another hippie musical with nudity. Big yawn.

FOUR ON A GARDEN. The opposite end of the dazzling theatre spectrum, a dreadful comedy with Sid Caesar and Carol Channing, excruciatingly dull.

GODSPELL. A total piece of shit... which 99.99% of the students vastly preferred over all the other shows.

FOLLIES. Universe shaking. Not a day goes by (sorry) that I don't visualize (escape to) some moment of this show. Please take me back to that world!

NO, NO, NANETTE (REVIVAL). Spectacular fun. The epitome of beauty for its own sake, light and innocent for its own sake, and joy abounding. Oh, and tap dancing! Tap dancing! Tap dancing!

ON THE TOWN (REVIVAL). Choreography-wise, it was disappointing, but I wouldn't have missed it for anything. The cast? Bernadette Peters! Donna McKechnie! Marilyn Cooper! Laura Kenyon! Sandra Dorsey! Zoya Laporska! Even Phyllis Newman was okay.

PURLIE. Could have missed it. Could have missed it all three times Densmore booked it. Gospel singing and screaming on high Gs leaves me cold, first time, every time.

IRENE (REVIVAL). Failed at everything *No, No, Nanette* had achieved. Loud, gaudy and insincere.

CYRANO. One of a string of snoozer songfests based on this dreary play. Why, why, why do they keep doing it? I hear Frank Wildhorn has another version waiting in the wings. Jesus God, have mercy and spare us!

ANNIE. Dorothy Loudon's show, and a well-crafted piece of storytelling, although uninspired musically.

CANDIDE (REVIVAL). Dreadful ruin of a great musical (at least the 1956 original cast album was great). The revival cast recording is deadly, as was this stage version. Deadly, I say. I saw it! Hal Prince and company tried to combine *Hair* with real theatre and real music and all we got was straw on the floor and picnic benches to sit on. Not for my $12.50!

CHICAGO. Shiny, bright and empty. Great performances, but "hard as nails." That only goes so far. God bless scenic designer Tony Walton... and Gwen Verdon (Lenora Nemetz was on for Velma).

A CHORUS LINE. Exciting and ultimately about nothing (show business).

HELLO, DOLLY! (with Ethel Merman). A classic, beautiful production worn out by a seven-year run. Can you imagine what *Phantom of the Opera* is like now after thirty years?

A LITTLE NIGHT MUSIC. Beautiful to look at and pleasant to hear. And funnier than the original cast recording led me to think... but an odd musical.

LORELEI. Terrible, and a foreboding look forward to the *Crazy For You*s, *Nice Work If You Can Get It*s, and *The Gershwin's Porgy and Bess*es. In other words, bad "revisals."

OVER HERE! One of the greatest nights of my life. The cast? Ann Reinking, John Travolta, Treat Williams, Marilu Henner, and the two surviving Andrews Sisters, and a great big, fabulous swing orchestra that rose out of the stage. Funny, exciting... Where is this show today???

PIPPIN. A rock musical that just squeaked by for me because of the musical theatre know-how of Bob Fosse. He was actually able to do something with those songs. Miraculous!!!! His staging should have been thoroughly archived and copyright-protected so no other production could be done without it.

RAISIN. A completely forgotten musical with one of the few contemporary scores that I found—and still find—enjoyable, moving, and appropriate to the story. One of my favorite CDs. Lost, gone with the wind, forgotten, and ignored.

SEESAW. One of the biggest pieces of shit I ever sat through. Unbelievable. The original play had two characters! I have never seen so much junk piled on a stage... one outrageously inane number after another.

SIDE BY SIDE BY SONDHEIM. Too precious, too British, and way too soon in my then 23-year-old opinion.

SUGAR. A drag, literally, with terrible sets and (gulp) Elaine Joyce as Marilyn Monroe???? Even Robert Morse couldn't save it.

JACQUES BREL IS ALIVE AND WELL AND LIVING IN PARIS. Made me want to kill myself, and no, not in a good way. I really wanted to take a fork and stick it in my eye at the start of each song.

THE CHANGING ROOM. Only great because I saw it with 80 high school kids. Our fearless director, Billy Densmore, mistakenly booked this play thinking we were seeing *That Championship Season*. This had lots of FULL-FRONTAL MALE NUDITY! The sight of their first real penis on stage sent up such a "whoop" from our black teenage girls, it can still be heard echoing around the universe.

THE WIZ. Colorful and well-done.

SHENANDOAH. Dumb, somber, overly earnest, and worthy of the *Les Miserables* discard heap.

I LOVE MY WIFE. Dumber. Wife swapping? Funny? Musical? How about sad and pathetic... how about being an off-Broadway musical masquerading as a Broadway musical? An early example of a shocking practice today—putting tiny, intimate, no-production-value-whatsoever shows onto Broadway stages and charging overly bloated ticket prices... a rip off!

THE WOMEN (REVIVAL). Unfortunately, an interesting cast wasted in a bad revival. I had yet to see the 1939 movie. Some things are best left alone.

Plus, my dad drove me to Garrison, New York, where *Hello, Dolly!* had just been filmed! The cobblestones were still painted on the streets and the building used for Vandergelder's Hay and Feed Store still had "Vandergelder's" etched in the glass of its windows. In 2010, on a repeat visit, nothing had changed 40 years later!

This list and my opinions might sound as if I don't like Broadway musicals... but I do. If they are good! It's simple!

As is evidenced, three of the shows seen on these trips were the core of Sondheim. In retrospect, these three were never bettered... I was blown away by this Sondheim guy *now*!

The work, discipline, and exposure to life I received from this school were life changing and eye opening, but I ultimately had to leave for two reasons: I was completely and utterly exhausted, and when something got in the way of my drinking, that something had to go. I walked into Densmore's office one morning and quietly tendered a two-week notice. His words to me were, "This is career suicide!" and "If you leave, I will never see anything you do ever again!" He made good on his word. I still cannot fathom that he actually could have sat in the audience of *Sunday in the Park with George* and not come down to the pit to congratulate me. Such was the case. Ah, well... every day a little death. I still feel traumatized, abused, and punished by this. Years later, when he retired from the school, one of his many secretaries called me in New York asking me to come down for a farewell celebration. I chose to stick to my trusty "self-righteous anger" guns and didn't respond to the calls. He died a homeless coke addict on the streets of Atlanta.

I had a lot of fun back then and received a great deal of valuable experience and I'm grateful for it. But THAT was over.

5. Collecting Cast Albums and Soundtracks... and Rape

Starting with the LP of *Flower Drum Song*, I became a voracious collector of many things. Every birthday and Christmas from age 10 to 17, I had a list of "must haves" for my parents. I did not (and would not) accept clothes or toys or bicycles or sports equipment or anything other than sheet music and LPs. I paid for some of them, too, with chores and good behavior. My aunt

Kathleen came to visit us once thinking that she was going to *fix me* by interfering or, as we say today, "intervening." She brought me a record of the music she felt was more appropriate for my age, *The Birds, the Bees, and the Monkees*. I listened to it, as I had listened to the Beatles' first album. Then I put it out with the trash, along with the Beatles and all such horrid nonsense.

When I got my driver's license, I was off to the races. Every weekend I would drive around Atlanta to every shopping center, K-Mart, Woolworth's and used-book store, and go through their record sections and dollar bins. I found unbelievable bargains and came back with a "take" of ten or twelve albums each time. It was my drug, my "Kool-Aid." I'll never forget one vacation with the folks when I found the original cast album of Harold Arlen's mammoth flop musical *Saratoga* and the soundtrack of MGM's *Hit the Deck* in Biloxi, Mississippi, or finding the London cast recording of *Bye, Bye, Birdie* in a K-Mart in southeast Atlanta. The Capitol Records label was eliminating all of its Broadway music, so everything was everywhere for a dollar—*Skyscraper*, *Tovarich*, *The Gay Life*, *Ben Franklin in Paris*, *Walking Happy*. I discovered what the term "out of print" LP meant. What it meant was "I had to have it!" But don't think I was just a hoarder. I listened to each recording, read the liner notes and memorized names. I listened and listened and learned... and absorbed. I was not interested in playing with the neighborhood children, although anyone was welcome to listen with me, but the takers were never there. When one neighbor friend came over and announced that *Hair* was the only good album I owned, I gave up on people completely and closed the door on the world. I also tossed out the *Hair* album.

I found ads in the back of magazines such as *Stereo Review* for rare-record sellers. I wrote away for the lists from some of these sellers and immediately made "goal" lists. Stephen Sondheim's *Anyone Can Whistle* (what the heck was this show?!?) was $25, *Tenderloin* was rare at $35, *Greenwillow* was super-rare at $60, and the RCA Television Cast of *Lady in the Dark* was a whopping $75! I... had... to... have... them... all! I don't know where the money came from except the generosity and indulgence of my parents and an allowance for chores... and begging! And doing without my own car or dates or clothes or anything extraneous. Bargaining and wheeling and dealing got me my collection... and being the best boy ever! I would order a few LPs from sellers and wait breathlessly by the mailbox.

One seller started calling me on the phone asking for a "want list" and I sent it. This person, whom I shall call "Ratso Rizzo" (even though I remember his name) suggested that the next time I come to New York with my parents, we should get together and he would show me his "collection."

On a Christmas trip visiting my sister, we were at the Howard Johnson's in New York City on Eighth Avenue and going to shows, and I was scouring Carroll's and Colony Music and Schirmer's Music. Oh, and the Interesting Record Store in the Chelsea Hotel—what a place that was! Ratso said that he would pick me up and drive me to his apartment in Somewhere, New Jersey. Mom and dad were not happy, but I was determined to pillage this guy's merchandise and I had my dollars in my pocket. Ratso drove me out and I looked at his collection and it was impressive. He showed me his "for sale" goods and I mentally noted what looked interesting. It was getting dark, so he suggested—or whined—that perhaps I should stay over as he "didn't wanna make the looooong drive back to New Yooowuk." I called the hotel and my folks said okay (reluctantly). Ratso ordered in food and I started to collect my thoughts about what records I wanted to buy. I think I was 18... but I'm not sure. Finally, I settled on three albums, one of which was the soundtrack to a strange-looking movie called *Three for the Show* with Betty Grabble... Grable... Grubble? That was all I could afford. "How about these?" I said. He offered to give me a discount, but only if I would let him... *fuck me.*

This was a dilemma. I was somewhere in New Jersey, 18 years old (not a virgin—that is another horror story), vulnerable, and inexperienced. He started whining (not threateningly) that he had "gwooone to ooooaaallll the trouble of driving ooooaaaall the way from New Yooowuuk and bwooooought me dinnah, and was doooin' me a big favah, and I should give him what he wooooooaaaaanted." I stood still and let him begin. I couldn't sleep all night, and in the morning he wanted moooooore. How did I know he would ever take me back to the city? He didn't seem like such a terrible person, just ugly and sniveling and whining and *old* (in his 30s). So, I rolled over and kept thinking about how the $20 he was going to take off the price of the records wasn't nearly enough. I didn't really want the records anymore. He drove me back to the city that morning. I still like the music from *Three for the Show*, but I get the creeps when I hear someone speak in a thick New Jersey accent. And if you don't know the name "Ratso Rizzo," just rent *Midnight Cowboy* and imagine what having sex with *that* was like.

6. Someone is Waiting

COMPANY

I continued my mad show-album collecting but was slow in getting around to listening to Stephen Sondheim's *Company* because I was allergic to anything that looked remotely modern, and I hadn't been impressed with what I had heard of Sondheim's music for *Forum*. The year 1970 marked the first time I traveled to New York City to see shows with the Northside Performing Arts School group. On that first trip, we saw *Hello, Dolly!* It was thrilling to see Ethel Merman, but it was true, as legend has it, that she walked through the show, marking everything except the singing (I saw her twice and she did it again). We also saw *Applause* (lots of fun and very gay), *Touch* (a terrible off-Broadway hippie commune, feel good, sing-along bore), *Hair* (another dreary hippie commune sing-along bore—"Leeeeeet the suuunshiiine in" my ass), *Two By Two* (my friend turned to me during Danny Kaye's song "You" and said, "This music is terrible," and I thought, "You know... you're right!"), *Purlie* (entertaining, but I'll take Lena Horne over Melba Moore any day), and *Company*, the original cast (with Dean Jones's replacement, Larry Kert).

My life changed that night at *Company*. The highlight of any musical for me was always the dancing, as was Donna McKechnie's dance solo, "Tick Tock," but the entire show was thrilling—modern in a *good* way. I didn't mind the new sounding music. It actually felt more Latin, more Burt Bacharach in rhythm, and harmonically it was way beyond monotonous rock music. When I got back home, I ripped the cellophane off the LP and wore it out. I ordered the vocal score and started practicing "Another Hundred People," "Company," "You Could Drive A Person Crazy" and, of course, "Tick Tock." It was all very hard, but great. Three years later we did *Company* at the high school (!) with a double-cast "Bobby"—Caucasian and African-American—pretty advanced for Atlanta in 1973. And there were 100 married couples on stage. That was a lot of company! We might have even had the first 15-year-old to sing "The Ladies Who Lunch." I saw the Broadway production again the next year with another Bobby replacement and a new cast, including Jane Russell in Stritch's role. She refused to curse on stage, so every "Jesus Christ" or other such expletive in the lyrics was rewritten, substituting, "My, oh my" and such. (Jesus Christ, Jane! Get over yourself!) And I saw a National Tour of the show play Atlanta with Allen Case and Julie Wilson. One of my college professors lambasted the music in class one morning. Needless to say, I disagreed.

For a long time, *Company* was in the "perfect show" column for me, but after seeing one poor revival after another, the glow has dimmed. Also, what was once daring or extremely funny in the book, barely gets a titter these days. The two stories told by Bobby and April (the "stewardess" in 1970) were riotous. I don't think the actors these days know that these monologues are supposed to be funny. And my favorite part of the show, "Tick Tock," is often cut. It's there for a reason—to give the audience a fresh moment that is different from everything else. That is what makes a musical exciting!

Since that electric night when I was 17, I've had the honor and privilege of working with many of the original cast members of this legendary show. There was Larry Kert (Bobby in *Company* and Tony in *West Side Story*) who played a leading role in the musical *Rags* in 1986. A very nice man. For those who care, he can be seen backing up Marilyn Monroe in the "Diamonds Are a Girl's Best Friend" number in the film version of *Gentlemen Prefer Blondes*, alongside his future *West Side Story* alumnus, George Chakiris. After *Rags* closed, I received an odd phone call from Larry asking if I would play "Being Alive" for him at a benefit. He said he was sick but wanted to make a go of it. I didn't realize how ill he was. He died of AIDS shortly after, without my hearing from him again.

I've had the pleasure of playing "Another Hundred People" for Pam Myers on many occasions at auditions, and I worked with the handsome, funny John Cunningham in the pre-Broadway San Diego production of *Into the Woods*. I also had the pleasure of working with the hilarious Merle Louise on *Into the Woods*. Charles Kimbrough was in the original cast of *Sunday in the Park with George*—a great and hilarious guy—and I'd often see Steve "Today is for Amy" Elmore on the street and at auditions.

The first words ever spoken to me by Elaine Stritch are immortalized on the *Follies in Concert* DVD. "We're gonna take this a little sloooower, pleeease," she growled at me as we rehearsed "Broadway Baby" for the 1985 Lincoln Center concert version of *Follies*. People would say to me, "You must feel terrible about that!" My response: "What? Are you kidding?"

During the early years of my playing for Mandy Patinkin, we were asked to do a benefit performance at Hunter College. Mandy had two ideas to liven up our concert. First, a children's choir would sing "Anyone Can Whistle" and the ragtime chorus of Irving Berlin's "Play a Simple Melody." The other idea would be for Elaine Stritch to sit in the audience and start shouting, "You don't need analyzing, it is not so surprising..." and then come onstage to finish Irving Berlin's "You're Just in Love" duet with Mandy. She pushed him upstage and took over, making a long speech about this "talented boy." Often when playing for Mandy in New York City, I would glance into the wings and there would stand Elaine Stritch, dressed all in white including her white rain hat, watching from the wings. How did she get in? What was she doing there? Who cares?

I played a televised PBS concert called *My Favorite Broadway: The Leading Ladies*, directed by Scott Ellis (a highly enjoyable program). During the orchestra rehearsal at the Manhattan Center, it was Elaine's turn to run her number, "The Ladies Who Lunch." These rehearsals can often be chaotic. Elaine had a rehearsal method to calm everyone down. She stood next to the conductor, slooowly stripped off her blouse down to her bra (she was in her 70s) and slooooowly changed into a "rehearsal blouse." The room suddenly became very quiet and all attention was focused where it should be—on Elaine. Good for her!

She called me a few years before her death to say, "Paul, I'm coming over. I have to learn 'I'm Still Here.' IT'S TIME." She showed up in a yellow raincoat with shopping bags and her omnipresent rain hat. It was a hot, sunny, summer day. She asked to use my bathroom and disappeared into the other room, shopping bags and all. A few minutes later, she emerged in nothing but a black leotard, ready for rehearsal! We began plowing through the song. She got stalled on the phrase "I've gotten through Herbert and J. Edgar Hoover" for at least 30 minutes. "I gotta get these notes right. Jesus Christ, Steve'll kill me! 'I've gotten through Herbert... I've gotten through... I've gotten through Herbert... I've... got... ten... through... Herbert'..." over and over and over. Two hours passed and she put on the raincoat and rain hat and left. Oh, she didn't pay me. She never paid me. She never has paid me... for anything. Since it was a hot summer day, my windows were open the whole time. I'm on the first floor looking out on a lovely air shaft. After Elaine left, my intercom phone rang. It was my friend Denise Nolin on the sixth floor. "I've gotten through Herbert and J. Edgar Hoo-oo-oo-vah! *I* can fuckin' sing it, for Christ's sake!!!" We screamed with laughter.

Some of my favorite moments in theatre, as I've said before, involved the dancing of Donna McKechnie. I finally got to play for her in a Sondheim concert called *Beautiful Girls*, originally produced in Colorado Springs, Colorado, for a summer music festival. Directed by Lonny Price, the cast included Donna, Marin Mazzie, and Jenn Colella, and was hosted by Zoe Caldwell. The song lineup featured women's songs from Sondheim shows. For my money, very little was included that was interesting, new or significant. "I Know Things Now" from *Into the Woods*, "Some People" from *Gypsy*, "Everybody Ought to Have a Maid" from *Forum*, and "There's Always a Woman" (cut) from *Anyone Can Whistle*, were a few of the more interesting items. This was a smooth production and was received very well by the Colorado audiences, and Steve was there to collect an award.

Patti LuPone made a special appearance singing "Being Alive" and presented the award. As they walked off the stage, passing me at the piano, Steve made a fake stumble pretending to almost drop the glass award. Oh, that Steve!

The shows that featured Donna McKechnie's dancing, *Promises, Promises, Company, On the Town* and *A Chorus Line*, all benefited tremendously from her participation, and the time I got to spend with her was sincerely precious to me.

I also spent some fun time with Wally Harper when he coached me on the piano score for *A Day in Hollywood/A Night in the Ukraine*. He did the dance music for *Company* and was Barbara Cook's musical director until his death. And *Company*'s orchestrator, Jonathan Tunick, was and still is the best orchestrator on Broadway. His charts play themselves and he doesn't resort to weird hybrid keyboards and tricks, and never gets in the way of the vocals. I was blessed to play his work many times. But as Phyllis in *Follies* said to another ex-showgirl, "You never liked me." And Jonathan, unfortunately, did not like me. Ah, well. Speaking of *Follies*...

FOLLIES

In 1971, I bought (or once again, my parents bought) the next Sondheim original cast album, *Follies*. Columbia Records had done such a fantastic job on *Company* (it virtually jumped off the record at you), that I thought it odd that *Follies* was on the Capitol label. Columbia was king of the original cast LP. Columbia's "king" was producer Goddard Leiberson (later Thomas Z. Shepard would ascend the throne). There were no liner notes on the back of *Follies*, so it was hard at first to have any notion of what the show was and what was inside. There was an insert inside the sleeve with small black-and-white photos and a long list of song titles. I played through it once and was not impressed with any of the songs. They were all short, hurried and sounded tinny and far away. Once again, I was doubtful about Sondheim.

Our next Northside School trip to New York was scheduled. Some of the shows lined up were a repeat of *Applause*, *Company* with Jane Russell in for Elaine Stritch, *No, No, Nanette* (I could not WAIT!), something grimly amateurish sounding called *Godspell*, and a musical based on *Cyrano de Bergerac* starring Captain von Trapp. The rest of the scheduled shows included a couple of plays, and that new Sondheim musical, *Follies*.

Applause had Anne Baxter playing Margo Channing, beautifully. Unfortunately, *No, No, Nanette* was missing Ruby Keeler, with Penny Singleton serving as her vacation replacement. (I was able to see Keeler on a later trip.) *Godspell* was a little horror about Jesus with hippies dressed up like clowns, and I slept through *Cyrano*. I hate classics musicalized, and sword fights onstage make me nervous. In movies they just bore me. Of all the shows on the schedule, for me, the big unknown was *Follies*.

The Winter Garden Theatre is huge with a very wide stage. (I haven't set foot in that theatre since the original run of the loathsome *Cats*, more than 35 years ago!) From our seats, I noticed debris on stage and the curtain was dark and musty looking. When the lights went down there was a low timpani roll and a blast of horror movie music. The curtain whooshed up and a flash of lightning briefly illuminated a bombed-out theatre set. All very sudden! No warning! No Overture! An eerie waltz began. There was movement on the bare stage. A single figure in a classic black gown began to move slowly through the shadows. Great! I immediately sat up in my seat! My first horror musical.

Two intermissionless hours later, I couldn't breathe. All I can say is how grateful I am today to have seen Ethel Shutta's "Broadway Baby," Mary McCarty and choreographer Michael Bennett's epic production number "Who's That Woman?" Yvonne DeCarlo's "I'm Still Here," Gene Nelson's "The Right Girl," Dorothy Collins's "Losing My Mind," Alexis Smith's "The Story of Lucy and Jessie," and in the freakiest moment of theatre I have ever witnessed, John McMartin's nervous breakdown in the middle of "Live, Laugh, Love." After having seen many other productions of *Follies* over the past four decades, none have been able to capture what happened that night in 1971.

Since music, for me (at age 18), had forever been ruined by The Beatles and the electric guitar/drum set garage band, I sensed that the end of my kind of theatre (glamour, sophistication and innocence in entertainment) was upon us. The specific atmosphere hovering over this particular show is something that can never be captured again in any production of *Follies*. After more than a half century, the end of a form of entertainment unique to New York and America which could never be equaled—that brilliant musicians and writers slaved to refine and redefine—was upon us. It was all dead. Gone that evening were innocence, dreams, belief in a better life, glory, grandeur, love, triumph, pure joy and, most of all, sheer physical beauty. And the actors delivering this message to us were the very people to whom this was happening.

The stars of the original *Follies* were authentic inhabitants of the world described in the story. They had lived through it and experienced the decline of their own careers. Not only the characters in the show were breaking down, but the real actors were teetering on the edge of a drastically changing world. No longer would charming gentlemen wear a clean tuxedo, no longer would there be beauty and drama captured in a dazzling tap number, no longer would there be a statuesque, truly sophisticated star of yesteryear leading a sea of red-tuxedoed dancers, no longer would a torch song be put forth with such will and determination (and, yes, joy), no longer would there be a stage spilling over with people, an orchestra pit full of all kinds of musicians, colors and sounds. The harsh ugly electronic Roxichord keyboard creeping into the natural, beautiful, acoustic music in the *Follies* orchestrations, signaled a new era of fake, synthesized, over-amplified noise. This world was truly falling to pieces before our very eyes as the show unfolded. For those who really cared, it really was the end. All you had to do was go and see *Hair*, in which dirty hippies were screaming all night long, to see what was not just being phased out, let go, dispensed with, but burned, like bras and draft cards. In other words, to really have seen *Follies*, you had to be there in 1971. The weight and impact of that original production will never be duplicated in future productions.

Failures in other recent productions of *Follies* usually are the result of economics. There are never enough people on stage, costumes are skimpy, the design is out-of-period or a mix-up of periods. The 1987 London production of *Follies* does not even count, because the script is completely different, and several key songs were rewritten or dropped, particularly (God help us) "The Road You Didn't Take."

In 1985, I was honored to play rehearsal piano for the first all-star New York concert version of the show featuring the New York Philharmonic. The whole purpose behind the production was to correct the big mistake made by Hal Prince in 1971. (Jesus Christ, male egos! Sorry. Male SHOWBIZ egos!) The big mistake on the Capitol original cast album was that literally every other page of the score was edited. Everything was edited—every two bars of the Prelude, second choruses of songs, the deletion of three complete numbers, dance music cut to shreds, show-stopping numbers trimmed to a minute, pages of brilliant lyrics left out. The way the *Company* recording "jumped off the record," the *Follies* recording just sat there. Yes, a few classic performances were captured, but the dance music and production numbers were simply not there. It takes all of it to make it work, and a two-record set was really required.

The concert would be the first new recording, featuring all the music in the show. On two records! But, again, all of the dance music was cut, production numbers were truncated, and the recording basically was a repeat of the 1971 debacle with the exception of the songs "Rain on the Roof" and "Loveland." It was a wonderful legendary concert, but still no complete recording! It took the Paper Mill Playhouse production in 1999 to finally get a complete recording of the show. Unfortunately, the vocal performances are a mixed bag, but at least you can hear for the first time what rabid fans had been relishing over the years through a pirated tape of a complete live performance that had been circulating among collectors since 1971. I personally obsessed over said tape, which had the voices recorded on one track and the orchestra on a separate track. Not perfect, but it was all we had.

I personally cherish the memory of every second I spent on that concert, but I still felt disgruntled and dissatisfied, and could not understand why no one else felt as I did.

After the millennium, I played all of the auditions for the Roundabout Theatre revival of *Follies*. Everything about that production was a mistake, from the puny-sized theatre chosen (the Belasco), through severe miscasting, and uninformed inept production design. (Georgia O'Keefe roses as a backdrop for Loveland?) And bad choreography, unusual for Kathleen Marshall. Plus, a tinkly little seven-piece band. The Paper Mill Playhouse production had an evocative first half, but simply went to the scenery warehouse and dumped everything they could find on the stage for "Loveland." No style, no rhyme or reason. A chandelier here, a staircase there, a column, a drape, your grandmother's army shoes... The final blow was replacing "Lucy and Jessie" with the weak "Ah, But Underneath" (written for the London production). There was no payoff to the show. The dream-like Loveland sequence that ends the show looked pretty much like the rest of the show. And as much fun as Ann Miller was, she was the wrong kind of show business for "I'm Still Here." And really, the best they could do for "Who's That Woman" was the smaller-than-life Phyllis Newman? She also was in the Lincoln Center concert. No one learned their lesson?

The Encores! concert that followed the Paper Mill production was an afterthought, and strictly amateur, with overwrought performances. But now to the 2011 Kennedy Center revival.

I caught up with this production when it moved to Broadway. The good news was that the first act was well done. The bad news was that there never should have been a first act. The show has to be played with no intermission. The intermission ruins this show. The cast was okay, but the Loveland sequence was (sigh) once again, a bomb. The design was a mash-up of movie musical images, cruise ship staging and someone's uninformed and unresearched idea of what a *Follies* show looked like. The showgirl costumes for "Loveland" were stolen from MGM's *The Great Ziegfeld*, the quartet following "Loveland" was done in dull street clothes in front of a tiny proscenium with running lights (cruise ship style), "Buddy's Blues" had no mini Burlesque prop car (essential), "Losing My Mind" was directed as a *sad* song where it should be a song of jubilation and defiance, "Lucy and Jessie" had eight - count 'em - eight chorus boys when there should have been 28 and no one—I repeat, NO ONE—should ever touch the character of Phyllis during "Lucy and Jessie." Not lift her, not throw her around, not TOUCH her. She is untouchable. She sings, poses, points, manipulates, dances a little, but is never tossed around like a sack of potatoes. And neither she nor anyone else should ever break the fourth wall by yelling "Hey" or "Go" or "Hit It." The only person who gets to break the fourth wall in this sequence is Ben when he breaks down. Everyone else's number is in limbo and they must not elicit contact with the audience.

And there must be a cacophonous "chaos" as indicated in the script to revert back to reality for the final scene of the play. Nothing happened in this production. The cast meandered off the stage and rose petals dropped from the flies exemplifying Sally's "tears." I was told this was the director's "concept." OY VEY!!! And as with the inept Roundabout production, "Loveland" is supposed to be a *Valentine*, not a bunch of Georgia O'Keefe roses, or in this case 4,000 pink toilet brushes glued to a backdrop.

Never again would there ever be the glory that was once Broadway, with the possible exception of the Tommy Tune series of musicals in the 1980s and early '90s. If people found *Follies* depressing (or epic tragedy) in 1971, it was because it was signaling the end. Now, *Follies* is purely a period piece with no weight. For the idiots and hippies (and those who thought these creatures were cute) in the '60s and '70s, *Hair* signified a new beginning—of what, I couldn't tell you. Irresponsibility? Bad hygiene? Complete and total ignorance? But *Follies* had a supreme impact for people like me because it was the end of what we... well... I... had grown to love so much in my short lifetime. There was no more humor, or grace in music or theatre after the '70s. All gone, replaced by crude noise, aggression, vulgarity, hostility, and anger. But that's life… and history. And that's why *Follies* has very little impact today, because no one remembers or gives a shit about what was achieved in the 1900s. The 21st century is now here, and everything else is gone with the wind.

Follies was the greatest production of any musical I have ever seen onstage— unsurpassed. It is my second favorite musical (*Gypsy* is the first). It was a hard act to follow and boosted Sondheim to the top of my theatre music heroes. I may have just been 18, but I knew what I was about and what was what.

A LITTLE NIGHT MUSIC

Continuing our twice-yearly school trips to New York, we were privileged to see what made *A Little Night Music* the winner of all those Tony Awards. The Awards broadcast that year showed "Magic to Do" from *Pippin*, but other than that, no other musical number or word or moment from *A Little Night Music* or any other show nominated that year was on display. The music played when Sondheim, Glynis Johns, and others connected to *Night Music* accepted their Awards, sounded like some bad '70s pop tune. (It turned out to be a Vegas-ed up arrangement of "Send in the Clowns!") I was able to purchase and listen to the cast album well in advance of seeing the show, giving me a head start. The cover design was beautiful and intriguing, but the music was classically oriented and did not grab me right away. No swingin' jazz band here! We were scheduled to see the show and, as always, our director bought blocks of tickets in the top-most balcony. Our heads touched the ceiling! This is the show I tell people about when I get into a conversation about today's ticket prices. I took my back-of-the-balcony ticket to the box office and was graciously offered a front row center seat for the added cost of three whole dollars, making my expense twelve whole dollars, instead of the original nine whole dollars. Yes, you were *allowed* to upgrade at the box office by paying the price difference, and you *wouldn't* have to pay your next month's rent with a credit card. *A Little Night Music* was a gorgeous show to look at and unexpectedly hilarious in places. (Without humor a show is dead.) But I found some of this show a slog. Not remotely as grim and off-putting as *Sweeney Todd* would be, if only because it was so beautiful to see and hear, *A Little Night Music* would, nevertheless, never become a desert island disc for me. But I was glad to see it twice, once with Len Cariou and then with William Daniels replacing him.

I played a few rehearsals for an Atlanta summer concert version with Atlanta local talent. What a disaster that was! Fortunately, for me, the antidote to that experience was a 2005 concert version with a wonderful cast and the Philadelphia Orchestra, in which we included the cut song "Silly People" (my personal favorite) and the movie version of "The Glamorous Life" (my other favorite). These two songs, plus "A Weekend in the Country" and the "Night Waltz" instrumental, are about all I can take from this score, although I greatly enjoyed playing "Liaisons" for Mandy Patinkin in our *Celebrating Sondheim* show. But I have never fallen in love with the "Now/Soon/Later" trio, or "Every Day a Little Death," or "You Must Meet My Wife," or (yawn, I'm getting sleepy thinking about it) "Remember," and definitely not "The Miller's

Son!" And the "Clowns" song has been so thoroughly mangled by everyone over the years, that I can only take it when Mandy Patinkin does his definitive version, or a legitimate theater actress/singer like Barbara Cook makes it work. Our cast for the concert included the divine John Dossett, his beautiful wife Michelle Pawk, the heavenly Marc Kudisch, and the late Irene Worth.

The less said the better regarding the 2009 revival, with that "movie star" and a miscast, over-qualified Angela Lansbury. So minimal (cheap) in every respect, let's just say that Ethel Merman's description of her marriage to Ernest Borgnine in her autobiography accurately sums up that production for me.

I also saw the New York City Opera version directed by Scott Ellis and choreographed by Susan Stroman. This was neither here nor there, with no sets and the central figure betrayed by that coldest-of-the-cold British musical theatre stars, Sally Anne Howes. I think that production improved during the L.A. stint, thanks to recasting, bringing in Judith Ivey and Victor Garber.

Finally, sadly, the beautiful Natasha Richardson came to my apartment to rehearse Desiree for a one-night-only benefit concert of the show at the Roundabout Theatre, which also included her mother Vanessa Redgrave as Madame Armfeldt! The stories from this brief outing were very amusing, but you would have to go to pianist Tony Geralis, who actually played it, for the facts. Unfortunately, Ms Richardson's death occurred shortly after this, but I had the pleasure of making her laugh before she left my apartment that day. A couple of years earlier, I had met her husband, Liam Neeson, at their Upper Westside apartment to run him through the score of *Camelot* for a proposed concert. I arrived, we chatted a bit, and since we were in a huge sprawling apartment, I looked around and said, "Well!... Where do you hide the piano?" He looked me squarely in the eye and said, "Well... I thought you would be bringing one." Honestly, these Hollywood types! We planned to reschedule, but I never heard from him again. Ms Richardson howled at my story once she realized the apartment with no piano I was talking about was her own!

Oh, and then there was a movie version of *A Little Night Music*... set in Vienna... and not Sweden... the first of a hundred million mistakes.

A Little Night Music. 1973. I was 20 years old. You had to be there. Never equaled in opulence, casting and design (the polar opposite of *Pippin*), it swept the Tony Awards, as well it should have. But I missed the showbiz of *Company* and *Follies*. The original cast recording is perfect and with the advent of CDs more material is included.

WEST SIDE STORY and DO I HEAR A WALTZ?

Speaking of Sweden, at the Midnight Sun Dinner Theatre in Atlanta, I did a terrible production of *George M* with the terribly miscast, but genuinely nice, *West Side Story* alum Russ Tamblyn. He told me stories about the making of the 1963 film *The Haunting* and autographed my soundtrack album of *West Side Story* in which he gave the definitive performance of Riff. (Although the original Broadway Riff, Michael Callan, was an awfully sexy, young teen star.) A few months later at the same theatre, I did a terrible production of *The Pajama Game* starring *Do I Hear a Waltz's* Elizabeth Allen. Her voice still rings in my ears as being a true gift to the theatre. Her reprise of "Hey There" rivaled Doris Day's from the film and almost made the "from hunger" production we were doing bearable. *My* moment with her was when she graciously signed my cast album of the wonderful Richard Rodgers-Stephen Sondheim musical, *Do I Hear a Waltz?* (more loved by me than *A Little Night Music*) and told me how "that man" (musical director Frederick Dvonch) tried to ruin her performance. Both her title song and Sergio Franchi's "Take the Moment" on *The Ed Sullivan Show* are priceless treasures—seek them out on YouTube! And, personally, I loved ending Mandy Patinkin's *Celebrating Sondheim* show with "Take the Moment," the only song in our show with music by someone other than Sondheim.

I had now seen the original productions of *Company*, *Follies*, and *A Little Night Music*. As a child, I had not been very impressed by Sondheim, because I thought he was just a lyric writer (albeit a good one), and then I saw *Forum*. It was such a funny show, but God help me if I could remember anything but "Comedy Tonight." Then, there was a flop show the parents of a friend of mine had seen and said was terrible. My friend said there were lyrics such as "grass is green, sky is blue," and that Sondheim couldn't really write music. He was better off just writing lyrics. That show was *Anyone Can Whistle*. (MUCH MORE on this show later!)

When I bought the *Company* album, I was afraid of it. It looked pretentious and odd to me (and it wasn't *Dames at Sea*, another item in that same purchase). But when I saw the show on Broadway with the original cast (minus Dean Jones), I suddenly needed to own and hear everything with Sondheim's name on it. I urgently sent my sister, who happened to live in Ridgewood, New Jersey at the time, to all the record stores in Manhattan to find *Do I Hear A Waltz?* and *Anyone Can Whistle*. They were already collector's items at $25 a piece! I couldn't wait to get them. I went through the record collectors in the back of *Stereo Review* magazine and told my sister that there was a guy in New Jersey (not the rapist) close to where she lived who had a monaural copy of *Do I Hear A Waltz?* for sale. I asked if she could go buy it for me. She went driving at night up to this creepy house in a neighboring town... went up to the door... passed $15 to the guy and was handed the record. When she got back in her car and looked at the record, it was stamped "property of the Ridgewood NJ Public Library" on the cover... which was where she worked! She sent it to me and I'm sure that I was the only kid in Atlanta who had a monaural copy of *Do I Hear A Waltz?* and a stereo copy of the astounding, mind-bending *Anyone Can Whistle!*

PACIFIC OVERTURES

Unfortunately, I never made it to New York to see the original *Pacific Overtures*, but my Northside High School student/friend Michael West (star of *When Pigs Fly*) went to Boston to see the tryout and reported to me about what an interesting, beautiful show it was. He saw it twice and heard different versions of "Chrysanthemum Tea" and was awed by Boris Aronson's sets. I have seen the video tape of the Japanese broadcast of the final performance, and it is certainly interesting. (Why, oh why, is this not available commercially???) The recording has grown on me immensely (almost to desert island status) and one of my favorite Sondheim songs is "Poems," a song inexplicably ignored in all Sondheim retrospectives. I insisted Mandy Patinkin do it on his *Oscar and Steve* CD. The 1980s off-Broadway revival directed by Fran Soeder really fixed it for me. That performance became a personal favorite. A fulfilling show to rehearse and perform, even though the production I ultimately worked on was less than spectacular.

And now the Stephen Sondheim scoreboard...

WEST SIDE STORY. Brilliant, and I was fortunate to see a superb re-creation in the 1968 revival. Sondheim's work is simple, clear-cut, sexy, and poetic.

GYPSY. The greatest musical ever written, the greatest original cast recording ever produced, a legendary original production, and an honest, faithful film version. Sondheim wrote the greatest set of lyrics, capturing the showbiz slang and searing emotions all in one show.

A FUNNY THING HAPPENED ON THE WAY TO THE FORUM. A comic riot, my kind of show, but musically it did not grab me. Several wonderful songs, though, two of which are classics.

ANYONE CAN WHISTLE. My third favorite Sondheim show and in my top-five greatest of all time. The original cast recording is a template of *how* to do it, and the vocal score is full of dazzling material. I discovered this after seeing *Company*, *Follies*, and *A Little Night Music*, and it really put Sondheim at the center of my musical theatre fantasy world. I can't believe I've actually done three productions of *Anyone Can Whistle*!!!!

DO I HEAR A WALTZ? Initial reaction? Lovely. And as the years have gone by, my love for it has grown deeper. Beautiful music and wonderful, caustic lyrics by the pro. A musical for adults.

COMPANY. Every song is perfection. The show blew me away.

FOLLIES. Nothing more need be said about this production and material. The word "pastiche" is now a dirty word in musical theatre writing, but I miss it... this show has two scores—brilliant pastiche and brilliant character writing.

A LITTLE NIGHT MUSIC. A perfect musical *if* the right people are in it, the production design is sumptuous, and there is a full orchestra to do the score justice. All of it is required. Skimping ruins it. I, however, prefer my Sondheim *swingin'*.

PACIFIC OVERTURES. I have always adored the Asian influence... first with *Flower Drum Song*, then *The King and I*, and now this. A beautiful score, simple, uncomplicated, and with a touch of pastiche. And that blazing finale, "Next."

Exactly! What's *next*? At the moment, there is no greater person on earth for me than Stephen Sondheim. And I am 23 years old.

7. A Chorus Line

I've never played *A Chorus Line*. I'm not sure I would've wanted to, even though I was hooked on it for a long time. I never even got to see the original cast. But I've had some interesting adventures around it. I quit college in 1974 but was still friendly with my piano teacher, John Schneider. He once told me he was friends with a certain musical director in New York, a certain Donald Pippin. Don Pippin? *A Chorus Line* Don Pippin? *Mame* musical director Don Pippin? "Big Man on the Broadway Campus" Don Pippin? During one of my piano lessons (where I avoided playing any classical music), I played some of the *Follies* score for Schneider and he was unimpressed. He preferred *My Fair Lady*. Schneider told me he had been in New York on a trip and spent some time with Don Pippin, playing through some music from Pippin's latest project. That was in 1969, so it must have been Jerry Herman's *Dear World*. Schneider didn't care for it, but I love the *Dear World* album... it's so over the top, so over-orchestrated, so abundant!

In 1976, my parents and I were going to New York to see *A Chorus Line* and *Chicago*. I didn't immediately ask, but something told me to speak to Schneider before we left. John said, "Well, let me call Don. You two should meet." Gulp! Pippin set it up for me to sit in the pit for a performance of *A Chorus Line*! We already had tickets, but this was a real "in," I thought! (It turns out it happens all the time.)

I met Pippin in Shubert Alley and he led me to the pit, which was completely covered and out of sight of the stage and audience. Oh! Bizarre! "We watch the show on TV monitors," he said. Oh! Bizarre! Since I was seeing the show in its second year, the new cast was onstage. Leland Palmer had been playing Cassie but left the show suddenly and luscious Ann Reinking (from *Pippin* and *Over Here*) was brought in. Pippin introduced me to the acoustic pianist/assistant conductor on the show, Fran Leibergall. "She has GREAT time," he whispered to me. (Mental note to myself: "Have... great... time... hmmm. Well, so far, I'm having a WONDERFUL time!") What he meant, of course, was *rhythmic time*. (I don't have it and never will. That kind of thing requires a lifetime of playing with a metronome, and that was not me!) Pippin was conducting and playing a crappy-looking plastic electric keyboard, and really went to town on "Hello Twelve, Hello Thirteen." I thought the plastic keyboard was going to break in half.

"The Music and the Mirror" was very exciting. Even the dialogue before it had drama. Pippin was listening closely to Ann Reinking and since she was new to the timing of the long dialogue scene leading into the song, it was still bumpy. She started to rush ahead and Pippin had to race through the underscore to meet her on "God, I'm a dancer..." Sweating, he mumbled "Jesus Christ." This was one of my first Broadway examples of what I like to call "show business emergencies." He was actually sweating nervously. What if... what if... just what if... he had been three seconds late with that chord? What would have happened? I shudder to think. The destruction, the chaos, the anarchy, the end of the world... After "Music and the Mirror," all the musicians got up and left the pit. It was time for Paul's "waa waa waa" poor-me-I'm-a-homo-drag-queen monologue onstage (the only part of the show I never cared for—oh, stop whining, go to school, and get a job). I was praying the musicians would come back in time for the rest of the show. The musicians called it their "intermission" since the show was done in one two-hour-plus act. After the show, I thanked Pippin and went to meet my parents. The next night we saw the show. It was terrific, if ultimately just one great big fat melodramatic "show business emergency" onstage. That was my first time in a Broadway musical orchestra pit, but it was a foreboding sign, what with the covered pit. An ugly notion to hide the orchestra. Since then, orchestras have been piped in from backstage, other rooms, even other buildings. The sense of community and "live" theatre has been greatly diminished because of this. Starting with *A Chorus Line*, the average audience began to assume the music was pre-recorded. Like I said, an ugly notion.

In 1983, my Atlanta college friend, Victoria Tabaka (Judy Turner on Broadway for a while), gave me a ticket to see *A Chorus Line* on the night it became the longest running musical. This was one of the two greatest theatre experiences I've ever had—the original *Follies* and that one-night-only extravaganza, especially re-staged by Michael Bennett.

8. Who's That Woman?

MY VISIT WITH DOROTHY COLLINS

During my last year in Atlanta, a big gay disco called The Magic Garden opened and the managers wanted to set up a cabaret room there. Fine, but first they needed to do some soundproofing, which they didn't. A couple of members of our cabaret group went to see Barbara Cook (an Atlanta girl). She cut her show short because of the thumping bass coming from the dance floor. (God, I hate that noise!) We went back a few times to see other people such as Marcia Lewis and the problem had been resolved somewhat. But nothing was going to keep me from going to see Dorothy Collins's nightclub act. Four of us made a reservation on our night off from our show, and we went to see her. We arrived at The Magic Garden to find that we were the *only* reservation and that they were canceling the performance. I felt so terrible for her that I asked if I could speak to Ms Collins. I was led to her dressing room where she was sitting with her pianist, Sand Lawn. (How about that name!) I introduced myself and my three friends and told her how sorry we were, and that we would definitely be back the next week. Then a lightning bolt went through my head. "Could we take you to dinner tonight, you and Sand?" They looked at each other and said yes! We took them to a late-night gay gathering hole/restaurant. I thought we had a very successful evening, and she chatted about *Follies* and how all the old dames used to go in the bathroom and cry after they rehearsed the "Mirror Number." I hung on every word! We went back the next week and brought more people and thrilled to her "Losing My Mind." I swapped information with Sand and they came to see our little cabaret shows. Sand was enthusiastic about my playing. They came back to Atlanta later that year to do *I Do! I Do!* at the Harlequin Dinner Theatre. Her costar was Larry Shue, author of *The Foreigner*. Her version of "What Is a Woman?" was gorgeous. Not as great as "Losing My Mind," but it was a nice alternative. I seriously talked to Sand about my coming to New York and he encouraged me. Sand would eventually allow me to sublet his apartment (for free!) on 82nd and Columbus for six weeks when I made my final move to the city, and he suggested that I take any jobs that came through *his* telephone. I did! I kept up contact with Sand for quite a while until he left New York for good, but I never got to see Ms Collins again. What a wonderful singer and actress and person she was.

SIDE BY SIDE BY SONDHEIM

During one of the school trips, I saw *Side By Side By Sondheim* in New York City. It was fun, but a little precious for me, and I never cared for Julia McKenzie or her wimpy version of "Broadway Baby" or any of the British interpretations of Sondheim. I much prefer Dorothy Loudon's sock it to me take on the 1984 Tony Awards. She reclaimed the joy of that song for me. The British really do drain the fun and the humor out of everything. They ruined Broadway with *Cats, Evita, Les Miserables* (I know, they were French), *Phantom of the Opera, Miss Saigon, Aspects of Love, Sunset Boulevard*, etc. Not a moment of fun, happiness, joy or laughter anywhere in the whole bunch... I enjoy using Sondheim's song title "Every Day a Little Death" in describing British musical theatre.

I left Atlanta in the spring of 1977 for a few weeks and lived in a basement room on East 90th between Second and Third. The apartment belonged to director Jack Allison and I sublet it from a mutual friend. I went back to Atlanta for the summer to do *Side By Side By Sondheim* at the Alliance Theatre. Directed by Fred Chappell, it starred Diane Findlay (fantastic voice), Jack Blackton (an original standby for the show in New York), and local gal Jackie Alder, who was unhappy and left in the middle of the run to be replaced by Betty Glynn. The direction was so-so, Diane was great, Jack refused to sing "Marry Me a Little," preferring "Being Alive." Smart man, since "Marry Me a Little" is a terrible song—too much work and no payoff—and not up to the quality of the rest of the *Company* score. Jackie was just unhappy working at night in show business—she had done it and was finished. Betty Glynn, her replacement, was funny, but could never get the vocal intervals on "Oh no,

Anita, no" in "A Boy Like That," which was hilarious every single night. She developed such a phobia to it she finally had to just speak it.

During our run, the Broadway production auditioned replacements and Jack Blackton thought the two women (Diane and Betty) were so good they should be seen. Diane, Betty, and I flew to New York on our day off and auditioned. Sondheim was actually there! We did "Getting Married Today" with no Paul sections. My first "note" ever from Stephen Sondheim came that very day. He said, "Slow down the wedding sections and speed up the patter sections." He said to Diane, "Do the patter as fast as possible... because I know you can!" She was fantastic, but we flew back with no promise of anything.

During that summer while Dorothy Collins and Sand Lawn were in town doing *I Do! I Do!*, Sand suggested I take care of his apartment in New York. My parents didn't know what to think of any of this. I was 25 years old and had lived at home that summer. I was told much later that my father had gone to Jeanette Lang, my childhood piano teacher, and awkwardly asked her opinion of the move I was planning. She couldn't really advise him, and he shuffled away mumbling, "Well...maybe he'll be able to get some kind of job..." I heard this story when I was 58 years old and felt such compassion and love for my dad, knowing that he had been worried about me. He had good reasons to be worried, but... miracles do happen.

9. Who Wants to Live in New York?

People, upon meeting me or seeing me after an absence, sometimes let out a sigh and say, "Isn't it great. You've lived your dream, doing what you were born to do" or "You came to New York to pursue your destiny and have sustained such a great career doing the thing you love the most." This is exactly what director-choreographer Randy Skinner said to me as we were on our way into a staged reading of a musical called *Hurricane* (all together now, OY!). I looked him in the eye and studied his face to see if I thought I could tell him a little 21st Century-style truth. I decided I could. I smiled and said, "Well actually, Randy, I moved to New York City in 1978 because I was so obsessed with a dancer's cock that I thought I couldn't live without it." He chuckled because, I do believe, all people can do impulsive things when they are young. But after years of therapy, AA meetings, rehab programs, and gay group therapy (sheesh! what a nightmare, THE WORST), I have been relieved of much of the fantasy world whirling around in my head and have let go of as many secrets as I could. I can honestly say that I have NOT lived out any kind of romanticized showbiz dream.

The true story of how I ended up in New York City—the basic facts were—I was in lust with a hot 20-year-old dancer and I was not going to let him out of my sight. At 25, I was already deep into alcoholism, sexual-obsession, and not living in reality, so when the *amour* planned to return to New York City, BOOM! I was going too. He found himself a sublet apartment and I found one, too. It didn't occur to me that when he told me we would not be living together, I was also being told that the whole fling was over. Making a long story short, I was in a remote basement apartment on the upper Eastside for six weeks before I went back to Atlanta to do *Side By Side By Sondheim*. Then in denial, I officially moved back to New York and was given the old heave-ho!

After leaving Sand Lawn's apartment, I sublet a dreadful hole-in-the-wall on West 79th Street for two months. I finally settled into a sublet at 438 West 45th Street, just across the street from the tiny park where Salvatore Agron murdered two white teenagers in 1959 (thus becoming the inspiration for Paul Simon's atrocious megaflop 1998 musical, *The Capeman*). I have not left West 45th Street since. When my parents helped me move from Atlanta, my only material possession of importance was my 2,500 plus original cast/soundtrack vinyl record collection. I had a single bed in a room the size of the bed itself and just enough room for a chest of drawers and the record cabinet. Since my mother has taken photos of every moment of my life for which she was present, the pictures of me standing in the little apartment on West 45th Street next to my records help me realize that I must have been in an alcoholic blackout and was just coming out of it to discover myself alone in New York City. What was I doing here? What was I going to do? I felt completely abandoned and very much alone.

The answer was at the Wildwood Tavern on Columbus Avenue at 75th Street, or Boot Hill on Amsterdam Avenue, or Cahoots Bar at 79th, or any other dark bar I could find. The answer was to continue to get drunk every night and sweat off the hangover every day. I had enough money, unemployment insurance and savings to last a year, but I was just going to have to recover from the "geographic" I had just pulled; get over all of the heartbreak and sweat it out for a while. I managed to magically get work, but the most important daily project was to find a new love-of-my-life and drink lots and lots of wine and vodka tonics. In the fall of 1978, I was living in New York City, alone and hung over, with only those goals in mind. Now... did someone suggest something about my living my dream?

10. Take the Moment

Okay, okay... I *did* move to New York City for *one* other reason. Every club, dinner theater and community theater in Atlanta was going bust. The job I was currently doing was going downhill and I was drinking regularly during the three shows we did every night. I worked two jobs for three months to compile money. When it was time to make the move to New York, I had a whopping $600.00 saved, plus unemployment insurance, which went a long way back then. The "boyfriend" and I checked into our separate sublets on a Sunday night, and on Monday morning he had his first audition. Since I was not going to let him out of my sight... ever, I told him I was going with him.

The rehearsal studio was in the far West 40s and the audition was a dance call for the Jones Beach summer production of *Annie Get Your Gun* starring Lucie Arnaz and Harve Presnell. We walked into a lounge full of dancers. After they went into the audition room, I was left alone to look around. My intention was to wait, even if it took all day, just to make sure the "boyfriend" didn't run off with one of the other dancers.

About ten minutes passed and a man burst out of the studio and ran to the pay phone. He frantically started speaking to someone, saying, "Why aren't you here? It's 10 o'clock!" I put two and two together quickly and went over to interrupt him before he hung up. I asked him if his audition pianist had not shown up and he said that that was correct. I told him, "I can do it." He blew the other person off and led me into the dance hall. The boyfriend just stared at me as the man introduced me to everyone in the room, including Bert Michaels, the choreographer (an original Jet from *West Side Story* and a Farm Boy from the movie of *Gypsy*! I recognized him immediately) and Jay Blackton, the original conductor of *Oklahoma!*, for God's sake! I certainly knew who *he* was! I played the whole dance call, which used snippets of "I'm an Indian Too" (yes, they did that song back then; none of this politically correct crap they do nowadays) and "There's No Business Like Show Business." The boyfriend was cut from the audition very early. So much for my keeping track of his whereabouts! But this was very exciting for me. I had a job to do! I had to continue to play for the guys' singing auditions after the dancing was over.

Once through with that, Jay Blackton, the conductor, came over to the piano. He was a tiny man, walking with a cane. He looked at me and said, "You're my kind of piano player." Jesus! He gave my phone number to the musical contractor of the show, John Monaco, who was responsible for getting me my jobs on *I Remember Mama, Dancin', A Day in Hollywood/A Night in the*

Ukraine, and *The Rink*. And to top it off, Lucie Arnaz herself walked into the room at the end of the day, chatted with the guys behind the table, then came over to me, slapped the top of the piano and said, "Well, I hear you just blew into town today!"

Yes, it was my first day in New York. And I got paid. And I met and worked with several unbelievable Broadway luminaries. And I even had sex with the boyfriend that night. Life was good. For a minute.

11. Next

SWEENEY TODD

During my first year in New York City, I saw the original production of Stephen Sondheim's *Sweeney Todd*. Saw it three times. Not because I necessarily wanted to. I went with friends, my mom, etc. I thought that it was perfectly legitimate, valid, well produced and performed... but grim and long and ultimately... boring. Once you've seen *Sweeney Todd*, there are no surprises, and yet you still have to sit through "The Worst Pies in London," "Poor Thing," "Johanna," "Greenfinch and Linnet Bird" (that title! Jesus Christ, or as Jane Russell would say, "My oh my"), "God That's Good," "Kiss Me," "A Little Priest," which was barely funny the first time, and (gulp) "By the Sea" with its yoo-hoos. I did like the title song and "Not While I'm Around" was well written, but that's a lot of earnestness to sit through. Give me *Follies* any day. Or *Hello, Dolly!* I don't like opera and this was opera.

I always forget about *Sweeney Todd* when I start going through the list of the Sondheim canon in my head. There are very few moments that I cherish the way I cherish so much of his other shows. And inexplicably (to me), *Sweeney Todd* appears on more people's favorite lists than you can shake a stick at. Go figure. I don't understand how people can sit through it over and over again. I've seen other productions of it, none of which held a candle to the original, and found myself wishing they were over. I wouldn't trade my three trips that year to *Ballroom*, Michael Bennett's beautiful flop musical follow-up to *A Chorus Line*, for a boatload of *Sweeney Todd*s.

I've never had to do the show and never will. Sondheim was now on the back burner for me. He was becoming (dare I say?) pretentious. But not for long.

12. A Smattering of Shows
(and Some Lessons Learned)

I always loved playing auditions. In 1978, audition calls were still all-day affairs, and ANYONE could show up. This is my very favorite audition story from that time. Now, people are generally required to learn material from the show for which they are auditioning. They are given "kits" of recordings and music from the casting director. The auditionees then learn this material, usually on their own, and just show up. In 1978, however, it was different. Actors went to coaches to find suitable material, work through chosen songs, and prepare a "book" to include various styles and moods of songs to show off their best qualities. Often actors couldn't afford or didn't bother to seek out this kind of help. This is a funny story of what often happened under those circumstances. A young woman (probably in her teens) came in and handed me what looked like a brand-new song sheet straight from Colony Music (an infamously overpriced sheet music store in Times Square, now unfortunately gone) of "I Cain't Say No" from *Oklahoma!* The music looked so new that I could smell the ink drying on the page and it creaked when I opened the pages. This immediately said to me, "This young lady has probably never seen this sheet music before." I asked if she wanted to start at the top, and she politely said, "No, just the chorus." As everyone knows (right?), the lead-in to the chorus of "I Cain't Say No" is a two-bar vamp in the style of a country hoedown. I started the vamp and she began. Right away I thought, "Oh Lord, this child is really tone deaf." When we got to the bridge of the song, she stopped and asked if we could start over again. No problem. The same thing happened, but I was starting to recognize what she was singing. We had to start a third time, and I figured it out. She was not tone deaf. She was singing the melody perfectly… the melody to "I Enjoy Being a Girl" from *Flower Drum Song!* So, try the following at home (don't worry, no harm will come to you).

1. Sit at your piano with the music for "I Cain't Say No."
2. Start playing the chorus.
3. Sing the words to "I Cain't Say No," but sing them to the tune of "I Enjoy Being a Girl" while you are playing "I Cain't Say No."
4. Stop after the lyric "just when I ought to say nix" or you will go into a seizure.

The audition table, finally, after three attempts, told her thank you and she left the room baffled, as were the people behind the table. I explained to them what was happening. They didn't know what I was talking about (or care), but I never forgot it! I wonder if she ever figured it out. Lesson learned? Know the name of the song you are singing, who sang it originally, who wrote it, what show or movie (if any) it is from, what key you sing it in, what the sheet music sounds like, and make sure it is the same as what you want to sing. Are you taking the repeats written in the music or not? Are you old enough to be singing this song? Young enough? Do you know the song, do you like the song, do you know the words, do you know the words are called "lyrics," is it in a good key for you? If you changed the key to suit *you*, is it written in *that* key for the pianist and do you know what that key is? Do you know anything about music, can you count to 4, why are you here, did you bring your music with you…?

I know these are just sarcastic questions and not answers, but this is still fundamentally a problem today. I have dozens of stories such as this, but that is another book. And like I said, none of this research, study, and preparation is required anymore. Just use the materials sent to you, memorize "Defying Gravity," sing it *exactly* like Idina Menzel, and go home.

One of my first jobs in New York was a small 1978 revival of the 1954 Jerome Moross-John La Touche musical *The Golden Apple* at the York Theatre in the Church of the Heavenly Rest on Fifth Avenue and East 90th Street. We had to set up and break down the set before and after *every* performance. The cast included future Broadway star Dee Hoty and soap opera star Peter Boynton. This was hard work, but the results were worth it. Not only was it directed by York Theatre producer Janet Hayes Walker, who had appeared in the original production of *The Golden Apple* (and also played June in the original *Anyone Can Whistle*), but our musical director was Philip Fradkin from the original *Golden Apple* orchestra. I was starstruck.

During breaks, I would practice some of the dance music from *Follies* for fun and Phil would ask, "Why do you like that music so much?" Because it was the greatest show I had ever seen (and would *ever* see), I replied. He said, "Well, you know I was the original pianist for *Follies*." I didn't believe him. I thought he was trying to get into my pants. But I found out I was wrong… on the first count. He WAS the original pianist on *Follies*!

We had a choreographer, whose name I forget, who always wore white vinyl skirts, white vinyl Carnaby Street hats, and white vinyl go-go boots. She couldn't choreograph a step. (What was it with these New York choreographers? And the directors who hire them? I would get involved with a whole series of kooky choreographers over the years, many of whom never planned anything in advance and made up everything as they went along.)

But it didn't get in the way of *The Golden Apple* being a totally fulfilling theatre experience. Phil and I played two pianos and we had a percussionist. Phil was a fantastic pianist and it was easy to play with him. He was a great leader! What a thrill, and I think I got paid $25.00 for the entire thing (bus fare). For the life of me, I cannot recall how I got this job!

Nine years later, composer, musical director, dance arranger to the stars, David Krane (how do you like that plug, David?) asked me to assist him on my next York Theatre "apple" show, Bock and Harnick's *The Apple Tree*. I've always loved that show. And it was great fun with cast members John Sloman and Kathy Morath (who in the Passionella act was the spitting image of Patty Duke's Neely O'Hara from *Valley of the Dolls*). I played piano and synthesizer on this. Even after having played *Sunday in the Park with George*, I was still not comfortable with synthesizers and I was left on my own to figure out what to do. I always felt that the "stops" I chose sounded like a harp and bamboo pole, combined! The next show at the York should have been the operetta *Apple Blossoms*, but it never happened. Lessons learned on these two shows? It's simply a miracle to work with people who are trained musicians (rare), and greatly talented to boot. I was in awe of Phil and David.

Years later, Janet Hayes Walker hired me again to play for a huge York Theatre tribute to Hal Prince performed in the sanctuary of the Church of the Heavenly Rest. It was quite an evening, and I played for everyone except Liza Minnelli, Chita Rivera and Barbara Cook. That was Louis St. Louis and Wally Harper. Oh, and Janet asked Paul Gemignani to musically supervise the evening, which meant that *he* got *all* of the credit… and I did all of the work. But I was still in my "I'll do anything, just love me" phase.

I loved working with Linda Lavin, who was the first person to introduce me to Joan Lader, vocal therapist to the stars. Linda sang, what else, "You've Got Possibilities," which she originated in Hal Prince's *It's a Bird, It's a Plane, It's Superman*. My show queen head was about to burst! Maureen Brennan and Barbara Cook, two Cunegondes on the same bill. Maureen took the "Glitter and Be Gay" spot and tore the house apart and Barbara sang "In Buddy's Eyes" from *Follies*. Kevin Gray sang "Music of the Night" from *Phantom of the Opera* but croaked his way through it (he was vocally exhausted from touring with the show), making fun of the slowness and the length and the boringness of it all. I *loved* it. So did the audience. When he went for the last "…mee-use-ick of thah… (breath) naaaaaawwwww…" his voice cracked gloriously, causing him to giggle and the audience to cheer. It was a travesty… and perfect! The only time I EVER enjoyed an Andrew Lloyd Webber song.

Sorry for the detour, but speaking of Andrew "Void" Webber, the closest I ever got to him personally was having to do two song-exploring-sessions in his Trump Tower layout with his once and past wife, Sarah Brightman. She was very nice and he was nowhere around. This was for her first CD, which was eventually recorded in London. I recommended "I Remember" from Sondheim's television musical *Evening Primrose*. Approach this CD with caution. Especially her "Mr. Monotony."

And this reminds me of the session I had in my apartment with Renée Fleming running through songs for her "show tune" CD dueting with Bryn Terfel. Paul Gemignani would conduct, but he left me alone with her to sift through songs. Her repertoire was already pretty much set, but I couldn't help playing for her some things I thought she might enjoy. After each tune, her response was "Sweeeeet!" So, I gave up. She did record my suggestions of "Loving You" and "I Wish I Could Forget You," both from the new Sondheim musical, *Passion*. Approach this CD with caution, too! Especially "All the Wasted Time" from the Jason Robert Brown debacle, *Parade*. Not so sweeeeet! In fact, pretty heeeaaavvy-handed, if you ask me. Opera singers and show tunes are rarely a happy pairing unless the material is operetta.

Well now, this reminds me of the CD I worked on with Gemignani and opera legend Marilyn Horne. She wanted to do her own version of Eileen Farrell's "I've Got a Right to Sing the Blues" pioneering crossover "opera singer does popular songs" album, but with several guest opera stars of the male persuasion. It was titled *The Men in My Life* and was frankly a hoot to rehearse and record. My favorite track was Cole Porter's "Friendship" opera-singer style! I suggested all the ad libs for it. There was some Sondheim on this one, as well. Approach this CD with caution... No, actually, don't. Look for it on eBay. It's really kind of a hoot.

Back to the Hal Prince tribute. Len Cariou sang "These Are My Friends" from *Sweeney Todd*, and I think there was a *Pacific Overtures* number, "Pretty Lady." (Why not "Poems!?!") It was a festive evening with all the Sondheim material, and I felt that I did pretty well with all those personalities. There was a cast party at some club downtown and against my better judgment I decided to go. When I got there, my name was not on any guest list, so I was turned away. So much for the "music" of the night!

Lesson learned? You may have accompanied almost every single star on the bill that night, but you, the accompanist, do not exist. Just do your job and *go home*!

13. I Remember Mama

In the Spring of '79, I received my first call from that fateful first day when I stumbled into those *Annie Get Your Gun* auditions. John Monaco, musical contractor (the union guy who hires all the musicians for conductors), called and asked if I was available to play for three weeks of rehearsal for a new show coming to town.

I Remember Mama would be the last Richard Rodgers musical produced on Broadway before his death. It had lyrics and direction by Martin Charnin (an original Jet from *West Side Story*!) and starred Liv Ullmann and George Hearn (who would take over the title role in *Sweeney Todd*). There had been typical out-of-town trouble, resulting in a heart attack for and the firing of director Charnin, the replacement of the choreographer, and the firing of many ensemble members. Charnin was also relieved of his duties as lyricist. His replacement for lyrics was Raymond Jessel, and as director, Cy Feuer. New choreography would be by Danny Daniels. My old "pal" Jay Blackton of *Oklahoma!* fame was conducting.

I walked, terrified, from my 45th Street walkup to the Majestic Theatre on 44th Street and was escorted onto the stage by the stage management to meet conductor Blackton, director Feuer, lyricist Jessel, and choreographer Daniels. The set was already loaded in and I found myself standing at a real piano (part of the set design) in the middle of an old family house "unit" with a staircase and various levels. I sat at the piano and looked around at the activity. I was given the music to a brand-new song, "A Little Bit More," handwritten by a copyist. It was very straightforward, and I had to play it through for Blackton and Daniels. People were very busy and no one was paying attention to us. I kept studying the music, when there was a tap on my shoulder. I turned around and looked up and (gulp) was introduced to Richard Rodgers towering over me. I politely said hello and he moved on. I never met the other rehearsal pianist on the show and I was put on the sidelines and used very little.

Waiting in the wings at one point, I saw Liv Ullmann sitting patiently. I quickly introduced myself and told her how much I loved the film *Lost Horizon*... seriously and sincerely, I meant it. She was very nice. Twenty-five years later, I would be touring with Mandy Patinkin out west and Mandy's wife brought Ms Ullmann backstage to see him after our concert. At an appropriate moment, I re-introduced myself and reminded her of our brief encounter on her one-and-only Broadway musical venture. Ms Ullmann literally threw her head back and shrieked with laughter. "No-no-no-no-no-no-no," she said, laughing hysterically. She probably thought no one would remember that period of her career and certainly not cross her path. That's all she could do was laugh and say "No-no-no-no-no," as if to say, "Please don't remind me it ever happened!" (I keep doing this kind of thing—reminding people of their most unpleasant theatrical memories. It seemed that every time I enjoyed someone's performance, it turned out to have been a traumatic experience for them. It never failed. What the hell is wrong with me, for Pete's sake?)

Over the three weeks of rehearsal, I rarely played but got to observe. I did have to play one staging rehearsal in the lobby of the Majestic for a song called "Easy Come, Easy Go" sung by the character of Uncle Chris, played by George S. Irving, and the children in the show. It was meant to be a sort of ragtime charm song. Danny Daniels was devising a simple cakewalk for them and I must have played for an hour. At one point the stage manager (damn him!) questioned my tempo, but Daniels said, "Leave him alone, it's perfect."

After that day I was free to watch. The most exciting moment was the orchestra call for a new piece of dance music in the production number, "Ev'ry Day (Comes Something Beautiful)." This was my very first Broadway experience of being involved with an original Broadway show while it was going through its growing pains. It was incredibly exciting to hear a new piece of dance music orchestrated and played for the very first time, a Norwegian folk dance that brought the number to a climax. Thrilling to be present for it.

My job was done, but I was given an opening night ticket. Wow! For me? I showed up for the performance and found myself seated next to a familiar woman. I thought for a second and said, "Aren't you Annie McGreevey? I saw you sing 'Another Hundred People' in *Company* and oh!... you were part of that great duo in *The Magic Show*!" (Terrible show, but I didn't say that.) I think she was happy to be recognized, so we chatted it up. It turns out she was married to Bob Gunton, the soon-to-be-star of *Evita*, and that they lived on West 45th Street near me. We checked out our seats and wondered if a mistake had been made. We were third row orchestra center and looking back into the auditorium we saw Michael Bennett and Donna McKechnie *behind* us. An usher came down and checked our tickets. We had been seated incorrectly! We ended up in the back row of the balcony. "That's more like it!" we said. The show started and the first big family number led by Liv Ullmann was the new song, "A Little Bit More." At the end of the song, Annie whispered to me. "Those kids! They sing so sharp!" It was true. Check out the Tony Awards broadcast from that year.

I Remember Mama was never a piece of material I was interested in as a play or film. Those warm family comedy-dramas did not make for interesting stage musicals. The movies *Meet Me in St. Louis, Centennial Summer,* and *Summer Holiday* were finely detailed, pastel Technicolor pieces of cinema, enhanced by a handful of ditties, but *I Remember Mama* did not lend itself to being blown up to a full 2-hour 45-minute, 20-song evening. The show got mediocre reviews and ran only a few months. Sitting next to Annie reminded me of my first school trip to New York and sitting through Richard Rodgers's *Two by Two.* Even after that production, I still couldn't believe that a show by an old master might not be up to par. I had not paid much attention to Rodgers's lesser works—*Allegro, Me and Juliet,* and *Pipe Dream*—and I still couldn't stay awake for side two of the *Rex* original cast album. But it was disconcerting to sit through another live performance of a Richard Rodgers musical flop.

This might be a good time to share my favorite Rodgers and Hammerstein shows, songs, and moments. Of course, the movie of *South Pacific* blew my five-year-old mind. I still want to find my own Bali Ha'i and live there. And I love Mary Martin's crystal-clear diction and pitch-perfect performance on the original cast recording. After that, the Atlanta Theatre Under the Stars productions of *South Pacific, Oklahoma!, Carousel,* and *The Sound of Music* did not make as big an impression on me. But as I said before, the original cast recording of *Flower Drum Song* was my breakthrough into learning to play the piano. I finally saw the movie version of *Oklahoma!* in a Todd-AO re-release at the Georgia Cinerama movie theatre in the mid-1960s. This for me was a perfect movie musical and the Agnes DeMille dream ballet is haunting and erotic and gorgeously filmed.

The movie version of *The Sound of Music* was a life-changing experience, and I particularly loved the two-piano arrangement of "My Favorite Things" as Maria and the von Trapp kids run around exploring Salzburg. Inspired movie musical making. The movie of *Carousel* has always been a rather drab sit-through, although the music is beautifully sung and tremendously played by the 20th Century Fox orchestra. Finally, Nicholas Hytner's 1994 Lincoln Center revival made *Carousel* work for me, with its fanciful settings and brilliant staging. *The King and I* has always been a satisfactory theatre experience for me, from Ann Blyth at Theatre Under the Stars to the 1979 revival with Yul Brynner and Constance Towers (with a vacation replacement by Angela Lansbury), and even the redesigned revival starring Donna Murphy and Lou Diamond Phillips. Both Broadway revivals honored the original and brought new delights. I played all the auditions for the Donna

Murphy production. And of course, the film version is another perfect movie musical. No other movie is like this movie—a one-of-a-kind extravaganza—especially with its "Small House of Uncle Thomas Ballet." In fact, all the filmed ballets and extended sequences in the Rodgers and Hammerstein films would make a splendid feature film—*That's Entertainment: Rodgers and Hammerstein Style!* In addition to the ballet from *The King and I,* I'd include the *Oklahoma!* dream ballet, the *Carousel* numbers "June is Busting Out All Over" and "Louisa's Ballet," the Bali Ha'i sequence featuring "Younger Than Springtime" from *South Pacific,* the two contrasting dream ballets from *Flower Drum Song* (the dramatic "Love Look Away" and the thoroughly musical comedy "Sunday Ballet"), and end with the Salzburg montage "Do Re Mi" number from *The Sound of Music.* Twenty years of the best of musical theatre/movies in ninety minutes.

But back to *I Remember Mama.* The score for *I Remember Mama* was not recorded for a long time and eventually featured Sally Ann Howes and some of the original cast. I have never listened to it.

It was wonderful to meet Richard Rodgers, Jay Blackton, Danny Daniels, Liv Ullmann, George Hearn, and George S. Irving, but the person from *I Remember Mama* who had the most impact on my life was not present. That was original lyricist-director Martin Charnin. I would be amazed at how much time I spent with this colorful, earnest man. More to come!

14. Gwen Verdon

As a child, I saw on television such movie musical masterpieces as *Meet Me After the Show* with Betty Grable, *The "I Don't Care" Girl* with the super-bubbly, effervescent, eye-popping (her eyes, not mine) Mitzi Gaynor, and *On the Riviera* starring the always annoying Danny Kaye. I was not aware at the time, but there was a wonderful dancer backing up all three of these stars who would soon become Broadway's greatest dancing star. Her one starring musical role on film was, of course, *Damn Yankees.* I never saw Gwen Verdon "live" until the 1975 Broadway production of *Chicago.* Prior to that I knew her strictly through original cast recordings of *Damn Yankees, Can-Can, New Girl in Town, Redhead,* and *Sweet Charity.* There was little chance of my seeing her perform, but thanks to YouTube and DVD releases, I have now seen her in many Ed Sullivan featured dance numbers and various television specials. My personal favorite Verdon moments are the numbers in *Damn Yankees,* the Can-

Can number in the 1952 *The Merry Widow*, "Beale Street Blues" from the Mitzi Gaynor film, the "No Talent Joe" number from the Grable film, the hilarious "Mexican Breakfast" dance from *The Ed Sullivan Show*, and the "I'm a Brass Band" number from *Sweet Charity*, also shown on *The Ed Sullivan Show*. There are some wonderful color clips from the "Garden of Eden Ballet" in *Can-Can* that were hiding in someone's private collection, but can be seen on the special edition DVD release of the film version of *Can-Can*.

After my fifteen minutes of work on *I Remember Mama*, John Monaco asked if I wanted to do some afternoon put-in rehearsals for replacements on Bob Fosse's *Dancin'*. Since I had been sneaking into the second and third acts of that show for quite some time, I was familiar with the music and gladly accepted. I was to show up and get trained by Sande Campbell (the legendary Broadway pianist) who was moving on from the show. Sande dumped the gargantuan 11" by 14" rehearsal piano books in my lap, my first Broadway score direct from the copyist's office. (Had no one ever heard of 8.5" by 11" paper?) Sande had notated all of the choreography in the music, so the pianist could quickly find where the dance captain wanted to begin. In this case, dance captain and Fosse right hand, Kathryn Doby, was putting in two new dancers. I barely played for the first couple of weeks, which gave me time to practice. I particularly loved the "Sing, Sing, Sing" number. I just kept my ears open to hear anything these Broadway professional dancers had to say. Fosse had recently filmed *All That Jazz*, so there was a lot of discussion about the film and occasionally a dancer would drop by and Doby would tell me, "He's in *All That Jazz*."

As it would turn out, Kathryn Doby had a huge part in the movie, as well. One day she was talking to the dancers and I overheard her say she was leaving for Los Angeles. During a break, I asked her if she was leaving the show and, if so, who was taking over for her. She casually said, "Oh, Gwen…" Oh! So, I would be spending the next few weeks in a studio with Gwen Verdon? Is that right? (DEAD FAINT!)

Ms Verdon was very quiet, slow, and methodical in teaching. We went to various dance studios over the summer. Of the two dancers initially rehearsing, one was Terri Treas, who would go to Los Angeles and do some film and television work in the 1980s and '90s. And for a few days a young ballet dancer, Robert LaFosse, came in to do a couple of solos from the show. Fifteen years later he had begun choreographing after a career as a ballet star. We would see each other again in 1995 when he choreographed the "Cookie Ballet" for Herb Ross in the concert version of Sondheim's *Anyone Can Whistle* at Carnegie Hall. Another decade would pass before we found each other sitting together at the Prince Theatre in Philadelphia for *Lady in the Dark*, which he had also choreographed.

At one point I had to go to the Broadhurst Theatre, where *Dancin'* was playing, to do a short put-in rehearsal and audition. I was under the stage, so I only *heard* the voice of Bob Fosse. I had been instructed on the traditional Bob Fosse audition routine. It was danced to the song "Tea for Two," the first eight bars and a two-bar tag of my choosing. Very short with a lot packed into it for the dancers. I would later notice that in the film *All That Jazz*, the opening sequence, although set to the tune of the obnoxious pop song "On Broadway," was actually built on the "Tea for Two" combination—a beautifully edited montage. The reason I say the "obnoxious" pop song "On Broadway," is because that particular piece of music, although about making it on Broadway, has lyrics such as "...play this here gee-tar," which is not only unsophisticated and poor grammar but, frankly, no one ever "made it on Broadway" playing a "gee-tar." (Of course, now we have Elvis and Jerry Lee Lewis impersonators on Broadway. Broadway catches up with 1950s Vegas in the 21st century! Way to go, Broadway!)

Dancin' had a lot of contemporary music (not my favorite), including a disco "Yankee Doodle Dandy," but the big band "Sing, Sing, Sing" number put the show over for me. Eventually I was asked to try subbing on actual performances playing the second keyboard part. This would be my Broadway debut. I called my mother in Atlanta before I left for the performance. "Light the candles! Get the ice out! It's today!"

It wasn't a hard book to play, except that this was the early days of synthesizers. In the pit, I was mostly on my feet, playing one of four plastic electric keyboards stacked on top of each other. There I was, my Broadway debut, reaching to hold one finger down on one key while reaching to punch buttons on another keyboard. Frankly, I couldn't discern what I was playing—the keyboard sounds were all indistinguishable from each other. I lasted about ten performances and they stopped calling, which was just fine and dandy with me.

Back to Gwen Verdon. I couldn't help it, but I felt I had to engage her *somehow*. So maybe for the first time, it occurred to me that I could "hint at" or "speak to her" by playing a one-fingered phrase of some obscure music from her theatre career. I thought about it and during a break played quietly and unobtrusively (or so I thought) the "Pickpocket Tango" music from *Redhead*, her Tony Award-winning show from 1959. She was warming up before rehearsal and looked up in shock. "What *is* that you're playing?" I had the sense to refrain from being rude and saying "Guess!" and told her. She responded with a slight smile but seemed to be amused by it. I thought I was very clever and teased her a few more times over the weeks, staying away from the tunes from *Damn Yankees*—much too obvious. This little routine would become habitual for me over the years (more about this later).

Ms Verdon gave me one piece of advice which I have never forgotten and am always aware of when I play. I had always been afraid of "rushing" or not being able to keep a steady beat, but she told me one day, "You slow down when you play softer. Don't do that." Words of wisdom from Gwen Verdon—to the point, direct, and very helpful. I can still hear her saying it. I was horrified, but it was great coming from her. I would like to say I saw more of her after that summer, but that was the end of our association. An early quick brush with greatness and one piece of good advice.

I love the dancing in old films, and particularly love it any time a dance company re-creates original choreography from films and Broadway shows. The American Dance Machine did that in the '70s and '80s and there is some wonderful film footage available. Gwen Verdon assisted the fabulous choreographer Jack Cole before her Broadway career with Fosse. Some of my favorite Jack Cole film sequences are Rita Hayworth's Greek ballet from *Down to Earth*, all of the numbers in *The "I Don't Care" Girl*, Marilyn Monroe's "Diamonds Are a Girl's Best Friend" and Jane Russell's "Ain't There Anyone Here For Love," both from *Gentlemen Prefer Blondes*, "No Talent Joe" and "Betting on a Man" from Betty Grable's *Meet Me After the Show*, the title song from Cole Porter's *Les Girls*, and the many dream sequences and dances from *Three For the Show*, also with Betty Grable. Of his Broadway work translated to the screen, we are lucky to have the 1955 *Kismet* as a record, but not much more of his theatre work exists. I have always been curious about his work on the legendary flop *Mata Hari*.

I was first aware of Bob Fosse in the film of *Damn Yankees* and love all the numbers from that film, especially "Whatever Lola Wants" and "Two Lost Souls." I was disappointed in the music used and the choreography (not the dancers' performances) in the film *All That Jazz*, so my hat is off to the faithful "to a tee" film version of *Sweet Charity*, a much more complete representation of his style. That film, if nothing else, is one great Fosse number after another, my favorites being "The Rich Man's Frug," "I'm a Brass Band," "There's Gotta Be Something Better Than This" and, of course, "Big Spender." Fosse's film appearances as an actor gave us the wonderful dream dance in *Give a Girl a Break* with Debbie Reynolds—where the film runs backwards at one point, so the confetti is falling up!—and the two great *Kiss Me, Kate* numbers, "Tom, Dick or Harry" and "From This Moment On."

I've always wondered what the dancing was like for his Broadway shows *New Girl in Town*, with the infamous "Brothel Ballet," and the most obscure Best Musical Tony-winner ever, *Redhead*, with its specialty numbers, dream ballet, and "Pick Pocket Tango." Fortunately, his work on *The Pajama Game* is preserved in the film.

In 1973, on one of the school trips to New York, there was a show I was not looking forward to on our list. I was not excited by the cast album, which was very rock-oriented and badly sung and, like the original *Follies*, was heavily edited. Quite to my surprise and delight, thanks to the wonderful work of Fosse with his orgy ballets and the soft shoe "Manson Trio," and the magical work of set designer Tony Walton, the original production of *Pippin* was that rare amalgam of all that is wonderful and classic about Broadway, with just enough contemporary edge without being the bland, ugly, desperate messes that *Hair* and *Jesus Christ Superstar* were. It became one of my favorites for a long time and the only work of Stephen Schwartz that I can tolerate. Fosse's 1975 follow-up, *Chicago*, was so completely under-appreciated that year because of *A Chorus Line*, that it is a vague memory in my mind. But I do know that it was far more beautiful, with its great Tony Walton neon scenery, than the rip-off revival that has been running for more than 20 years now.

Fosse's last *somewhat* original show, *Big Deal*, had only one number worthy of him. Publicly, Fosse had expressed his impatience with collaborators and chose to use old 1930s songs instead. So, no original music here, but if he was going to cheat at least he was drawing from good sources. However, Gordon Lowry Harrell's contemporary disco arrangements dashed that hope and left a weird, colorless hybrid of a show with only faint re-creations of other more famous numbers.

One comment on the film version of *Cabaret*. His work was based on Ron Field's stage version and, unfortunately, because of that film no one can figure out what to do with this show now. Every bit of subtlety, charm, warmth, and care has been sapped from this show since its original production closed on Broadway. And the attempts to impose the ugliness of the film onto recent revivals have made this show look worn-out and no longer the subtle, often lovely show that it could be, with Alan Cummings' performance as the MC being the nadir of its history.

One more Fosse-related favorite for me is the beautiful, remote, throaty-voiced wonder, Ann Reinking. I didn't notice her in *Pippin*, except in photographs, went wild over her in *Over Here*, missed her in *Goodtime Charley*, third-acted *Dancin'* multiple times to see her trumpet solo dance in "Sing, Sing,

Sing," chuckled when "She Got Annie" in that film, and loved her playing herself in *All That Jazz*. I had the great pleasure of meeting and working with her on Mandy Patinkin's original *Dress Casual* concert and again on the Patti LuPone-Mandy Patinkin concerts. I am proud to have a dance arrangement choreographed by Ms Reinking to Murray Grand's "April in Fairbanks" on rolling desk-chairs mocking an ice-skating ballet. One of my favorite preserved pieces of choreography on video is the "Charlie's Place" number from *Over Here* on the 1973 Tony Awards broadcast. I never hear any talk about this performance and have had a tough time finding a watchable copy, but there is a perfect knockout jitterbug with John Mineo backed by (and get this list) Treat Williams, Marilu Henner, the Andrews Sisters, and a baby John Travolta! There are other brilliant captures of Ms Reinking on video—"Me and My Baby," "I'm a Brass Band," and even a *pas de deux* on the Oscars. I was thrilled to get to work with these top dancers no matter how briefly.

15. It's the Hard Knock Life

ANNIE

I greatly enjoyed working on three shows with director-writer-former *West Side Story* Jet, Martin Charnin. The first was the 1979 Third National Tour of *Annie* starring Harve Presnell (the best of all Daddy Warbucks), Patricia Drylie (a terrifically understated Miss Hannigan, straight from a terrific turn as Dorothy Loudon's pal in *Ballroom*), Deborah Jean Templin (never was there a better Grace Farrell, she got every laugh and more, a terrific performer) and Michael Leeds, a super-sexy Rooster Hannigan. I even liked our child star, Roseanne Sorrentino. This was my first National Tour, a solid year, 26 cities for two weeks a piece. An old-fashioned show business tour. Everyone in the company—adults, children, dogs, and mothers—had a footlocker that we placed outside our motel (and I do mean *motel*) rooms to be shipped to the next city.

I was hired as the rehearsal pianist, pit pianist, and assistant conductor, even though I had never held a baton in my hand. Let's get the depressing part over with. I had to conduct a total of two weeks out of the whole year. And that, folks, was the end of my conducting career!

Harve Presnell was very encouraging about my conducting. I tended to flail my arms wildly when conducting, and I think he liked being able to see the motion out front. Other than that, the tour was a wonderful experience, full of hangovers, sex in every port, close friendships, family values, trips to local health clinics for social diseases, trips to Disneyland, the fabulous gay Parliament House Motel in Orlando, the "whoopee!" night life in Cleveland, pot brownies in Milwaukee, the Melrose hotel in gay Dallas, the gay Montrose area in Houston, the most bizarre Christmas ever in Indianapolis in a Chinese Restaurant with the entire cast (dogs and mothers included), a snowy winter in Baltimore, conducting the show in front of my family in Atlanta, my first and last car accident (driving got in the way of my drinking, so I quit driving), my first sleazy guy with tattoos in New Orleans, waking up in an Oklahoma City suburb with a gun pointed in my face (it was just lying there on top of a basket of *House Beautiful* magazines next to the bed of my previous night's assignation), my "lineman for the county" in Pittsburgh, trying to get high on over-the-counter codeine-laced 222 tablets in Hamilton, Canada, *You Can't Stop the Music* and the death (hallelujah!) of disco in Buffalo, midnight at the *Rocky Horror Picture Show* in Jacksonville with a hippie woodwind player from our orchestra pit (who could have been the love of my life if I had only been paying attention), attempting to read Theodore Dreiser's *An American Tragedy* while snorting poppers and waiting for a trick to arrive at my room, living on peanuts and orange juice and diet pills (oh, and did I mention alcohol?), seeing *Cruising* in Columbus, Ohio with two gay cast members who were appalled by its depiction of gays (why be appalled? It was an accurate depiction of our behavior!), and 416 performances of *Annie*, counting the matinees during which I fell asleep.

Putting the show together in the burnt-out dilapidated Broadway Arts rehearsal studios (where *All That Jazz* was filmed, or at least replicated on a soundstage) was exciting and a not too difficult job. Meeting Charles Strouse (a wonderful songwriter, more on him later) and choreographer Peter Gennaro, legends all!

Near the end of the rehearsals, before we left town, we participated in something I had faintly heard about, but took as a casual thing until the day came.

"Come down to the Alvin Theatre at noon. We're going to do a gypsy run-through of the show for some of our friends," said Annie Sullivan, the stage manager. "Great! My mom's in town. Can I invite her?" "Sure!"

I showed up with my mom the next day and there was a line stretching down the street.

"What's going on?" I asked.

"Oh, just the gypsy run-through for some of our friends..." and 1,500 other top echelon people from the theatrical community! What?!? Oh no! I couldn't possibly! And Arthur Greene, the conductor, as conductors always do, thought it was a good idea for me to be ONSTAGE at a beat-up rehearsal piano while he conducted FROM THE ORCHESTRA PIT! BRILLIANT! I couldn't see him from where I was seated but was expected to follow his every move. There was a perfectly good piano in the pit, but nooooooo! That would cost money for a sound man. Though terrified, I got through it, not without many ugly scowls from the conductor. The show was spectacular, the audience great, and my mom loved it. I'm just glad I didn't know what I was in for the night before. I might have disappeared into the Hudson River at dawn.

Martin Charnin, warts and all, was a good old-fashioned director with a huge ego and personality, a great sense of humor, and an absolute insistent control over the company with no interest in taking "guff" from actors. It was his way or the highway, thank you very much! I felt led by him, even as a rehearsal pianist. There was a lot of grumbling and unhappiness among the twelve-person ensemble, so at the end of the first six months of the tour we lost eleven out of the twelve. Dick Decareau was the only one who stayed. Fortunately, for the second six months, we had a new, spirited, happy-go-lucky group including my old, old, old, old, old, old friend J.B. Adams, Gail Pearson, the hilarious Chuck Rule (never sober onstage, not once, he hated children, begged stage management to fire him; "No, Chuck, we love you too much," was the answer to that), several Jills and Saras and Davids. The show kicked into high gear onstage and off and we were in Florida for the spring.

Charnin stepped in to direct the new ensemble in Jacksonville. My new-old pal J.B. had told me he sang for his audition the lovely "The Good-Time Girl" from *Over Here* and I said "Oh, I loooved that show." The song is also known as the "V.D. Polka." J.B. also told me that at the end of his audition, Charnin said "Never... ever... ever sing that song again! It's distasteful!" I thought this was hilarious. After all, he got the job! So, on a break during the put-in rehearsal, I started playing "The V.D. Polka." J.B. frantically motioned from the stage for me to shhhussshhh. But all the way from the back of the house came Charnin's voice on the microphone, "Paul, what's that song you're playing?" and being so grateful for the attention from Charnin, I yelled back, "J.B.'s audition song, 'The V.D. Polka!'" J.B. and I are friends to this day, but I believe this was the moment that my horrible tradition of "theme songs" was solidified. Thirty years of making up theme songs from people's most dire theatrical experiences and grabbing their attention by serenading them with them. Boy, did I need attention. Needy and how!

My final city on the tour was Hartford, Connecticut, and I rode home on the train to New York with Michael Leeds and Katharine Buffaloe, our Lily St. Regis. I looked like a shriveled up, Cajun-blackened lizard from booze, dieting, and over-tanning. Exhausted, but grateful to be going home, I had paid my rent a year in advance to preserve my room and my record collection. It was only $75.00 a month, so it was worth it.

By the way, the *Annie* tour had one notable link to Stephen Sondheim. Peter Gennaro's assistant choreographer was Mary Jane Houdina, who played young Hattie in the original *Follies* and provided the tap dancing in the basement of the Winter Garden for one of the greatest musical numbers of all time, "Who's That Woman." This supreme production number, staged by Michael Bennett, not only used a "click track" (pre-recorded voices) but utilized the show's dancers tapping on a hardwood floor in the basement and piped into the stage speakers in order to enhance the aural impact of this mighty musical number. I was so excited to meet her and kept playing the dance music from the number for her. She would do all the Michael Bennett choreography for me right there. All for little me.

UPSTAIRS AT O'NEALS'

I next met up with Martin Charnin in 1982, when I got a phone call while in Atlanta taking a long-needed break. It was from composer, musical director, dance arranger to the stars, David Krane, who wanted to interview me as a possible second of two pianos that would accompany a new revue, *Upstairs at O'Neals'*, directed by Charnin.

I flew back up to New York and agreed to meet David at my apartment. He came in and told me he would be arranging two piano parts for a collection of songs and sketches collected and directed by Charnin which would play the O'Neals' restaurant on 43rd street... upstairs! Great location for me. I was "in" already, ready, willing and almost sober. David said that he had heard me play *The Golden Apple* at the York Theatre and, I believe, I got a recommendation from Martin Charnin himself. As we were sitting on the sofa talking, the scene became the classic comedy bit where Krane kept leaning closer into my face and moving closer to me. I would shift an inch or two, and he would shift an inch or two. He kept talking, giving me his background and credentials, but moving closer and closer until I got to the edge of the sofa. I held my ground and went nose to nose. I had never been on the "casting couch" before and I wasn't about to be now. Fortunately, I got the job and David and I have compared notes since then. He has confessed that that *was* exactly what was happening that day. We've laughed about it. I don't care, and I wish to God someone would try to seduce me today!

The cast for the revue was already chosen: Michon Peacock, Richard Ryder, Douglas Bernstein, Sarah Weeks, Randall Edwards, and "Baby Bebe" Neuwirth. Mary D'Arcy would replace Edwards in the middle of the run and Neal Benari, Bob Freschi, and Kate McAteer came into the company, as well.

The show was a delight to rehearse. The writers who contributed a third of the show were on hand, namely David Crane with a 'C' and Marta Kauffman, who would go on to make a fortune from various sitcoms including *Friends*. The original show was in two acts and was recorded on the Painted Smiles label. After fantastic, unbelievable reviews, we had to battle for audiences with another little show that opened at exactly the same time uptown at Palsson's Supper Club on West 72nd Street. A little show called *Forbidden Broadway*. *Upstairs* ran for nine months. *Forbidden* ran for 99 years!

We had trouble getting an audience for *one* performance a night, so, of course, Charnin cut out a quarter of the show, pushed the two acts together, and we did the show *twice* a night… two seatings… which cut our already meager audiences in half. At times we played to only two or three tables. It was still a great show and we had an occasional celebrity like Elizabeth Montgomery in the audience. One night, Kitty Carlisle Hart and Irene Selznick sat right down front. Whoopee! When Richard Ryder did his "Morosco Blues" number (about the demolition of Broadway theatres) and came to his line about "Cee-leste Holm being out front picketing," I saw the two *grande dames* turn to each other, put their hands up to their mouths, and "tee hee" at the little joke about their fellow dame. But mostly we played this extremely sophisticated little show to early '80s out-of-towners who had never been out in a public place, let alone known anything about culture. The performers very often had to stop and lecture the audience. This was bad, sad, and a sign that the Jerry Springer generation was about to take over the world. One night, Doug Bernstein had as a guest one of the crown princes from "Franistan" or some such place and it was very exciting. I wanted to at least be introduced, but Doug said that only Mary D'Arcy would be given the honor. I whined "whhyyyyy?" and he said that I "would only scare the prince." WELL!

David Krane moved on to other jobs and I took over on first piano while D'Arcy's husband Karl Jurman took over my part. (Jurman has been the conductor of *Lion King* all these years.) And finally, I left to take my first and last summer stock job. Jimmy Roberts, who made a fortune from co-writing *I Love You, You're Perfect, Now Change*, came in to finish the run.

I was still drinking "a little," knocking them back at the bar now and then, but had been on better behavior throughout the run. I went back to see the show a couple of times and became one of those loud, belligerent drunks sitting in the front row. Charnin was there one of those evenings and came face to face with me on the stairs. He looked me in the eye and said, "You're a drunk!" Ouch! Caught!

After the show closed, Charnin took all of David Krane's piano vocal charts and "disappeared" them. David had not copied them and ever since, when someone asks me for some of the music, I have to say "sorry, doesn't exist!" Oh, and Baby Bebe married our bartender, won a Tony Award for the revival of *Sweet Charity*, went to Hollywood, got on *Cheers*, divorced the bartender and became the Bebe Neuwirth of Bebe Neuwirth fame.

The best thing about *Upstairs at O'Neals'* was that after we opened, I only rarely tied one on. But on December 22nd, I wandered into the Crossroads Bar, a sleazy neighborhood gay establishment on Ninth Avenue at 55th Street, to drown my sorrows. My father had died (more on that horror later) and I was lonely and depressed. A couple of nights earlier a guy across the bar had gestured with his hand for me to *smile*. I blew him off, but this night he was there, and I decided to smile. We chatted, went to his place, and after a night of bad sex were "married" the next day. Thus began my 12-year relationship with Charlie Stramiello, my Italian Jew from the Bronx. We had a great time for six years and, after his HIV diagnosis, another torturous six years until his death in October of 1994. He courted me at the show, sent me flowers, sent me a stripper(!) on my birthday (witnessed by the entire cast *and* Martin Charnin), brought his best friend Brenda to meet me... So, what more could a guy want? I was his. My one and only true love. To this very day there has been no one else!

BACK ON THE TOWN

A couple of years passed, including *The Rink* and *Sunday in the Park with George* (these stories to come), and conductor Paul Gemignani asked me to do a new project—a new Broadway revue called *Back On The Town* starring Nancy Walker and directed by Martin Charnin. There would be a leading man. Anthony Holland (from *All That Jazz*) was mentioned but never brought up again. The material for the show was being commissioned and auditioned by Charnin from many young writers. And finally, there would be an ensemble of twelve versatile actors auditioned through the casting office of Shirley Rich, former casting director for Harold Prince, specifically for *Company*. Rich did many, many screening auditions for people, having them pull out all their comedy stops. These auditions were sublime. It was the mid-1980s and there were still remnants of ancient vaudeville performers coming out of the woodwork.

My two favorite auditions were by Myrna LaBow and Lon Hoyt. Myrna had always come to open calls and was probably in her 60s. She was a blonde ex-showgirl type who loved to strip down to a leotard and put a little crown of feathers or a tiara on her head and sing some endless piece of special material, all meant to show her sexy, Ann-Margret, kittenish side. On this audition, I believe she chose "Adelaide's Lament." All of it... with props... lots of them. It came across as Edith Bunker in a blonde wig singing on her vocal "break" for eleven minutes. Shirley Rich let her do the whole thing! Lon Hoyt, young handsome composer-musical director, came in with a piece of his own material he wished to accompany himself on. He sat down at the piano and started to sing a "funny" song about a devastating romantic breakup. A very early precursor to the dreary Jason Robert Brown stuff. When he got to the gist of the number he was wailing the lyric, "You're an asshole..." Shirley Rich jumped up from her seat, started screaming at him, and ordered him out of her audition. Lon looked at me with "uh-oh" in his eyes and ran out of the room. Shirley paced and sputtered, "I will not put up with that trash, that is not funny, these people don't know what funny is...!"

As we got to the callbacks, Gemignani, Charnin, and Nancy Walker herself were all in the room. These went on for days and days. I made a lot of money. Some of the contenders were Barbara Walsh (whose audition material Charnin wanted to buy for the show), Lauren Mitchell (of the upcoming *Into the Woods* and future producer of *High Society*), and Walter Bobbie (possibly the luckiest man in show business; he directed the still running revival of *Chicago*). But most auditions were greeted by a chorus from Charnin or Walker (or both in tandem) of "Do you think that's funny?" or "Do you think the misfortunes of others are amusing?" or "What makes you think filthy language is funny?" as one auditionee after another slinked out of the room with his tail between his legs. Eventually, a cast was picked and a few offers went out.

Now came the big confrontation. Charnin had assembled, auditioned, or commissioned a lot of material, but no one—I repeat, no one—had heard a note of music or one word of dialogue. Not even the Shuberts or Nancy Walker herself. He was determined to keep it all under wraps. One day after auditions he brought young composer-lyricist Jonathan Sheffer in to play an opera spoof for everyone. The number would have Nancy Walker as a charwoman mopping up after a Met performance. An impresario would discover she had a glorious voice (dubbed from offstage) but could only make those glorious sounds while clutching her mop. Sans mop, she would revert back to sounding like Nancy Walker, so she would have to make her Met debut with a mop in her hands. After about 40 minutes of opera spoof by Sheffer, Nancy Walker stopped the audition, stood up and announced "This is NOT FUNNY! What makes you think this is FUNNY? I can't do this material! I demand to see the material in this show before I continue another minute!" A couple of days later, I found myself in a private room with Charnin rehearsing and being the first to hear the material. He and I alone worked on the songs and prepared to do a special presentation for Nancy Walker, the Shuberts, and other backers. The day arrived and Charnin began reading *every* word of the script (in defiance) from the page numbers to the copyright dates to the stage directions to the periods at the end of sentences. In other words, "She wants to hear the material, she's going to hear ALL of the material!" Two hours later, we finished Act One and Charnin put a little black plastic box on the piano and opened it. Out popped two little plastic hands clapping while the sound of roaring applause played. The Shuberts got up and left and Nancy Walker proceeded to make a speech. "This is crap. What the hell makes you think I could or WOULD do such lousy material? I cannot and will not do this!" THE END. Show over. Not another day or minute was there of *Back On The Town* starring Nancy Walker. Well, at least I made some dough off the auditions.

But it was not the end. Charnin and I auditioned this material for a year in some spectacular living rooms around New York—plastic applause box and all—before he finally let it go (and I was freed). Some of the material ended up a while later in his Off-Off-Off-Off Broadway revue, *The No Frills Revue*. And one night, I was watching that wondrous 1980s phenomenon, late-night New York City public access cable television, when cabaret writer and performer John Wallowitch sang his title song for *Back On The town* entitled... "Back On The Town." I had played this ditty for a year, so I called the station and got him on the air and said that I had been involved in the initial stages of the show. His response was, "What the hell happened to that?" Before I could give him the lowdown on the air, the show's time was up. Probably for the best. Some of the material I recall from the show included a sketch about a priceless, valuable item kept in lockdown in a vault being sold to a salivating young couple. Finally, they decide to make the purchase and are handed from the vault *two tickets to CATS!* BLACKOUT! There was a sketch of various musicals composed in a "what if" style by other composers, hence an *Annie* spoof done in the style of Sondheim's *Sweeney Todd*. "Good evening, frieeeends" was the best line. There was also an endless patter song about food which Charnin tried to get me to teach to the multi-talented deliverer of clever lyrics, Liliane Montevecchi (who was also being considered for the cast). We never got past the first verse in two hours. And a reprise of the "Yma, Ava, Abba, Oona, Ugo, Ida, Ullu" tongue-twisting monologue written by Thomas Meehan for an ancient Anne Bancroft television special. (*She* did it very well, but where did Nancy Walker fit into this?)

I made money and had a great time but... moving on. I rarely saw Martin Charnin after this, but I must say I had a great time on *Annie, Upstairs at O'Neals'* and all the private time spent with him on the revue material. I came away admiring him and his valiant efforts. A fun time.

16. A Day in Hollywood/A Night in the Ukraine

I first saw Tommy Tune in the movie version of *Hello, Dolly!* playing Ambrose Kemper and shortly thereafter in Ken Russell's brilliant, psychedelic movie version of *The Boy Friend.* Tony Walton furnished the fantastic set and art direction for the Ken Russell film and I'm sure that this was the beginning of a match made in heaven. The match? Tommy Tune musicals adorned by Tony Walton's imaginative sets. In 1974, Mr. Tune won a Tony Award for Best Featured Actor in one of the worst musicals I have ever witnessed. *Seesaw,* by Cy Coleman and Dorothy Fields, was an overblown, noisy, absurd musical about romance in New York. There were hooker numbers, barrio numbers, pink-bewigged Motown numbers, tap numbers, and a first act finale which had a grating Michelle Lee (with a thick Brooklyn accent) having an emergency problem with her uterus as the curtain fell. And, yes, Act Two opened with a hospital number called, "We've Got It." But the over-the-top horrendous spectacle that took the cake and won Tune the award was "It's Not Where You Start, It's Where You Finish," a loony production number featuring the 6'- 6" dancer in white stretch pants, red vest, and shoulder-length Rita Hayworth hair dancing up and down staircases while the ensemble, wearing balloon costumes and top hats, did ballet *en pointe.* The star ensemble member was petite Baayork Lee, who danced with Tune. It was a surreal freakshow signifying and celebrating... what exactly? I adore crazy musical numbers tossed in from left field in most musicals, but this was just ridiculous. Besides, it followed a dozen other numbers just like it, rendering it exhausting for the audience. This was a troubled disaster of a show taken over by Michael Bennett with lots of casualties, including the career-crushing firing of Lainie

Kazan. (I'm told that the National Tour starring Lucie Arnaz was a vast improvement.) But from this arose a wonderful directing career for Tommy Tune. Well, two actually—Tune's and Bennett's, the last two great geniuses of the Broadway stage. There would be no others.

A few years later, I saw an off-Broadway musical directed by Tommy Tune that became a long-running success, *The Best Little Whorehouse in Texas*. There was one good moment, the Aggie dance with the high school football players. The rest of the show was geared toward the not-as-yet-identified Jerry Springer crowd. Whores, madams, crooked politicians—basically unsympathetic country morons who, God help me, the American public finds amusing. And simplistic unexciting country music and lyrics. I would have the distinct misfortune of having to do this show in Las Vegas for the summer and it sent me to more booze and more cocaine than I could stand. Doing this show twice a night helped this alcoholic hit bottom faster than crystal meth does for your average gay man today.

Tommy Tune's next Broadway show was a little jewel. Not perfect, but unusual and stylish. *A Day in Hollywood/A Night in the Ukraine* was a tiny London import reshaped and outfitted with some new songs by Jerry Herman. Act One, *A Day in Hollywood*, took place at Grauman's Chinese Theatre (courtesy of Tony Walton), while Act Two took us to a red and gold palace for a snowy *Night in the Ukraine*. The first act was a tribute to Hollywood in the 1930s with old and new songs, clever medleys, and tap dancing. A revue with no story. One hour in length, it gently celebrated many Hollywood icons. The genius here was that we often saw only the feet of those icons, especially in an extended number, "Famous Feet." While the cast sang, two mysterious dancers performed high above on a little stage that exposed only the lower part of their legs. There was Judy Garland's Dorothy, Sonja Henie on ice skates, Mickey and Minnie Mouse, and finally a beautiful ballet for Fred and Ginger to Cole Porter's "Easy to Love," arranged by Wally Harper. Cast member and co-creator Frank Lazarus led the cast at a shiny black piano, while the rest of the orchestra was merely two upright pianos off stage played by Rob Fisher and Allen Cohen. Wally Harper did all the charming arrangements.

This was a magical little show but, for some, the main attraction was the Marx Brothers send-up in Act Two, for which the cast members transformed themselves into the Brothers and all the usual suspects. Lazarus played Chico at the same piano used in Act One, while the two guys on the backstage pianos got a 45-minute break. What a job! The cast included David Garrison as Groucho, and Priscilla Lopez (*A Chorus Line*) who would win a Tony Award playing Harpo Marx. When I went to see it, there was a loud bang during the

"Easy to Love" ballet. I would later discover from my own experience that the backstage pianos tended to break strings, which when amplified sounded like gunshots. I much preferred the first act but was awed by the splendor of Tony Walton's second act set.

This show opened while I was still on the road with *Annie*. When I called contractor John Monaco to let him know I was back from the road, he told me to go check out the two piano books from the show.

But before I did that, he threw another tidbit at me. I was to play the Fred Astaire arrangement of Gershwin's "Slap That Bass" for Tommy Tune on *The Dick Cavett Show*. Thrilling! We rehearsed and showed up at the studio to tape it twice through. This was my introduction to Mr. Tune himself. Having survived this, I started to learn the *Hollywood/Ukraine* score. I sat and watched the pianists and decided to sub on the show. I was called quite often. Rob Fisher had already left the show, Allen Cohen had moved up to Fisher's chair, and a funny character named Rod Derefinko was playing the second piano. I was in awe of Rod because he turned out to be the dazzling pianist on the original cast recording of Jones and Schmidt's *Celebration*, which I adored. When Rod moved to first piano, I would play second piano. Pretty soon, Allen Cohen decided to leave permanently, which left a spot for me for almost a year's run.

My first Broadway run! I thoroughly enjoyed everyone in the cast and saw many replacements come through. Tudi Roche took over for Lopez, Celia Tackaberry played the Margaret Dumont role, John Sloman was the male ingénue.

David Garrison left the cast, but six months later was rehearsing and going into *Pirates of Penzance* up the street. One of our Groucho understudies was on vacation, and the other one overslept for a Sunday matinee. The stage management ran to the Minskoff Theatre, yanked Garrison out of his rehearsal, and threw him onstage. Garrison remembered all the tapping, all the clarinet playing and, most important of all, the incredibly nonsensical Grouchoisms in Act Two. What a pro! Amazing and hilarious! The show must go on!

The mega-hit *42nd Street* was vacating the Winter Garden Theatre for *Cats* (a pause here to mourn the death of the American musical theatre as a result of the British imports that would monopolize Broadway and suck the life out of it for the next 35 years) to move to the Majestic Theatre on 44th Street. Our show was at the Royale on 45th Street so our stage doors were literally feet from each other in the alleyway that snaked under the Milford Plaza Hotel. Once *42nd Street* was moved in, I started hanging out in the alley chatting with Tammy Grimes, Lee Roy Reams, and the hordes of dancers. Philip Fradkin, musical director from *The Golden Apple*, was now their conductor. (Sad note:

Phil was struck by a taxicab after a cast party one night and killed instantly.) Since Rod and I had a 45-minute break in Act Two, I started to sneak in backstage at *42nd Street* and watch the last part of the first act. It was so much fun watching all those dancers line up in the wings and run onstage for the "We're in the Money" number. The real show business! I never missed my cue back at the theatre, but Rod Derefinko sure did! He would take walks in Times Square and his "watch would stop" (Ha!) and he'd come running in just in time to play the curtain call music. This was when Broadway was fun. Not so horribly urgent, everyone having a good time. Some of the crew members would put porn magazines in my music. I loved the attention.

Composer John Kander's longtime partner, Albert Stephenson, was the dance captain and the male pair of the "famous feet." He was being given an opportunity to stage the next Tony Awards, so our whole cast (including me) came in early to be bodies for him to work out his staging. We also were flown to San Francisco to perform in Union Square for the "I Love New York" campaign and Lucie Arnaz was hosting the event. I reintroduced myself as the "guy who just blew into town" at her *Annie Get Your Gun* auditions three years earlier. She said she remembered, but in 2011 when I befriended her on Facebook it had been 30 years. I again thanked her for being there on my first official day in New York. She thanked me for the story but didn't remember.

Two years before all of this, I was lying on my single bed in my 8' by 10' room looking out over the airshaft in the next building feeling blue. I wasn't sure I should be in New York. I'd worked some, and the *Annie* tour was lucrative, but would I ever really be able to walk up the street, into a stage door, into an orchestra pit, and be a real part of a real first-run Broadway show? It looked grim. But here I was replacing someone in the middle of a real Broadway run—though *no* orchestra, *no* pit, and only *eight* people in the cast. Nevertheless, I was there.

One more funny *Follies* coincidence. When I was on tour with *Hollywood/Ukraine*, I was going to a gym in L.A. just crammed full of West Hollywood gay men and I was trying to pick up this sexy guy in the whirlpool. There I was in the whirlpool expounding on Broadway at the top of my lungs (which were alcohol-soaked and peppered with cocaine by now) and the sexy guy said, "Oh, I was on Broadway."

"Really? What did you do?"

"Oh, *Applause* and I was part of the dance team Vincent and Vanessa in *Follies*." His name was Michael Misita and he danced the Vincent and Vanessa bolero with Graciela Daniele. Well, that shut me up! I shrank to the size of a pea. I was immediately humbled and put in my place by him and, believe me, he was not about to be picked up by this loudmouthed drunken musical comedy queen that day! Me and my big mouth!

17. Booze and Broadway Part 1

We shall now step aside from the glamorous world of show business into deepest darkest reality.

When I was 4 years old, my family took me to Owensboro, Kentucky to visit my father's side of the family. His mother, sister, and youngest brother, John, lived in a roomy craftsman-style house in a middle-class neighborhood. When we pulled up in front of the house (and yes! I remember this as if it were five minutes ago), Grandmother Ford, Aunt Christine and Uncle John came down the path to greet us on the street. As Uncle John got near to us, he vomited all over himself. He was in a bathrobe that was already covered in dried vomit. My mother exclaimed, "Oooohhhh, Uncle Joooohhhhnnnnnn! Paul, honey, don't look at Uncle John. Come with me." She took me into the house and into the front bedroom. She explained to me that Uncle John "is an *alcoholic*. He drinks liquor and cannot stop and is doomed to live down the hall in that little bedroom, while his mother and poor Aunt Christine take care of him. Poor Aunt Christine was never able to get married because Grandmother Ford forced her to stay home and help take care of John. He's a drunk and cannot stop drinking. Look at me when I tell you never, ever, Ever, EVER TAKE A DRINK, DO YOU HEAR ME? IT WILL RUIN YOUR LIFE!!!"

I heard her... but to me, Uncle John looked like he had a pretty good deal. For another 13 years, I white-knuckled it, while everyone around me in good ol' Hotlanta drank beer, whiskey, stingers, wine, bourbon, and my peers in high school smoked pot and dropped acid. I hung on to my abstinence for dear life while everyone else seemed to disagree with mother and have the time of their lives, bonding and joining the party and going through the "rites of passage" together. I was always outside looking in.

My first hangover. I was 18. *Hello, Dolly!* Northside High School in Atlanta, Georgia. The cast party. My first teenage party... ever. It was a magical evening. I was having such a good time for the last six months of my senior year with this incredible High School of the Arts program. There were lots and lots of people there. Lots of students and no parents. I decided to just sit in an armchair in the family room with plenty of people around. I actually felt so comfortable and thought, "I'm just going to sit here and breathe and relax. This is heaven." The kid that lived in the house came up to me and said, "Paul, do you want a drink?"

I said, "Oh my God, no, I don't drink."

He said, "You don't want a beer?"

I said, "Oh my God, that stuff is nasty. I don't drink."

He said, "Well, let me fix you something you might like."

And he brought me back a tall glass with what looked like Hawaiian punch with a straw. A "sloe gin fizz." And I sipped it and it tasted like Kool-Aid. And I sucked it down. It was tasty.

"Well great, I'll have another one."

He put another one in my hand and I sat there and everything went soft focus and I started feeling really, Really, REALLY good. I'm pretty sure that he came and screwed a glass into my hand six times. By the time the parents came home to greet the students (it was a wild, raucous party by then), I got up to go over to meet them. I was introduced to the host and the hostess and immediately fell on the floor. Just passed out right on the floor, but I remember the woman saying "Well, hello to you, too!" I was looking up at her from the floor, but I don't remember anything after that. I woke up in the middle of the night in a strange bedroom in a strange house with another senior from the school. I realized that I had been taken to his house and had thrown up in his bathroom... violently. It was all red because it was that sloe gin red fruity stuff. I went back and fell asleep. The next day I woke up and my friend said, "Why don't you call your parents to come pick you up." I did, and they were just horrified.

But I was ecstatic. It was the happiest day of my life. I'd gotten drunk. I'd had a good time. I'd passed out. I'd slept over at somebody's house. I'd thrown up. I had a hangover. I had ARRIVED! I was now a member of the human race. And the next step was to do it again as soon as possible and as often as possible. I had a lot of catching up to do!

That was 1971. By 1976, I was playing the piano for the local cabaret shows. We were doing our Irving Berlin show. There was a piano onstage, as well as over on the side. I had to get up, go up there and be a part of the show onstage. We were doing an Irving Berlin medley. I was playing along and all of a sudden the piano jerked. It was because a cast member had kicked the piano, saying to me, "Get it together." Right in the middle of the show. Lately, I had been having a glass of wine between each show. I was pretty schnockered by then and was dozing off during the medley. I kept a glass of wine on the piano at all times from 1976 to 1978. I had been drinking during every performance I did. I was drunk every night at the piano. When I moved to NYC and started to work there, I decided that I shouldn't drink when I was working. Only after. So, I proceeded to show up and play auditions and rehearsals at 10 o'clock in the morning for the next couple of years with a raging hangover. I was not drunk, but I was hung over. All right, yes, I would still be drunk! Because that is what being hung over is. DRUNK!

When I went on tour with *Annie* for the entire year of 1979, I was drunk every single night. Hung over every single day. Not eating. I weighed 160 pounds. I was determined to be the thinnest gay man on the planet. And we found the bars in every city. We were in each city for two weeks for 52 weeks, 26 cities. Every time we had a matinee, I fell asleep during the show and the conductor would have to rap his baton on the piano. He was not happy. When I left the tour in Hartford, Connecticut, I got on the train looking like I was on the train to a concentration camp. Hung over from a year of drinking and drugging and touring. I was only 27 at the time, but a self-diagnosed (is there any other kind?) major alcoholic.

I continued to drink at the bars every night for the next year. I played every performance of *A Day in Hollywood/A Night in the Ukraine* for eight months with a grinding hangover. My next big fight with the hangover was going on tour with that show. We toured for eight months. We were in Wilmington, Delaware for two weeks, Toronto for six weeks, Los Angeles for six weeks, Seattle for four weeks, San Francisco for six weeks. I never drank so much alcohol in my life. I would swallow anything anybody put in my mouth in pill form. I did a lot of cocaine. When I was in San Francisco, on our day off I went with a guy I had met to the Russian River. We had Sunday night, all day Monday, and I had to be back at the theatre Tuesday night. I did so many drugs and drank so much during that day-and-a-half period, I literally couldn't play the piano when I got to the theatre, and I had to ask my co-pianist on the show to cover me in case my hands wouldn't function. For most of that tour, when I would show up on Tuesday night for the first show of the week, I would not only be so hung over that I could hardly play the piano, but I would turn to him and ask, "Could I borrow $200 until payday Thursday?" He would lend it to me, and then I would pay him back. But it was because I had spent all my money on booze and drugs. I crawled home from that tour. It was 1981. This was a year for the books, literally. I had made a decision to be bad, and I was extremely BAD!

Upon returning, I almost immediately got a phone call from the pianist-musical director for the National Tour of *The Best Little Whorehouse in Texas* which was playing at the Desert Inn Hotel in Las Vegas. He asked if I would come out and finish the run for him for eight weeks... July and August in Las Vegas. I didn't know how to say no. I didn't need the money, I didn't need the job. What I needed was a fucking rehab. But I said yes, and immediately turned around and went out to Las Vegas and found the bars. We had to do two shows a night, six nights a week. We started at 6 o'clock and finished at 11. And then I would go to the bar. I would stay out until 6 in the morning every single night. I bought cocaine from a member of the cast almost every night. I'd buy $100 to $200 worth of cocaine a night. I even slept with Joan Rivers's hairdresser.

About five days before the show was done, I went to a little party at one of the cast member's apartments. I was drinking Stolichnaya straight up, no ice, no nothing. Just big water glasses of Stolichnaya. Warm! We all decided to sit up and watch *All About Eve*, which started at 3 in the morning. At 6 in the morning, the party broke up and a cast member, who I owe amends to today, helped me down the concrete stairs outside of this two-story apartment complex. Well, I fell, and I fell on him, and all I remember was him saying impatiently, "Oh, Paul!" He got me into his car. Fortunately, I didn't rent a car there or drive in Las Vegas! He drove me to my apartment complex and helped me get to my apartment. I gave him the keys and he went to unlock the door. Then I realized, "Uh-oh, this isn't my apartment." So, what did I do? I turned around and walked away and left him, because it was 6 o'clock in the morning and he was trying to open someone else's door at the wrong apartment. I just walked away and found my apartment. He found me and again said, "Oh, Paul!" He opened the door, handed me the keys, and pushed me in. The next thing I knew it was 4 o'clock in the afternoon. I woke up with a show to do in two hours. My hands were scraped from falling on the concrete stairs. The shower was on. The bathroom was completely steamy, and completely wet, but I don't think I caused any flooding downstairs. I was lying on my bare mattress because I never bothered to buy sheets or rent sheets or ask for sheets. And I was so sick I could hardly move. I looked at the clock and walked into the living room and the whole dining room set was knocked over. I must have fallen all over it when I came into the apartment that morning. I took a shower and got dressed. I'd had nothing to eat, so I was sick as a dog.

I called a taxi and went to the Desert Inn and wolfed down some food. I went to the stage door... barely able to move... hurting all over. I looked at the call board and there was a little wicker basket stapled on it with a sign that said, "Donations for the Paul Ford Home for Drunken Pianists." There was a quarter in it. I walked in the green room and people were snickering at me. I apologized for my behavior. For the next two nights on stage, I was playing with scraped, scabby fingers, and it hurt, and since the piano was onstage, and under the hot spotlights, and I was in fucking cowboy drag, it was triply miserable. Every time somebody walked or danced by the piano, they would bump into the piano, and say, "Oh, I'm sorry," as if they were drunk and falling all over themselves. They did this in the middle of the show... *everybody* in the show did it... laughing of course. I thought it was really, really endearing at the time, but underneath I was humiliated.

In the middle of our final week, I woke up in the morning to the phone ringing and my mother telling me that my father had died suddenly of a heart attack. I had three more days to go of this awful show. I couldn't get out of the show, so they had to delay the funeral for three days. I got on the last Sunday night flight out of Las Vegas to Atlanta... a red-eye, arriving the next morning. I showed up to my dad's funeral weighing 160 pounds, tanned a leathery black, and so hung over that I started crying during the service and couldn't stop. It was because of my dad, but it was also because I was completely bottomed out. I decided to stay in Atlanta indefinitely to "dry out," something only an alcoholic would say.

A year later, I was playing the piano for Martin Charnin's *Upstairs at O'Neals'* in New York City. I was trying some "controlled drinking." This was the night I was going down the stairs to leave and Martin Charnin was coming up the stairs. We stopped to chat, and he just looked me in the eye and said, "You're a drunk." I was so humiliated. And even though I continued to work for Charnin for about a year or so after that, I was always, always aware of him looking me in the eye and calling me a drunk. That was devastating. I decided to look into stopping drinking, went to one AA meeting and decided I would stop... but on my own, with no help from anyone... well, maybe a therapist. I just stopped cold turkey. Soon I would become what is known as a dry drunk for the next four years.

18. Back in Business

MERRILY WE ROLL ALONG

But what of Stephen Sondheim? After *Sweeney Todd* I had lost faith, plus I was so busy trying to just cope. Before I went on the infamous *Hollywood/Ukraine* bottoming-out tour, I participated in the current Sondheim bashing party as one of the "bitches" (his word), those who come to an early preview to jeer at his latest folly. *Sweeney Todd* had left a bad taste in my mouth, and I never really expected to hear or see anything, funny, bright, amusing, and "swinging" coming from him after *A Little Night Music, Pacific Overtures*, and the cannibal musical. I went to the Alvin Theatre, home of *Lady in the Dark, It's a Bird, It's a Plane, It's Superman*, and *House of Flowers*, to see what all the gossip was about—the gossip about his latest show, *Merrily We Roll Along*. The title, at least, made me hopeful for something back to "normal." The show began with a fantastic Overture, a graduation ceremony, and then the cast of teenagers began the play. The first scene was bewildering, a party scene ending with the character of Mary being pushed into an onstage swimming pool, which was a hole in the stage with blue paper covering it, simulating water. When she fell "in," ripping the paper, the cast gasped in shock, and someone near me in the audience said "Sheeesh!"

The next scene cued the audience into what would be the structural gimmick of the show. It would go *backwards* in time! I loved that, though most people today hate it and complain about it, using the utterly asinine phrase, "It doesn't work!" Immediately came two terrific songs, "Old Friends" and "Franklin Shepard, Inc.," socked over by the dynamic Lonny Price. The rest of Act One was messy with the original leading man, a rather dorky, schlubby, nondescript kid unable to live up to the charismatic nature of his character. At intermission, the atmosphere was indeed grim. But then came Act Two, and the show took off like a rocket with a string of incredible showstoppers and the youthful actors starting to feel at home in their roles as the show continued "backwards" and the characters got "younger."

Before going on the road with *Hollywood/Ukraine*, I bought the cassette tape (remember those?) of *Merrily We Roll Along* when it was released. The show closed quickly, but I became hooked. Especially with the song "Opening Doors," one of my all-time favorite Sondheim sequences. But I loved the whole recording, and Jim Walton had replaced the leading man. I first met Jim when I was living at 438 West 45th Street. I heard something bumping against our door and I went to investigate. When I opened it, there was this cute guy mopping the hall floors. He introduced himself as Jim Walton, new actor in town, living on the third floor and making extra money by doing some assistant superintendent work in our building. Two years later, he was starring in the most recent of controversial Sondheim musicals. I love Jim Walton and his brother Bob, and I always run across the street to grab him/them and hug him/them. We still live on the same street! The only other version of the show I have seen is the Kennedy Center version with Raul Esparza and Michael Hayden. As faulty as that first preview was at the Alvin, I still prefer the original version of the show to the jazzed up "improved" version. "Rich and Happy" is one of my favorite Sondheim songs and it is no longer a part of the score, and "Growing Up" is just dumbing-down the show for idiot audiences. However, I would sit through any version of this show before sitting through another performance of "Parlor Songs" or "Poor Thing" or the Wigmaker's scene ("There's tawny, and there's golden saffron. There's flaxen, and there's blonde!") Oy! *Sweeney Todd!* Oy!

I LOVE *Merrily We Roll Along* and have no problems with it going backwards in time. Just put it back the way it wuz!

And Sondheim was back on top with me. That year on the Tony Awards, the best nominated scores included the dreadful *Dreamgirls*, the glorious though lyrically dopey *Nine*, and *Merrily We Roll Along*. *Merrily* was by far the superior score, arguably Sondheim's best from that point on, but the Tonys were a lost cause. Not with me, however!

WEST SIDE STORY
JEROME ROBBINS AND ME

After the 1979 revival of *West Side Story* closed, many tours went out. I was hired to play rehearsals for a European Tour starring Brent Barrett and Josie de Guzman. I met David Stahl, the conductor, and *Pacific Overtures* dance music arranger Danny Troob on this show. Let's face it, I was out of my league here, so on the first of two run-throughs for Jerome Robbins himself, Danny played and there was a percussionist, as well. I watched and learned. It was thrilling, and I felt humbled. What I didn't know was that Danny and David were leaving for Europe the next day, leaving me to play BY MYSELF the second run-through for Robbins. Robbins only snapped his fingers at me once at the top of the Mambo, then left me alone after that. I broke a blood vessel in my finger at the beginning of the run-through. I managed. After it was over and my job was done, I went up to Jerome Robbins and introduced myself and told him what an honor it was to play for him. He looked confused and said thank you and I scurried away. I had no idea of his reputation other than as a God of the theatre.

IRMA LA DOUCE and ANYONE CAN WHISTLE

The Sondheim connection here was that one of the ensemble men on my summer stock tour of *Irma La Douce* was Sterling Clark, an original cast member of *Anyone Can Whistle*. I would work with him again on the 1995

Carnegie Hall concert of *Whistle*, in which he played his original part along with fellow original cast member Harvey Evans. On *Whistle*, Sterling pressured me to go to Paul Gemignani and make sure that he, Sterling, could say and sing his original lines and harmonies. I can't resist a pretty face. Gemignani begrudgingly said yes. On *Irma La Douce*, when he began to chat, I realized I was in the presence of a rarity. A performer who had really *been there*.

I started to get out my old souvenir programs from musicals and movies from the 1960s. There was this handsome, dark-haired dancer having a blast right behind Fred Astaire and Petula Clark in *Finian's Rainbow* and singing his heart out right behind Barbra Streisand in the big "Hello, Dolly" number. I found pictures of him backing up Angela Lansbury in "Me and My Town," and even as early as 1960 as one of Molly Brown's brothers, behind Tammy Grimes. I felt honored and in awe of this true Broadway-Hollywood studio system veteran. It also turned out that he was life partners with another veteran dancer, Buddy Vest, who (along with a baby-faced Lee Roy Reams) can be seen backing up the lead dancer in the "Rich Man's Frug," and Sammy Davis, Jr. in "The Rhythm of Life" in the *Sweet Charity* film.

When I got back from the *Irma La Douce* tour, I got a call from my friend Evalyn Baron from the *Hollywood/Ukraine* tour. She wanted me to play for her at a very early audition for a new musical at some place called Playwrights Horizons. It was for a workshop of a new Sondheim show called *Sunday in the Park with George*. I played for Evalyn for casting director John Lyons and that was that. It sounded like another weird idea for a musical and after *A Little Night Music*, *Pacific Overtures*, and the big yawn *Sweeney Todd*, I was sort of disinterested. Of course, little did I know that eight months later I would be in the middle of the greatest experience of my life.

19. The Rink

The Rink was a big career turning point for me. Again, it started with a phone call. I was in Atlanta, Georgia with Charlie, visiting family. I checked my messages back in New York and had a message from John Monaco, the contractor. He said, "I need a second rehearsal pianist for the workshop of a new show called *The Rink*—Kander and Ebb, Chita Rivera, Liza Minnelli, Paul Gemignani (Sondheim's primary conductor from *Follies* to the present) conducting." I gasped, then said "Ok...when?" He gave me the dates, I hung up the phone, and started screaming to Charlie. "Ohmigod, LIZA! CHITA!

KANDER AND EBB! PAUL GEMIGNANI! All in one show!?!" Of course, I was sweating bullets already. This was a turning point, the big job that resulted from my first day in NYC when I was hanging around that rehearsal studio where the audition pianist hadn't shown up and I volunteered to play, etc. etc. etc. This was THE phone call. I was to work with Paul Gemignani, who was to hire me for 27 years... 27 years. He was somebody whom I never thought I would ever meet, let alone work for.

My friend Ray Stephens from Atlanta, who used to sing in our cabarets, was doing *On The 20th Century* with Paul in 1978, playing one of the tap-dancing porters in the original cast. I asked Ray if I could possibly meet Paul Gemignani, and he said, "I tell ya what ya do... just hang out at the stage door... you know what he looks like... right?" So, I went and hung out at the stage door with my little phone number in my sweaty hand and stopped him as he went barreling out the door. I said, "I'm Paul Ford and Ray Stephens said I should speak to you and give you my phone number." He responded with a "mutter mutter grrrrr," took the phone number and hurried off. Since then, I've learned that he's actually very good when somebody approaches him that way... he will pay attention to you. But nothing happened for five years. He didn't call me, and I thought... "Well, that's that."

But the opportunity was now here and I had to show up and prove myself! But something was unsettling. It was the title of the show, *The Rink*. Something made me think "rank" when I said the title out loud. Oh well, who cares, I was excited!!! And I was NOT DRINKING, HALLELUJAH!

The first day of the workshop of *The Rink* was like any other (except this was my first time with a brand-new original musical, completely unknown territory). We sat around a table, introduced ourselves, and prepared to read through the script with John Kander, Fred Ebb, and Terence McNally the playwright. It was a real treat because John played every song brilliantly, and Fred sang everyone's part. The reading began and there were Liza Minnelli and Chita Rivera at the table. The choreographer was Graciela Daniele, and the director was A.J. Antoon.

It's so funny how there will be all these famous Broadway musical people in a room, and then there's this director in the room who has *never* directed a musical and I think, "Well... what's *he* doing here?" Antoon was supposedly a good director, and people seemed to like him but... I didn't get it then. Still don't. The guys in the ensemble were Jason Alexander, Mel Johnson, Jr., Ronn Carroll (catch him singing behind Ethel Merman on *The Ed Sullivan Show* in the "I've Got the Sun in the Morning" number), Scott Ellis, Frank Mastracola (one of Chita's dancers), and Scott Holmes (a soap star) as Chita's leading man. And... the swing dancer was future film director, Rob Marshall! All legendary in their own right today. Most of them had to do drag in the show playing female characters. There they all were, sitting around the table, reading the script, and I was just gulping air. The main rehearsal pianist and dance arranger was Tom Fay, a great guy, who played most everything in the rehearsals. I played only two numbers, "Ah, Ma" and "Gee It's Good To See You After All These Years." But I'm jumping ahead.

The reading reached the point in the second act where Liza's character has to say to Chita's character, "Fuck you, Ma!" And then Chita slaps Liza and Liza slaps Chita. I was thinking... this... is... absolutely... without... a... doubt... the most HORRIBLE show I have ever heard! All of the songs were horrible. I thought, I've heard all these songs before. They're rehashes of every Kander and Ebb song. Every ballad was "Maybe This Time" turned upside down or sideways. The same chord progressions. And if I heard "Fuck you" one more time in this script... it was the "gritty new Broadway," dontcha know. But I was HATING IT! None of the songs were inspired—"Colored Lights," "Chief Cook and Bottle Washer," "Not Enough Magic," "Marry Me" (...come on and marry me). My gut reaction was "How do I get out of this?" I never dreamed it would be such a mediocre, ugly, and depressing show. But there it was... and there I was!

The first time I had to go into a room with Paul Gemignani, all the guys were learning a song called "Gee It's Good To See You After All These Years." The first thing Paul said to me was, "Play it up a third." What?! I could barely make it through the slightly convoluted melody. I really wasn't expecting to have to transpose in front of all these people. The song itself is still director Scott Ellis's theme song... anytime he walks into the room I play the first phrase and he closes his eyes and shakes his head. My funniest memory of the song was of the guys rehearsing the number with a prop trunk. They were staged to throw Scott in the trunk and slam the lid. One day they tricked him by quietly leaving the room, leaving him alone in the trunk... waiting... and waiting... until we heard his little voice say... "Can I come out now?"

We were rehearsing a song called "We Can Make It" ("Maybe This Time" version 4!) with Chita. John Kander was asked to come in and listen to it. While he was listening, someone stuck his head in the door and motioned for him to come out of the room momentarily. He quickly got up and left the room. Chita stopped singing and said, "What the fuck! Where did he go?" John came back apologizing and she said, "You just got up and walked out right in the middle of my song!" Everyone was laughing and thought it was very funny. She was very good natured, funny, and charming... back then. Weeks later, when we got to the orchestra reading, Paul Gemignani set it up so that at that same point in the same song, the orchestra would put down their instruments and walk out of the room... which they did. We lost ten minutes of rehearsal time because of the laughter. That was really, really hilarious. Like putting on a show in a barn. Old-fashioned show business. Unlike now. There was still looseness and fun then. Unlike now, I repeat.

All through rehearsals, Liza was very remote. She hung out at the piano with John Kander and rarely made herself available. On breaks, the two would sometimes sing through a song not connected with the show. I got the impression one did not dare attempt to interfere, join in, or even make eye contact during these private moments, let alone comment on them or ask a question such as "What was that song you were singing?" or "How are you today, Liza?" I was TERRIFIED of her but couldn't stop staring. She looked away anytime I came near her.

She broke her toe! During tech rehearsals. We all went on dinner break and since I was now living across the street from the theatre, I went home. I was dreading playing anything at this point. The whole process was really new and overwhelming. This was my first show from the very beginning of a workshop all the way through tech rehearsals to opening night in NYC. I was overwhelmed and scared of my own shadow. And the show still sucked! I was also NOT DRINKING! That night I was sitting in the theatre waiting after the dinner break. It was 7:30... everybody was due back... 8 o'clock came, and we got the word that Liza was leaving a restaurant when somebody stepped on her toe and broke it. She was being treated and would be along soon. There was a lot of hubbub and we sat waiting and I thought, "Oh God, can't we just go home? Ya know... this is just... nothing's gonna happen tonight." Finally, everyone showed up and came onstage. I was in the house. Liza came hobbling onstage with crutches and her big old foot pointed up in the air. She said "We're gonna do a really great *rehearshal* tonight. We're *jusht* gonna keep doing the work tonight... we're gonna keep going... we're not gonna let a little thing like *thish* get in our way...c'mon, *kidsh, let'sh* go." And everybody walked off the stage. Ten minutes later, the stage manager came back onstage and said, "Everybody go home." I don't remember what happened the next few days. Standby Lenora Nemetz had to get up there and fill in... but she knew her stuff.

My one performance of *The Rink*. *The Rink* was a synthesizer-only show, but mostly piano sounds with a little organ for the you know what—the sound of the old rank RINK! Gemignani conducted while Tom Fay went out front to watch and take notes. I got through the whole thing... I didn't do badly. Tom Fay came back afterwards and said, "Well ya got everything." I'm sure it was good and loud. I managed to get through all my little solo moments. It was not an easy score. That was my first performance under Paul Gemignani's baton. Scary, but it was a big band with lots of loud playing which made me courageous. The thought of actually playing it a second time was absurd. Fortunately, I didn't have to. The toughest number was the rape ballet. The rape ballet was so brutal and so long and so uncomfortable to watch, I didn't even want to watch it, let alone play it. I have a live video of the show and I watched it once and thought, "You know I'm glad I didn't have to play that... or be in the rehearsal room for that scene... it was all Tom Fay's dance arrangement... really ugly music... and that's what the show was all about... everything on the boardwalk in Atlantic City (or wherever this play was set) was changing or had changed and not for the better. It was just so ugly. There were Jason Alexander and Scott Ellis all dressed up like street punks doing this "street" robot choreography. It was long and drawn out, and Chita literally was climbing up a metal fence to escape only to be pulled off, and thrown on the ground, kicked in the head and stomped on. It was just horrible. Two other guys lifted a third guy over her just like in *West Side Story* and simulated raping her. Then they picked up another guy and he raped her and left her lying there with her skirt over her head. Ron Carroll and Mel Johnson, Jr. (in drag as old ladies) were sitting on a bench stage right averting their eyes... singing "What Happened to the Old Days?" It was just... horrible. When the stock rights were made available the next year, I saw Lanie Kazan star in the show at the Coconut Grove in Florida. The way they did this scene was the punks laid Kazan on a box, colored lights whirled, and the guys twirled the box around in circles with Kazan kicking her legs up in the air. The music was cut down to about 30 bars... and that was the rape ballet. It was still ugly.

And that's what all the reviews said. An ugly show about ugly people. The set was ugly... even when it was all lit up and supposedly in its glory, it was ugly. There was roller skating... like sword fighting on stage, not something I want to see. It makes me nervous. I can't even imagine EVER sitting through *Starlight Express*.

Before a preview one night, I was told to go over on the far side of the stage and wait outside of Liza's dressing room to run through a little bit of the song, "All the Children in a Row." I had never been in her dressing room. She paid no attention to me... hadn't spoken to me at all during the entire process. But my favorite person on the show was standing outside her dressing room, her bodyguard Chuck Zito, who you might remember from *Oz* on HBO. He was a Hell's Angel. He had a tattoo under his tongue. He was a hot Italian body builder. Another night during a preview, I was standing watching the show and looked over to my left and there was a man in full Indian headdress and fringe jacket standing with his arms crossed. And I was thinking "What is Sitting Bull doing here?" It was Chuck dressed up in Native American drag! He was certainly an interesting person. I was terrified of him. Anyway, this one night outside of her dressing room, I was sitting there waiting to see Ms Minnelli. A funny old man in a suit and tie was waiting with me. Finally, the door opened and they told the funny old man to get in quick, quick, quick, quick!!! And the old man went in and I was thinking, "Who was that?" Then I heard Liza's voice... or something. It sounded like nothing I had ever heard in my life. Because she could barely sing at this point. She could barely sing at all during this show. She was just trying to get up to an A above Middle C. The man was honking and retching, then she would honk and retch. He was obviously her vocal coach. It was so frightening, and it just went on and on. Then, finally, she could grunt out a phrase of "Colored Lights." They shooed the funny old man out, then told me to get in quick, quick, quick, quick!!!! Everything was so frantic around there. I went into her dressing room and there was this little toy piano with no bass notes... and the one note I needed to play the most, didn't work. It didn't have a string on it. She kept nodding for me to play the downbeat on the one note that wasn't there. We got through it and I came out of there bewildered at the horrible sounds that were emanating from that dressing room. She never could remember the lyrics to "Colored Lights" and Fred Ebb would stand in the wings night after night with the lyrics trying to get her through the number.

Charlie and I went to the opening night party at the Roxy roller rink. It was my first big party and it was absolutely dull and boring. We left early. I didn't get to introduce Charlie to anybody and I didn't even see anybody. *The Rink* opened to hateful reviews across the boards.

During the run, I would be going out at night to see Charlie up at his place and come home very late. A limo would be sitting across the street at the Martin Beck Theatre (now the Al Hirschfeld). It would stay there *all night long*... and the stories I heard about parties in Liza's dressing room! Whoa! She was minutes away from Betty Ford. She left the show early to actually go to the Betty Ford Clinic. Stockard Channing came in and closed the show. (I asked Stockard during rehearsals of a dreadful revival of *Pal Joey* what her experience was like and she said, "Oh my God, it was an out-of-body experience. There were soooo many songs, I didn't know which way I was turning. I had so many lyrics and so many songs to sing!")

Oh, and the red dresses! The red Halston dresses! *The Rink* was not a show about any kind of glamour whatsoever. Liza looked like a shlub, dressed like a slovenly hippie. (Ever since the '60s and the hippies, I guess some women have settled on looking like that from here on out.) *The Rink* was something of a period piece in which Liza played a hippie who comes dragging her useless hippie ass home (no sympathy there), and she looked like shit throughout the whole play. Chita wore only one dress... one purple dress with polka dots on it, all night long. It was not pretty! I really hated this show. I thought it all was so dismal... the "new grunge" Broadway... the ugliest set, the ugliest music, the ugliest dialogue... ugly story... am I repeating myself? I went back one more night to observe the show from the house and at the curtain call, out came Liza and Chita in matching red Halston gowns! As if that could make up for the three hours of *drear*. "That'll get 'em on their feet," I'm sure was the thinking. Really absurd. And really bad.

20. Sunday in the Park with George

During rehearsals for *The Rink*, I received two of the greatest theatre gifts possible in my little showbiz lifetime. The first gift was a ticket to see what would become one of the most thrilling events I would ever witness, *A Chorus Line* on September 30, 1983, the night it became the longest running Broadway musical, courtesy of my friend Victoria Tabaka, who was participating in the event. She was one of the hundreds onstage that night and I am forever grateful to her. What Michael Bennett achieved that evening was a one night only, one of a kind, American legend. In my mind the history of the Broadway musical came to a close that night. Even though I have loved Tommy Tune's work since then, I believe the Broadway musical became a different animal after this show hit that historical marker. This was the end of the American musical theatre style and tradition so painstakingly and lovingly nurtured throughout the 1900s. The last great dance show celebrating life and spirit and, above all, individual personality onstage. And a complete original. I was screaming my guts out during the "One" finale with all those 300 gold-costumed dancers everywhere in the theatre... then... it was over. I walked up Broadway and saw the *Cats* marquee at the Winter Garden Theatre. It was like looking at a red flag with a swastika on it.

The second greatest gift was handed to me by conductor Paul Gemignani outside of the men's room during a rehearsal break on *The Rink*. I was coming out, when conductor Paul stopped me and said, "You got your choice here. You can either stay with this show after it opens and play in the pit, or you can come with me over to another little show called *Sunday in the Park with George*." I looked at him and wanted to say something really sarcastic like, "Can I sleep on that for a minute?" then nod my head, snore for a second, and then say, "Okay, I've made up my mind." But I think I just immediately said, "*Sunday in the Park with George*, please." I didn't want to sound too dismissive of the show we were doing at the moment, so the reason I gave him was, "I think I'll be ready to move on. "Yes! I think I would like to go do that little *Sunday in the Park with George* musical by Stephen Sondheim, whatever it is! I think I just might get a little kick out of doing a l'il ol' original Stephen Sondheim musical on li'l ol' Broadway. That just might be a fun li'l ol' thing for me to do! Tell me, does the sterling silver platter come free with the job it's being served upon?" I went home and screamed to Charlie, "I just got offered the next Stephen Sondheim musical!"

When I picked up the music for the show, voluminous doesn't describe it. Back then, Broadway music was printed on thick 11" by 14" accordion-style paper which made carrying around the two acts of a typical musical the equivalent of lugging two world atlases. I also received a cassette tape of the workshop that had already been performed at Playwrights Horizons. The workshop contained the following songs: "Sunday in the Park with George," "Yoo-Hoo," a very long version of "No Life," "Color and Light," the "Gossip" sequences, "Everybody Loves Louie," "The Day Off" (The Dog Song), a very long "Soldier Song," "Finishing the Hat," "Beautiful," "Sunday," "It's Hot Up Here," and pieces of something about art called "Gotta Keep Them Humming." I had recently moved to my very first New York apartment of my own on West 45th Street, and the show was to play the Booth Theatre... on West 45th Street. I purchased my first piano of my own, a Sohmer studio model, and on it I started to learn the score.

Right away, I discovered that the key signatures of the songs on the cassette tape of the score did not match the music in my hands. Surprise, surprise, surprise. Even though I had transposed on *The Rink*, this was something else altogether. I really didn't know to ask the powers-that-be if I might ever see the music written out in the correct keys. So, I started learning the title song, "Color and Light," and "No Life" in the keys from the cassette tape. Ouch! I had a couple of weeks before we started rehearsals but was left completely on my own to figure all this out. Paul Gemignani gave me no heads up—just the tape and the music—the keys for Mandy Patinkin and Bernadette Peters had not been corrected even during the long hiatus between the workshop and the Broadway rehearsals. Good grief!

From what I recall, we didn't do the typical first day of rehearsal read-through and Sondheim did not play the score for the company. We all just got acquainted and broke up into rehearsals. Ted Sperling, a young pianist just out of Yale, was my partner in crime, and to me (a just turned 30-year-old, dry drunk, non-college graduate), Yale graduate Ted Sperling was just a mite intimidating. Nothing he did was wrong, mind you, it was just... well, I really did not understand how the heck I got in the same room with these phenomenal people! Paul conducted, Lapine directed, Randolyn Zinn (who???) choreographed (more in the chapter on *Passion* about James Lapine and his cast of wacko choreographers), and Charles Blackwell was our production stage manager until he left to write the musical *The Tap Dance Kid*. (Charlie was in the original cast of *Fanny* in 1954 and loved to do the belly dance choreography from that show for me on breaks, for which I gladly provided the music. This was before texting, when people had fun on breaks during rehearsal without running and hiding in their corners to text text text text text their lives away!) We had one very abrupt cast change. Charlotte Moore, John McMartin's longtime partner, was quietly released from playing the second female lead, Yvonne. But after a spirited rendition of "I Can Cook Too," Dana Ivey, fellow Atlantan, stepped in. I was in awe of Mandy Patinkin from *Evita* and felt I was in the room with a genuine star in the making, and Bernadette Peters... well, she had this incredible new hairdo with cascading curls and was so unbelievably beautiful and charming and pleasant and nice and... ohmigod... *Dames at Sea!*... *Mack and Mabel!* I just couldn't resist playing "Love is Good for Anything That Ails You" from her film *Pennies from Heaven* (the last great movie musical ever made, with great choreography by Danny Daniels) for her. She would smile and "boop-boop-a-doop" back at me. Then there was the hilarious Charles Kimbrough whom I teased unmercifully with the first two bars of "Sorry-Grateful," his number from Sondheim's *Company*, and Robert Westenberg, who just LOVED (hated) to be reminded of his previous job, working with the "legend in his own mind" star, Anthony Quinn, in the *Zorba* revival. I would play the opening vamp of "Life Is" and he would playfully throttle me at the piano... in a good way (unlike the way opera diva Teresa Stratas would in my next show, *Rags*). Nancy Opel (dear Nancy Opel) and Brent Spiner (years before he released his *Old Yellow Eyes* CD, capitalizing on his *Star Trek* fame) were cast as German servants, Franz and Frieda. Nancy Opel would perform some memorably funny antics in tech rehearsals, climbing all over the miniature second act office building cutouts as King Kong. Funny! She and I rehearsed some Marc Blitzstein music from the opera *Regina* for a concert she was involved with that contained some pseudo-gospel music, which had repeated instances of "Certainly Lord, Certainly Lord" in it. We could not contain our laughter rehearsing this. I can't think of Marc Blitzstein anymore without Nancy Opel's sopranoesque Certainly Lords coming to mind. And on top of that, the versatile Nancy Opel had been one of Patti LuPone's standbys in *Evita*!!! Every time I see Nancy Opel, I feel good for a minute. What a versatile, dazzling, hardworking talent! Certainly Lord!

This was a time when fun was had in rehearsals and personalities abounded. We weren't caught up in our "texts."

Minutes before the first week of rehearsals began, fresh music arrived from the copyists–in the corrected keys. WHEW! So we were in gear. What a relief! I can't remember the first moment I *officially* met Sondheim, just around the rehearsal piano I guess, but my first work session was with him and Barbara Bryne on the song "Beautiful." Just the three of us. I had to play it in four different keys. It's a testament to Sondheim and the like (of which there are very few) when you feel trusted and comfortable enough to actually function in their presence. When they just ignore you and let you do your job and don't hover, get nervous, or panic, or correct you, or micro-manage you, it's easy! Barbara Bryne was the focus of the rehearsal, and my little mistakes didn't matter. This session set the tone for me to relax and be myself. That was Stephen Sondheim. And certainly not the case with most other composers.

There was a new Soldier Song in the new music arrivals called "The One on the Left" for Bob Westenberg, Melanie Vaughn, and Mary D'Arcy. It was a huge piece of music! Long! And full of intricacies. Since all three were good musicians, they learned it quickly. Not so another new piece of music called "Nowhere to Go" for Mandy and Bernadette. It had the germ of an idea in it but was unnecessarily rhythmically challenging. Lots of busy 8th note noodling with a 7/8 bar here and a 5/8 bar there. Very Andrew Lloyd Webber. That piece of music lasted exactly one read-through in a private room and was never heard again. Dana Ivey and Charles Kimbrough were given a new abbreviated version of "No Life," and Bill Parry, Opel, and Spiner were given revised "The Day Off" sequences. Lapine was having Randolyn Zinn lead the whole company in morning promenades to music, practicing graceful walking while I played "No Life" or "The Day Off." (These came to a quick halt. I like to think that the audible groaning on my part had something to do with it. Why do directors waste their time with these silly exercises?) I don't remember anything eventful or dramatic happening during the rehearsing of Act One as Mandy and Bernadette were already up on their material. We just proceeded quickly.

I believe that the first song to go was "Yoo-Hoo." It was a moment for Nancy Opel, Danielle Ferland, and Cris Groenendaal that really should be heard in a revival... today... RIGHT NOW! It was short and funny. This show needed short and funny. The first two bars still exist in the score, leading into "No Life." The next major surgery in Act One was the new Soldier Song, "The One on the Left." All but the first two pages ended up on the rehearsal room floor. Late in rehearsals, the spot in the show that was to have been filled by the Andrew Lloyd Webber-esque number "Nowhere to Go" was filled with a lengthy duet for the two stars titled "We Do Not Belong Together." What I was starting to notice was that, despite the difficulty of the music for the title song and the "Color and Light" sequence, Sondheim's new music was rolling out in an easier, less complicated style. The performers were having no problem absorbing it. This new song was a big dramatic moment for Bernadette near the end of Act One. As we were learning it, I was thinking, "Where have I heard this before? Uh-oh! Don't go there, Paul!" But it was simply that Sondheim had taken the beautiful bridge of the original discarded workshop "Soldier Song" and made it the dramatic climax of this new number. Fine. Why waste a beautiful melody?

Act One was in good shape. Just a few snips followed here and there.

On to Act Two.

"It's Hot Up Here," the opening number of Act Two was easy, already rehearsed and staged from the workshop. But next was to come something called "The Chromolume Scene."

Act Two was set in the present with a whole new set of characters and a whole new story. The Chromolume was to be a performance art piece that was not dealt with yet. What would it be? There was tinkly underscoring of the dialogue that Ted and I improvised but none of that lasted. Mandy, now playing the present day 1980s George, and Bernadette, as his wheelchair-bound grandmother, talked and talked and talked in the scene as they presented George's latest creation. Then the Chromolume (whatever it was) was to start up. There was to be an explosion, a technical foul up, followed by more talk, and Brent Spiner, now playing a geeky technical director would enter, start the Chromolume up again, and Lapine would say, "The Chromolume!"

In 1983, I was five years in New York City, two years on the road. I had no idea what "performance art" was (or what "downtown" was for that matter). I had never really been to Soho or Noho, couldn't stand the Public Theatre after experiencing Elizabeth Swados's *Runaways*, and something called La Mama screamed "STAY AWAY!" to me in big neon lights, so this whole aspect of the show around performance art was bewildering to me.

Following this Chromolume thing was a party scene with a new song. The moment came when Paul Gemignani did to me what he would often do for 25 years. Without a moment's notice, not a hint that it was coming, he said, "Play a long glissando from the bottom of the piano to the top." I did. "Now play cocktail music." "Oh, but I don't… (play cocktail music, I wanted to say)." So I tried to play whatever cocktail music meant to me at the time. You know, "As Time Goes By" without the melody, I guess. "Now jump to that new music… okay jump!!!" The new music he referred to was Part 1 of *457 thousand* parts of a new song called "Putting It Together" that was to follow "The Chromolume." And between each of those parts, Paul wanted cocktail music. Bossa nova, jazz waltz, regular cocktail, walking bass with tinkly chords… and on and on. I was not happy that day. I had to keep track of what I did. Thank God, I still had a memory. He didn't approve or disapprove of anything I did, and since I would be playing it in the show, I made myself happy by arranging them to be comfortable to play. I don't know if Sondheim was ever happy with this stuff, I'm pretty sure Ted and orchestrator Michael Starobin weren't. (Starobin later rewrote them for the published score!) But as long as Paul Gemignani didn't care, so be it. This was one nightmare of a number to play. But I really wish I had been given a heads-up before having to improvise in front of the whole company. Even a lunch break to prepare. But this number actually fell into place fairly easily with the actors (not so later, in tech rehearsal with the pop-up prop Mandys that would or would not pop up out of the floor on cue). Ted Sperling officially wrote the last bar of "Putting It Together." Sondheim hates writing buttons to songs and Ted's was perfect. But Ted also pointed out something to me that was never noticed, addressed, or corrected in "Putting It Together." Mandy and company for the entire run of the show sang, and the orchestra even played, incorrectly, the phrase, "Bit by bit… Putting it together" and any variation of it (there were quite a lot of them). I'm ashamed to say that I didn't notice it either, but rhythm was not exactly my strong point. The rhythm is written as quarter note "Bit," quarter note rest, dotted quarter note "by," eighth note "bit." But Gemignani kept demonstrating it "vocally" as a dotted quarter note "Bit," a dotted quarter note "by," and a quarter note "bit," and Mandy, the company, and the orchestra went right along. It is simply not written that way in the score. If anyone out there would like a demonstration, call me at home. It makes a HUGE difference. This drove Ted Sperling crazy for a year-and-a-half. But too late. "Putting It Together" had been put together.

In the script, after the "Putting It Together" number, came another scene with lots of talk. Then followed another scene and... more talk... then Bernadette re-entered with the whole company for the final scene and... more talk... then finally the company was scripted to sing a second act finale culled from the first act finale. Act Two now consisted of "It's Hot Up Here," (talk talk talk), "The Chromolume," "Putting It Together," (talk talk talk), "FINALE!" It was my first Sondheim show. I didn't know his history of procrastination with his writing, but I noticed no one seemed worried. Maybe director Lapine... a little.

I don't remember exactly when, but I believe it was just as we went to the theatre for tech rehearsals, Sondheim sent to us through the music copyists a huge pile of music, pages and pages and pages, all 11" by 14" heavy stock (what were they thinking?!) for a new song for Mandy and Bernadette. The 11 o'clock number. It was built on the vamp that was hinted at in the cut "Nowhere To Go," but instead of a jagged rhythm and time signature changes, the music flowed in a peaceful, gentle, fluid murmur. Sondheim had composed the glorious century-spanning love duet, "Move On." And that, folks, was how we went into tech rehearsal in the theatre! With a second act full of missing songs!

Sondheim wanted to "audition" some of Michael Starobin's orchestrations since he was using someone new after Jonathan Tunick had done the last long series of shows. The orchestra of eleven was assembled and we tried "Color and Light," the title song, and "Finishing the Hat." Starobin and Gemignani wanted to try an experiment with the piano (oh, great!). The idea was that my piano was to be tricked up with a mechanism that would muffle the strings to create a *doink*ing sound to accompany Mandy/George's brush strokes during "Color and Light." An observer that day was asked to press his arms over the strings of my piano on cue. It was certainly "doinky." Ted was playing a huge synthesizer book, but they wanted a real piano sound with the special attachment built in. My piano went through several treatments, but the device never worked, and I was stuck with a crummy, damaged piano for the entire run of the show! Next, we played through "Finishing the Hat" and, immediately, Starobin's original orchestration was sent back to the drawing board. Sondheim's rolling piano accompaniment figure in thirds is the motor of the song, but Starobin broke it up between the woodwinds and piano. It would never have flowed, so the figure was put entirely on the piano as a base. I practiced that song every night and never felt I did it justice.

As we approached the *sitzprobe* (the first official orchestra reading with the cast), the Chromolume music was at last taking shape. Starobin created a series of sequences and triggers that Ted released on his synthesizer which would play themselves. Paul Gemignani just gave him cues. Then I played variations on Sondheim's opening arpeggiated chords on my synth (yes, they finally did sneak a fucking synthesizer into my part!) on top of Ted's sequences. Our horn player would then play an expansive theme on top of that. Very much like Alexander Courage's fanfare in the opening credits of *Star Trek*.

We soon had a day when the special effects being created for the sequence were explained by Bran Ferren, about how and what to do in case of any runaway laser beams, and the Chromolume was unveiled. The Chromolume was a big white rocketship-shaped machine with a large white ball on top. It would be set center stage. A slide show was projected onto the white ball while Mandy and Bernadette did their performance art speech. Oh, and, of course (what else), the omnipresent dry ice fog would fill the stage. After the dialogue was done, Ted's synthesizer would sound a low ominous note and a green laser light show was projected out into the house. The music from Ted's synthesizer would burst into wild shimmering sequences, Ron would play his expansive horn melody, and I did my arpeggiated chords, waiting for my piano glissando cue into the "cocktail music." It was Show Biz Magic! During the run of the show we did have some fun with this. One night I dared Ron Sell, our horn player, to actually play the *Star Trek* fanfare on top of all of the Chromolume music. He did it! No one batted an eye.

The orchestra moved into the orchestra pit and what a set-up that was! Generous Mathilde Pincus, who was the legendary music copyist of the time, liked me and decided to do me a favor. She believed that my music was difficult to play (it was) and that I might have trouble with substitute keyboard players (I did), so she decided to keep my piano part on the same 11" by 14" paper as the piano/vocal rehearsal book, including the vocal line and lyrics. The subs could follow the lyrics and know exactly where they were at all times, but it meant that there were three times more page turns than there would have been had she written me a tight, no frills 8.5" by 11" piano part. I was speechless. I didn't know what to say but... thank you! I wasn't strong enough to ask for a piano part the size that everyone else was getting. Since my piano had to actually go underneath the audience to fit in the pit, and there was no room to the right or left of me, we were forced to place my synthesizer (you guessed it!) on top of my piano where the music rack would normally be. My big cumbersome music books had to go on my far left! On a rickety music stand! I played the entire run looking forward toward the conductor while my music was almost out of my peripheral vision on my left... and I had to turn pages, voluminous page turns, with my LEFT HAND AS I WAS PLAYING. This couldn't have been worse. A year-and-a-half of it. I had only three subs and the only one who played more than once was David Krane. Thanks to him, I got a vacation. He said it was the hardest thing he had ever had to do.

The first preview was up and running and going smoothly, unbelievably so. What a thrill. At the end, I got up from my piano and walked out into Shubert Alley and exhaled. Surprised and delighted, I saw two old friends from my hometown of Atlanta waiting, Lulu Downs and her boyfriend. I had kvelled at seeing Lulu in her Broadway debut in Tommy Tune's *Nine*. She was the "German at the Spa" who stopped the show in Act Two with her tambourine/vagina act. (And just to illustrate how Broadway has changed, the 2003 Roundabout revival of *Nine* simply cut "The Germans at the Spa!" The song *and* the characters. In other words, anything that is fun and imaginative and might take the audience on a little ride is now deemed extraneous and unworthy.) Back to Lulu. Happy to see them, I hurried over. Twenty-seven years of Alcoholics Anonymous has now taught me to expect absolutely nothing from anyone... *ever!* But after having encouraged and supported Lulu through her wonderful show for two years, I expected a big scream of congratulations. After all, I had just played my first preview of an original Stephen Sondheim musical under the baton of Paul Gemignani starring Bernadette Peters and Mandy Patinkin. This was a miracle for this kid from Atlanta, Georgia. What Lulu said to me was, "Ugh, how can you play that *terrible* music! That must be torture!" (And she *spat* on the ground. In Shubert Alley!) I trudged home. I never saw or spoke to her again.

Now for a brief rant. For forty-five years, I have had this experience. Friends, relatives, audience members, smart people, dumb people, strangers, and lovers have all done this. If you don't like the show your friend is in, please, think before you speak. Point up what you like and be supportive of their contribution. If you feel the need to be hypercritical and the person you are speaking to then rips your face off, do not defend yourself with the excuse, "Well, you didn't write it. You just played the piano for it (or made the costumes, or did the dancing, or sold the tickets). It's no reflection on you that it was the biggest piece of shit I've ever had to sit through and I want my two hours back! You're just too sensitive!"

Remember, if you are a host, waiter, or even a busboy, you don't want to have friends, relatives, diners, smart people, dumb people, strangers, and lovers say, "I hated my meal at your restaurant. It made me want to throw up!" Or if you're a heart surgeon or a nurse, you certainly don't want to come home to or leave the hospital encountering friends, relatives, smart people, dumb people, strangers, and lovers saying, "Heard the body count's up at your hospital. Don't take me to *that* emergency room!"

So, as I said, I never saw Lulu again. I never again saw my first boss, Billy Densmore, at any of my performances after leaving the Northside School of Performing Arts in 1975, in Atlanta or on Broadway. And people told me I was too sensitive. No, I just had high expectations of people. That is no longer true, and I am now a hypercritical, caustic, and take-no-prisoners cynic. Justifiably so.

The first preview over, there was now a lot of work to do. All of the existing music in the show was orchestrated, but since there was still a big gaping hole in Act Two, something new was coming soon. We started understudy rehearsals, and I was down in the men's room in the lobby where the sign for the enhanced hearing headphones was on display. In large print and quotations, the sign read "DON'T MISS A WORD!" Underneath that, someone had written "MISS AN ACT!"—meaning Act Two of our show! I was starting to hear that audiences were generally happy with the first act but confused over the second. At one performance, during the "Move On" scene, Mandy was being quite "intimate" on stage and someone from the audience yelled "Louder!" WOW! Stunning! Mandy just got softer and sang "Move On" in a whisper. (Yeah, that'll show 'em!)

A week before the critics came, I was called to the lobby and handed two new songs, one for Bernadette and one for Mandy, "Children and Art" and "Lesson #8," respectively. We barely rehearsed them. I had barely seen the music and yet they were going into the show the next night—UNORCHESTRATED! I had never dreamed of or heard of such a thing, but we did it. "Children and Art" went well, but I don't think Mandy and I were on the same planet with "Lesson #8." After the show, I sheepishly excused myself as I squeezed between Sondheim and Bernadette to leave the theatre. They were talking about her new song. She said to Steve, seriously, "Maybe we should keep it as a piano solo." As I squeezed past, I called back "NO!" Enough pressure was enough. Eventually, we had a fully-orchestrated score just in time for opening night. My mother came up from Atlanta. She and my roommate were given front-row seats for opening night. She LOVED it. We went to Sardi's for the opening night party. This was the first time I noticed that no matter how hard the musicians work on a show (and, after all, *what makes a musical is the music*), we were treated differently from the rest of the company. After entering Sardi's, we were immediately sent back outside and directed next door, where an elevator took us not to the second, but the third floor in order to keep us from mixing with the "real" people. I was disappointed and angry. This was the first time this happened. *It never happened again.* Because I never went to another opening night party at Sardi's again. I wanted to introduce my mother to everyone, but we were relegated to the third floor with the "help." For some reason (probably just because they were nice people), Mandy and Bernadette came up there and I got to grab them for a second, but it was *their* night, so I didn't intrude for long. The reviews were mixed, but we would run for a year-and-a-half, achieve cult status and win a Pulitzer Prize!

Since it was May, it was already Tony Awards time. We filmed the first act finale for the telecast. I gave my one and only Tony Awards party in my apartment. Most guests hated my show and *La Cage Awful* swept most of the awards. As they left my apartment, they were saying my show was not really worthy of any awards. This would never occur again. Nobody would be invited into my apartment and this remained so for thirty years. Then came the original cast recording.

Fasten your seat belts, this was going to be a bumpy ride. Sondheim and Lapine got together with record producer Thomas Z. Shepard well in advance to figure out timings, edits, cuts, etc. They got down to micromanaging tiny, tiny, tiny cuts of a bar of music here, a bar of music there, a vamp here, four bars there, especially in the long numbers "Color and Light," "The Day Off" sequence, and "Putting It Together." They gave all these cuts to Mathilde Pincus, the copyist, in plenty of time for her office to work up a new batch of orchestrations reflecting the changes. But in typical Broadway fashion, not one word, not one peep of any of this was told to the conductor or the actors until they were in front of the microphones on the day of the recording! Nonetheless it was an exciting day. But those long numbers had to be recorded in sixteen bar sections because Paul, Mandy and Bernadette couldn't absorb all the tiny changes. The orchestra had music to read, but Mandy and Bernadette didn't really read music, so...

And, as is typical in a recording studio at that time, the layout of the instruments was screwy. I was informed that for the best sound of the piano, my back would have to be to the conductor all day long. I repeat, my back had to be to the conductor all day long. One mo' time! MY BACK HAD TO BE TO

THE CONDUCTOR ALL DAY LONG! I guess I was supposed to pull a Linda Blair and spin my head all the way around. There were added strings and a real bass player. Ted Sperling had been playing the bass on his synthesizer for the performances, but now we had a real bass player... who didn't know this complicated score. The great high G on the French horn at the end of Act One was replaced by a trumpet. The trumpet is disappointing, the bass is never with the orchestra, and *I'm* never with the orchestra (did I tell you my back had to be to the conductor all day long?), and since so many numbers were edited together piece by piece, there are wildly varying tempo changes throughout. In other words, it's a mess! Listen to the first horn solo on the first track and note the terrible edit right after the first phrase. And when Mandy does his *a capella* "red red blue blue" stuff in "Color and Light," he is going very fast, but when the orchestra comes back in, the music is a third slower than where Mandy had been. The sound is too reverberant, and the orchestra sounds miles away. Despite all this, it was a thrilling day. However, I can never listen to it. I have a homemade CD of the soundtrack taken from the PBS DVD of the show and I listen to *that* whenever I want to hear this show, because I can't listen to the award-winning original cast recording.

We only won two Tony Awards because *La Cage Awful* ran off with our best musical, score, book, and performance Tonys. Ah well (to quote Sondheim), every day a little death.

Celebrity sightings! I was coming out of the theatre one night and rushing around the corner to go home when a woman burst out of the exit doors running across the sidewalk to a limo. It was Streisand. That stopped me in my tracks. She recorded several songs from the show on her *Back to Broadway* album. One song would have been sufficient ("We Do Not Belong Together") in order to make room for other great Broadway composers. Lerner and Loewe, Lane and Harburg, Leonard Bernstein, and Harold Rome were all recorded, but they didn't make the cut. For shaaaame!! Well, that was the closest I've ever been to her. Another night I was going up to Bernadette's dressing room to tell her how my mother loved her singing the old '20s song "Poor Butterfly" on the *Johnny Carson Show* and, as I was coming back down the tight hallway to leave, a 6' 4" man was coming my way. I had to squeeze by none other than Rock Hudson to get through. And it was wild to see Warren Beatty, who turned out to be a Sondheim freak, hanging out at the stage door.

During the summer, we settled into the run and I learned that I was going to have to submit a "sub list." A what? A sub list! What's that? Well, if you miss a show or are sick, someone has to substitute for you. Me? Miss a performance? Someone else play my Sondheim show? What, are you crazy? You have to, Paul, it's a union requirement, I was told. You have to take two weeks of vacation. What?!?!? NOBODY is playing my book! But I was forced to have a sub. I went to Jamaica with Charlie for four days and a sub played the book. When I came back, Paul Gemignani said "No" to the sub. So, I went to David Krane, who reluctantly agreed to do it. He made the grade.

I decided I wanted to see the show from out front, so I took a night off and stood in the back of the house. There were two other people standing near me, a young couple whispering and smooching all through the show. The house manager was keeping an eye on them. Toward the end of the show, around "Lesson #8," the guy of the couple suddenly yelled out to the stage, "YOU'RE BORING!" The house manager grabbed them both by the collar and shoved them out the exit. Bravo! I didn't have a good time seeing the show that night. I was disappointed in the thinness of the orchestra, but that's what you get with eleven instruments. (The Roundabout revival in 2008 had only five of the eleven players, and all were situated and playing from the house-right box seat area at Studio 54. It was like listening to your old stereo with the left speaker disconnected. I hate the Roundabout. Cheapskates! It's not a concept, it's just cheap!)

Word spread that Mandy was leaving the show. What? It was August! We had only been running three months! So, Bob Westenberg played George with Bernadette and then *she* left (ohmigod) and Cris Groenendaal played George for a bit and Betsy Joslyn played Dot, and then Harry Groener played George, and then Maryanne Plunkett played Dot, and then Mandy came back, and the original cast came back to film it for PBS right before it closed. (Thank God for that!) All in 18 months.

But let's talk about all the wonderful folks who auditioned for George and Dot. And one of my favorite theatre stories is courtesy of the wonderful Betsy Joslyn. Betsy was playing one of the Celestes and was very funny and often ad-libbed, to the pleasure of the orchestra. Then she played Dot, beautifully... for a while. She had black hair and intense blue eyes and a thorough command of her voice with no break. It was a unique sound that only she had. And she had incredible comic timing. But, alas, there were still auditions going on to replace Bernadette. Patti LuPone learned the title song, as did Maureen McGovern, Ellen Greene, Pam Dawber, Marilu Henner, and Maryanne Plunkett. Sondheim was most interested in Ellen Greene and at her audition came down to give her an adjustment on the song. He asked her if she could try the song without the accent. She said "What eeck-thent?" (Thunday in the Puawk wit Joe-wahge!) And the answer was, "No, she couldn't." *Little Shop of Horrors* meets Pawis, Fwance. She got to play Dot eventually in Alan Menken's rip-off musical, *Weird Romance*, singing the rip-off song, "Someone Else Is Waiting" ("Move On," Menken style).

No one else had the vulnerable ethereal qualities of Bernadette, so it was looking good for Betsy Joslyn. I was praying and keeping my fingers crossed. Then Maryanne Plunkett came in right under the wire and was so honest and commanding that you could see Lapine and Sondheim just polishing up that old silver platter. She got the job and was lovely. Sondheim threw one of his cozy parties for the company, my first time ever at his townhouse on East 49th Street, with Katharine Hepburn still next door. I was in heaven. Harry Groener was George and quite a few more replacements had come in. Frank Kopyc for Kurt Knudson, Bruce Adler for Brent Spiner, Jeff Keller for Bob Westenberg, Pamela Burrell for Dana Ivey, but Betsy was there looking all glammed up in her new floor-length Betsey Johnson-designed dress. It was black satin with big red tropical flowers all over it. Her figure was great, and the dress showed it off. Very Morticia Addams with a splash of color. She had just received the news about Maryanne Plunkett and was beating herself up over it. I was one of Betsy's biggest fans and tried to raise her spirits. The party was going on. Sondheim's house had so much interesting décor everywhere, all board-game-themed, with decks of antique playing cards framed and hung in rows on the walls and doors. We were mostly limited to the ground floor, a family room, with a dining area in the back with buffet looking out onto the gardens of Turtle Bay. The sun was still out, so we could wander in the gardens a bit. The second floor had the legendary music room with the piano, and an office with a metal vault that saved his original scores when there was a huge fire. The two floors above were not for our viewing. The music room had a wonderful stained-glass alcove where I'm sure Sondheim dreamed up much of his work. The place was lively that night. Most of us were newcomers. I was upstairs in the music room with Betsy as more people arrived downstairs. Suddenly, an entrance was made by our new leading lady, Maryanne Plunkett. She had on a new flamboyant dress with ruffled sleeves and a wide skirt with petticoats. Very old-fashioned and girly. It was designed by Betsey Johnson. It was made of black satin. With big red tropical flowers on it. The exact same material as Betsy Joslyn's dress! "This irresistible Paris original..." (And if you don't understand that musical theatre reference, close this book and throw it away.) Betsy spent the rest of the night standing behind a big armchair.

One of my favorite auditions was for Brent Spiner's replacement. Bruce Adler came in for the part of Franz. He sang "What Kind of Fool Am I?" Lapine whined, "Uhhh... well... hmmmmmmmmm... what else do you have... is that alllll?" Then he told Bruce to be a "bad lounge singer from New Jersey" and sing it again, but up-tempo AND with a German accent! He did. He got the job. I played many auditions for Lapine over the years and I loved it when he did that. I love it more when the actors are game and go with it without batting an eyelash. Another memorable moment was when Lapine asked a man to sing a souped-up Las Vegas version of "Johanna." We were *on* that day. One more audition that was interesting was John Rubinstein's for George. He was given the Dog Song and "Move On" (even though most of that is Dot's song). He came in with single-sided sheet music and was asked to tackle "Move On" first. He had much musical training and seemed a little put-off at being asked to display his wares in such a manner. As he half-heartedly crooned through the song, he tossed the sheets in the air and, when he was done, he just left them there for the stage manager to pick up. Nice. And that was a load of pages.

There was often great fun in the orchestra pit. We laughed a lot at the copyists who mistakenly mistitled "Move On" as "Move In" on our orchestra music. With our fabulous horn player nailing that high G on the horn next to me every night in the first act finale, we would often applaud him and then cheer his best subs when they would nail it. We were very proud of the show. Marilyn Reynolds, Karl Bargen, Eileen Folson, Ron Sell, Cecelia Hobbs, Les Scott, Al Hunt, Bob Ayers, Beth Schwartz Robinson, Ted Sperling. All great.

The comic highlight of that pit concerned a 14-note melody in the underscoring of the song "Putting It Together." Michael Starobin had forgotten to orchestrate it and just left it to the keyboards. I played the chords and Ted Sperling played the 14-note melody with a different synthesizer sound every night for the whole run. Eventually, Ted wrote the melody out for all the instruments and each person would take turns riffing on it. But the best was the night Ted gave each orchestra member one note a piece which added up to 9 notes. Ted took the first 5, and then it went around the orchestra like dominoes falling. (I, being the eleventh musician, of course, stayed on my chords.) It worked beautifully and we all screamed with laughter, barely recovering for the rest of the number. Show business USED to be fun!

I look back on this year-and-a-half (1984-1985) as the happiest, most golden period of my life, when I had a lot of what I thought should have made me happy. And much of it did. I was happy to be with my partner, Charlie. I was trying to take care of myself. I was not drinking. I was really settling in. I was playing THE MOST BEAUTIFUL music I would ever play in my life for two of the most talented people in the world. This all fell into my lap. I got my first original Stephen Sondheim musical by standing outside the men's room on the fourth floor of Michael Bennett's 890 Broadway rehearsal studios. I went to Jamaica, Monte Carlo, and Paris with Charlie, and we took pictures on the actual Island of La Grande Jatte. I stumbled onto my apartment where I would stay for more than 35 years and never pay over $700.00 a month (I now own it outright). I still had a waistline; I was 31 years old... but I really believed that this was all an accident and that I had no participation in it's happening whatsoever. It was all just dumb luck. It was all a series of miracles. Some great, some good, some in the form of future lessons to be learned. But all of it golden for little me from Atlanta.

A footnote on this show. In 1994, while previewing *Passion*, we did a one-night 10th year anniversary concert of *Sunday in the Park with George* with the original cast and the original orchestra, minus Karl Bargen, who had passed away. Bob Westenberg also didn't join us and Howard McGillin subbed for him. It was on the set of *The Who's Tommy* at the St. James Theatre and Lapine used the slide-show equipment to run a breathtaking series of photos as background for the scenes and then a personal, candid, rehearsal slide show during the exit music. The audience did not move a muscle or utter a sound during the exit music. They were that spellbound. The actors rehearsed very little and carried scripts. Bernadette was Bernadette, Mandy was Mandy, Dana Ivey stole the show, Charles Kimbrough was now celebrated for *Murphy Brown*, Danielle Ferland had grown up, Cris Groenendaal had gotten more amusingly curmudgeonly, Nancy Opel had never stopped working, Brent Spiner was a TV star icon, Bill Parry was his usual "great guy," and Melanie Vaughn and Mary D'Arcy were still sopranos. Even Kurt Knudson came back with the fabulous Judith Moore, tearing the house down as "Mr. and Mrs." And, of course, "our mom," Barbara Bryne. It was a flawless concert and the most surprising thing was that it became the musical COMEDY it always had hidden away inside of itself. Everything that was sardonic, ironic, satirical, sophisticated, and smart bounced around the theatre that night like the lasers in the original Chromolume. The laughs were long and outrageous, but always appropriate. It put all of us at ease. I have never seen such a reaction to a script like that in a concert reading. Brilliant. And as I said, Dana Ivey stole the show as Yvonne in the first act and as the morose modern composer, Naomi Eisen, in Act Two. Her hair even got laughs. This was my very own *A Chorus Line* longest-running-show night. I have never experienced anything like it before or since. When "Mr. and Mrs." (Kurt and Judy) came downstage with their pastries and their southern accents complaining about "Paree," Judy said her line, "I don't see any PASSION either," the audience screamed for two minutes just because of the connection to the mixed reaction that Sondheim and Lapine's latest show *Passion* was getting at the time. All the hard work on *Passion* was worth the payoff of that reaction to that line on that night! I bumped into Donna Murphy afterwards as she was coming backstage, and all she could say was "That was an UNBELIEVABLE experience!" I agreed. If I died today (if *only* I had died then), my life would have been worth it.

21. Bring On the Girls

FOLLIES IN CONCERT

I was not trusted enough, I believe, by conductor Paul Gemignani to handle the stylistic aspect of the *Follies* score and Tom Fay was hired to play the performances of the new Lincoln Center concert and recording of *Follies*. But I came away with the best possible consolation prize. I was the rehearsal pianist for three days in a brightly lit room with Barbara Cook, George Hearn, Lee Remick, Mandy Patinkin, Elaine Stritch, Betty Comden and Adolph Green, Carol Burnett, and a host of others for this historic event. I was completely oblivious to the filming that was going on, but when PBS aired the (disappointing) TV special of the concert, I was far from disappointed! I was EVERYWHERE in the documentary, playing for all of the above people, even having my very special moment with Stritch where she corrected me on the tempo of "Broadway Baby." (It would have been nice if conductor Paul Gemignani had informed me of that little detail ahead of time, but I was completely on my own, as always, for those three days accompanying that incredible crew, while Gemignani rehearsed the orchestra in the concert hall.) Something that didn't make the documentary was Carol Burnett singing "I'm Still Here" quietly into her tape recorder and then doing one of her trademark BWAH-HA! laughs as my music accidentally ripped apart and fell from the piano.

Also not shown was Lee Remick complaining about the Lucy and Jessie tempo, with director Herb Ross coming to my defense. This would be my shining hour on public television. I was thin, I was handsome, I was partnered, I was sober (dry), and I was having a blast with these legendary people. Little money and no credit, but there I was plastered all over the place and I absolutely cream every time someone says, "I was watching that Lincoln Center *Follies* DVD and was that... could that have been... was that REALLY YOU playing for that?" I swell up like a peacock. I don't care, I loved it and I'm proud of it. The finished product (the recording and the video) left much to be desired, though.

And now, in my personal showbiz tale the bottom falls out with the traumatizing four-month prison sentence I had to endure called *Rags*. At least the friendly, happy, funny star of *Company* and *West Side Story*, Larry Kert, was on hand to brighten things up occasionally with some all-knowing and welcome sarcastic asides.

There is a difference in putting together a big Broadway musical when you have a Stephen Sondheim (my hero for the moment). There is no guesswork with him. He COMPOSES his scores! He doesn't hum or sing into a tape recorder and leave the rest to the arrangers. He doesn't give us fucking lead sheets (melodies and chord symbols). He writes a full piano score with nothing left to the imagination. This is rare... and I was now spoiled rotten.

The next chapter illustrates what can happen when a Stephen Sondheim is *not* at the helm of the music in, of all things, a *musical!*

22. Rags

After *Sunday in the Park with George* closed, I took six months to relax, live on unemployment, bask in my own glory, and enjoy Charlie, but finally I needed a job. The conductor Eric Stern asked me if I wanted to play rehearsals and be the acoustic pianist in the pit for a new show entitled *Rags* slated for Broadway. I immediately said yes, knowing little more than the name of the composer. Charles Strouse was a hero of mine.

There are in my mind four composer-lyricist duos that I lump into what I call the '60s *craftsmen*. First, John Kander and Fred Ebb. I have a love/hate history with their show *Cabaret*, mild affection for *The Happy Time*, delight with the recording of *Flora the Red Menace*, and true admiration for *70, Girls, 70*, even after working on a troubled production at Encores!

Next come Tom Jones and Harvey Schmidt, who wrote four little gems, *The Fantasticks*, *I Do! I Do!*, *110 in the Shade*, and my favorite, *Celebration*, with its great collection of songs!

The successful team of Jerry Bock and Sheldon Harnick gave us *Fiddler on the Roof* (masterful, but unappealing to me, thus way down on my list), *Fiorello* (Pulitzer Prize-winning but dull to me), *She Loves Me* (which has grown on me a little over the years, but is ultimately just too academic and a bit dull), and two curiosities that I love and admire which are seldom done or done well, *Tenderloin* and *The Apple Tree*.

And finally, Charles Strouse and Lee Adams. *It's a Bird, It's a Plane, It's Superman* is a desert island recording for me, and *Bye, Bye, Birdie* comes close. *Golden Boy* is a great collection of songs but will never be quite the same without Sammy Davis, Jr. *Applause* has a terrible score but is absolutely terrific fun, and *Annie* was a mega-hit (though uninspired musically). One thing to be said for Charles Strouse, this man could write an infectious melody. Unfortunately, after *Annie* came a legendary series of instant disasters unrivaled by any composer ever—*Dance a Little Closer, A Broadway Musical, Charlie and Algernon, Annie 2: Miss Hannigan's Revenge, Bring Back Birdie, Nick and Nora, Minsky's,* and... *Rags.*

I was excited about adding a Charles Strouse show to my list of experiences, and grateful that Stephen Schwartz was only writing lyrics, though he seemed to have a big influence on Strouse (perhaps even composing some of the songs), leading to a weird eclectic score with that dreaded (and always dreadful) contemporary pop sound (example, the song "Wanting") creeping into what was struggling to be an authentic period score.

My first job was to play a few auditions, one of which was for a pre-adolescent Christian Slater! Eric Stern and I shared a cab uptown after auditions one day. He was groaning and I asked him what was the matter. He, with escalating panic, explained to me that Charles Strouse had not sent the score of the show (which had gone through several workshops) to be professionally copied into piano/vocal parts for the cast and staff. And Strouse had no intention of doing so. I had not yet seen any music, and Eric described the disastrous condition of the present rehearsal score—Strouse's original pencil scratches, an odd handwritten manuscript page, a few lead sheets, a piece of yellow legal pad paper, a napkin with chord symbols, etc. He told me flat out that he had one week before rehearsals began to sit down and write an entire vocal/piano book from the existing material, because Strouse "has the first nickel he ever made" and refused to spend the money to have his own music in professional condition. Throughout the six-week rehearsal period, Eric Stern confined himself for a majority of each day to a small cubicle at 890 Studios, writing simple arrangements of every song as fast as he could, as well as dance arrangements for the choreographer. Everything was handwritten in those days.

The creative staff of this show was headed by director Joan Micklin Silver (WHO??) helming her first musical. Once again, we had that strange phenomenon of hiring a staff with musical theatre experience and then putting someone with no experience whatsoever in charge. The powers-that-were believed Silver's little Lower East Side-set film, *Hester Street,* gave her the insight to helm a $3,000,000 epic stage musical. The rest of the team included Broadway veteran Joe Stein, book writer of *Fiddler on the Roof*, Ken Rinker (WHO??), another in a long list of downtown garage dance company choreographers doing his first musical, newcomer Michael Starobin creating the orchestrations, and Lee Guber and Shelly Gross, the masters of summer schlock, as producers. Sets and lighting were by opera designer Beni Montresor, designer of *Do I Hear a Waltz?* (Rumor has it that he never finished those sets either!) My fellow piano player was the ever youthful, brilliantly talented Scott Frankel, composer of *Grey Gardens*.

The cast was unbelievable—enough stars for three Broadway shows—opera diva Teresa Stratas (along with her reputation for tantrums and canceling performances), Larry Kert, Terence Mann, Judy Kuhn, Lonny Price, Dick Latessa, Marcia Lewis, Evalyn Baron, Michael Cone, Michael Davis (the original "Springtime for Hitler" tenor in the movie comedy *The Producers*—not the Susan Stroman version, the REAL movie), with Donna Murphy standing by for Stratas. Donna left after a few days to return to *The Mystery of Edwin Drood* to take over Betty Buckley's role. Donna missed quite a journey. She was succeeded by the beautiful and thoroughly professional Christine Andreas.

On the first day of rehearsal, Eric Stern gave Scott and me our photocopies of the first few songs in the show. He would barely stay ahead of the rehearsal progress by daily turning out pages of the score. My first moment (of many such moments) after the cast meet-and-greet, was to go into a room with Strouse, Schwartz and star Teresa Stratas, a tiny little woman with a roaring speaking voice. The stage manager gave her a photocopy of the first song, a duet for her and Judy Kuhn set on a boat on its way to Ellis Island. Stratas looked at the music and said, "What the hell is this? I can't read this! I need professionally copied music!" Wheeee! And awaaaaaaaaaaaaaaay we go! (as Jackie Gleason frequently declared). After singing the quiet, nostalgia-tinged ditty full out in her huge soprano, Stephen Schwartz immediately stepped forward and said, "Could you sing it more like this..." and proceeded to demonstrate in his best Art Garfunkel folk-rock-pop-*Godspell*-"Corner of the Sky" style. Stratas said, "If you want it to sound like that, why the fuck did you hire ME?" At that moment I had nothing but respect for this lady.

Three weeks of rehearsal passed with Eric feverishly writing in his little room, while I played the dance music for the title song for the choreographer, and Scott masterfully held down the big room.

One nice moment with Stephen Schwartz was our talking about film scores. He had a particular favorite, Elmer Bernstein's beautiful score for *To*

Kill a Mockingbird. I couldn't help but agree with him and during some of the grimmer moments on this show, I would play a few bars of the main theme and we would smile together.

Director Joan Micklin Silver stood for three weeks with her hands tapping her chin, unable to utter a direction or make a decision. We were all busy, but nothing was happening. The first cast member to go was actor Alan Manson who flat out quit, and then choreographer Ken Rinker was replaced (for exactly one hour) by Graciela Daniele.

I came in early one morning at 9:30 to find Graciela rehearsing some social dancing with Stratas. Stratas barked at me, "Get over to that piano and play that 'Yankee Boy' song." I did what I was told and started playing the foxtrot tune. All of a sudden, I heard a shriek from across the room! "When we stop dancing, YOU STOP PLAYING!! YOU'RE CONFUSING ME!" and Stratas tore across the room and put her bony fingers around my neck and started to throttle me. Graciela Daniele came over and ushered her back to her spot. My mother is the only person who had ever touched me in such a way (spanking me) so I felt assaulted by this event. An hour later I knocked on Eric Stern's door and asked to speak to him. "She put her hands on me and assaulted me! What do I do?" Eric sighed and shrugged his shoulders. I wanted to quit but I was 33 years old and afraid that I would "never work again in this town," so later when he came out of his room, I told him, "Okay, I will play dance rehearsals, understudy rehearsals, and pit performances, but I will not be in the same room or play for that woman again!" Eric sighed and shrugged his shoulders. I never played for, nor spoke to, Teresa Stratas again until the last matinee performance in New York four months later.

A week later, the entire company arrived in Boston for a four-week run at the Shubert Theatre. We were Joan Micklin Silver-less now, for a few days earlier Charles Strouse and Stephen Schwartz had stood in front of the company and informed us that *they* would be "co-directors" on the show until further notice. A terrible omen! We used every second and then some (including days off) because of this decision. Beni Montresor had made little progress with the physical production. Jules Fisher was now taking on the lighting and if anyone knows Jules Fisher, his lights are certainly worth waiting for, but Jules Fisher can make a company wait... and wait... and wait. Which left much time for the two co-directors to disagree on every aspect of the show.

Our new choreographer was the old pro Ron Field from *Cabaret* and *Applause* (and fired from Sondheim's *Merrily We Roll Along*). He and his assistant sat behind me at the rehearsal piano, which was in the house-right aisle of the Shubert Theatre for most of the tech period. We had a great time talking about a project he wanted to do, showcasing the work of the fabulous choreographer Jack Cole. I knew all the movies he was referencing, and on a day off in New York I copied my video tapes of *Down to Earth*, *The "I Don't Care" Girl*, *Meet Me After the Show*, and *Three for the Show* for him. He was very grateful, and we had a load of fun talking about obscure movie musicals. The one thing, though, that Ron Field *didn't do* was choreograph. I kept asking him when they were going to give him the time to work, and he said that they were not. "They won't let me do anything! Every time I make a suggestion or try to talk about staging, they say 'Not now, Ron.'" So, as far as I know, Ron Field never staged a number or choreographed a step on the show.

I was obliged (and paid) to stay at the piano, but when Stratas came onstage I got up and signaled Eric or Scott, and then left the auditorium to go work with the understudies in the lobby.

We had early morning meetings before noon rehearsals to discuss various musical numbers. One number, "Penny a Tune," was a lengthy montage scene that began with street musicians—a violin, a clarinet and a tuba. Charles Strouse's ambitions for this sequence were to not only introduce many characters and convey a passage of time, but to also show the entire evolution of how Klezmer music became jazz! All in seven minutes! The number was to end with a huge orchestral blast of fast, loud (and slightly anachronistic) swing music. By opening night in New York most of it had been cut. It was one of *those* numbers—a number worked on every day for hours before being slashed to ribbons or eliminated altogether! The big soaring ballad "Children of the Wind" was originally arranged and staged for Stratas, Kuhn, Latessa and the ensemble to build into the main anthem of the show. Then someone (Strouse or Schwartz) wanted to make it a solo for Stratas. Then Schwartz or Strouse wanted to put the family characters back in, making it a trio. Then Strouse or Schwartz wanted the ensemble back in, then Schwartz and Strouse wanted... and round and round and round it went. I was present for one table meeting when the whole creative team conferred on this number. The discussion would start with Schwartz saying, "I want it to be a solo." And each person around the table would say "Okay, let's make it a solo." Around the table we went and finally it was Strouse's vote. "You know, I think it should be an ensemble number." Back around the table, a series of "Well, maybe it should be an ensemble number." And finally, Schwartz would acquiesce and say "Okay, I see what you mean. We'll keep the ensemble." Then Strouse would say "Well, now that I think about it, it should be a solo." And around and around the table we'd go. Since we had two co-directors, every single issue and decision went through this process. By now it was obvious that Schwartz had a better grip and more experience as a director and was capable of keeping us afloat. Therefore, I started referring to Strouse as "Contrary Mary" because, like clockwork, he would always pick the opposite viewpoint on everything. Finally, I heard Schwartz say, "OH, SHUT UP, CHARLES!" and off we went. Up, up and awaaaaaaay! Somewhere around this time, the company got word that Teresa Stratas would *not* be performing for the first few preview performances. WHAT?!? This announcement followed what we heard was a hotel room dispute between the co-directors and Stratas that ended in a chair being thrown at Strouse and an ultimatum from Stratas that she would not perform until *they* got their "shit" together. Christine Andreas went on for at least ten performances including opening night! She had watched and studied (although she'd not been on the stage for one second) and got superlative reviews. The show itself received enthusiastic, encouraging reviews and audience comments.

What we had in the show now was an opening sequence (no Overture) minus the Stratas-Kuhn duet, a trio version of "Children of the Wind," a "Penny a Tune" sans the history of klezmer into jazz, oddities such as ensemble member Gabriel Barre walking around on stilts as a street performer (making everybody nervous), a comic Yiddish theatre version of Hamlet ("Sometimes it's hard to be a Prince!"), a beautiful bluesy romantic number for Stratas ("Blame It On the Summer Night," with lyrics that didn't rhyme), a montage of dances to Lonny Price's song, "The Sound of Love," Yankee Doodle rags, Victrola waltzes, political rags, a showstopping title song for Kuhn complete with a brief dream ballet, a showstopping duet for Lewis and Latessa ("Three Sunny Rooms"), a showstopping "Rose's Turn"-type soliloquy for Stratas ("Dancing With the Fools"), pop ballads ("Wanting"—"I must be wanting in my brain...!"), riot numbers, a union number ("Bread and Freedom"), a "Brand New World" song for Stratas that had one of my all-time favorite pop song rhymes ("world" and "whirl"), a "let's beat up the kid" mob scene, and the Triangle factory fire disaster with the death of Judy Kuhn's character. Not to mention, an opening number, "Greenhorns," a Cherry Street Café scene complete with a Texas Guinan-type chanteuse singing, what else, "At the Cherry Street Café," and scenically, a giant Statue of Liberty that rode across the stage, boobs to torch only, painted white, a few mirrored (mirrored?) panels and a few panels representing tenement buildings. A frightening, dangerous looking metal black bridge would descend from the flies like the mother ship in *Close Encounters* and then barely be used in the staging. *Sweeney Todd* also had such a contraption as part of its gargantuan set design.

There was no time, money, or interest in how to stage the climactic Triangle fire, Judy Kuhn's death scene, so Judy was told to run up on the top of the bridge, wave her arms frantically and pose as if she was going to jump from the top of the factory. Accompanying this was a loud chord from the orchestra and red lights on a wrinkled bare cyclorama followed by a blackout. Then the entire cast performed a Charles Strouse *Kaddish* in Hebrew! Let's see, according to my calculations that adds up to 76 major characters singing 371 musical numbers.

We did have a huge orchestra, and I played a frankly dazzling, challenging and satisfying piano part on a nine-foot grand, but Starobin had such an enormous amount of orchestrating to do (which I believe he did every note of; orchestrators often have outside help) that a percentage of the show remained unorchestrated all the way up to the final previews in New York. Marcia Lewis's "Three Sunny Rooms" remained a piano solo the entire run in Boston, and she kept literally crying for an orchestration, but Strouse held back several numbers for some unknown reason. Something tells me it was about... oohhhhh... money?

I found myself so traumatized by the goings on, from the choking incident to the big piano solos I had to play every night, I was dealing with stress in the only non-drinking way I could afford. Eating. Every night I was awake at 3 AM, unable to sleep, so I would go to the 24-hour pizza joint across from the hotel and order a giant pepperoni pizza and wolf it down. Usually, I would bump into Michael Starobin doing the same thing, only he was awake from trying to finish the orchestrations for this giant score. Sometimes after the show I would call the Legal Seafood Restaurant and order a "large fried clams with onion rings" to be delivered to the hotel by 11:30 PM. Needless to say, I gained 40 pounds by the time I got back to New York.

I had managed to steer clear and escape the clutches of Teresa Stratas. She returned to the show, giving a terrific, full-out operatic performance. It was safe in the orchestra pit between 8 PM and 11 PM. But poor Eric Stern. The day of our very first preview, he called me to come to his hotel room. He was lying on the floor with a big therapeutic girdle on. The stress had caused his back to go out and he could barely move. Our synth player was the associate conductor, but no one was prepared to do the show without Eric, so he conducted the whole Boston run with just his right hand, while his body was practically strapped to a chair.

Despite the over-plotting, the "co-direction," the half-baked set design, the unorchestrated numbers, the leftover unfinished Ken Rinker choreography, and the change in leading ladies halfway through the run, the show was playing like gangbusters in Boston, with huge ovations after many numbers and a justifiable standing ovation at the end. This was pretty exciting, and hope was building in the company. Many famous directors and choreographers from New York were spotted in the audience or backstage, but nothing came from them. We closed in Boston and headed for New York for a short break.

I heard very little during this break, but we were to start rehearsing again at the Minskoff rehearsal space (home of the worst pianos in New York since the closing of the Broadway Arts Studios), before heading to the Mark Hellinger Theatre. (Sadly, we were one of the last shows to play that beautiful palace—where *My Fair Lady* premiered—before it became a church. Shame on those theatre owners.) When the rehearsals picked up again, we learned that a new director, Gene Saks, had been brought in. Strouse and Schwartz were sulking in another studio down the hall, threatening to withdraw their score. Saks was as good a choice as any but there was very little time. Frankly, I thought we were in good shape, but Saks proceeded to re-order scenes, which meant hours and hours of additional tech rehearsals. Wasted time and energy.

The most bizarre moment with Gene Saks occurred when he asked for the whole company to gather around Eric Stern at the piano. He believed that there was one important element missing from the show. We were breathless with anticipation. What on earth could be missing from this show? It had the kitchen sink and your grandma's army boots and loads of mirrors (MIRRORS?). Saks asked Eric to play the standard Klezmer "hora" vamp. You know, the one that goes "bump-babump-babumpbabump-babump" that you hear all the way through *Fiddler on the Roof*. And... that was it. He believed the "hora" vamp had been left out of the score and must be inserted anywhere and everywhere possible! Well, he hadn't been listening, because that vamp was EVERYWHERE in the score. Eric put several vamps of "bump-babump-babumpbabump-babump" in what was left of "Penny a Tune" and we were all fixed.

At the Mark Hellinger Theatre it was discovered that the Statue of Liberty would not fit in the wings stage right, so the tip of the torch stuck out in full view of the audience throughout the entire show. And the statue itself blocked the only stage right entrance to the stage from the dressing rooms, so a door had to be cut between her breasts, for people to pass through. Of course, it was completely visible to the audience in its showstopping 60-second trek across the stage. By order of Gene Saks, all the mirrored (MIRRORED??) panels and tenement panels were switched around for different scenes, just for the heck of it, and yet ANOTHER song was added for a group of corrupt politicians in case you missed THAT plot possibility. The song "'What's Wrong with That?'" remained unorchestrated during previews.

The audiences were still responding well, but the cast was discombobulated from all the scene switching. We opened on a Friday night (the old "sneak it in" trick) as opposed to the traditional Thursday. The fabulous opening night party was held in the lobby of the Novotel down the street, complete with cash bar and a couple of plates of hors d'oeuvres. By the time I arrived from the theatre, the party was over, and Dennis Cunningham was panning the show on the bar TV, making fun of Michaels Cone and Davis in their "Greenhorns" number, saying sarcastically, "...and who the heck were THOSE GUYS?"

Closing was posted for the following Saturday night. The cast was in an uproar and on that final performance day marched between shows from the theatre into Times Square protesting the closing. I went home and took a nap, praying that it would be over for good that night. I trudged back uptown to the theatre and ran smack dab into Teresa Stratas at the stage door. She was in mourning and portraying the sad opera star who flops in a Broadway musical. "Heeeyyyy Paul..." she said sorrowfully. Then she said, "Would you come to my dressing room in a few minutes?" Uh-oh! She's going to finish the job. I was dead. I could hardly expect an apology. I knocked on her door and she ordered me in, ordered me to sit, and shoved a pair of Walkman headphones onto my head. "Listen to this." It was a Kurt Weill song that I loved! When Mary Martin sang it! "I'm a Stranger Here Myself" from *One Touch of Venus*. Stratas had a success with her first Kurt Weill album recorded by Nonesuch and was releasing a second volume. I listened. The orchestra was clunky, the fun '40s bluesy arrangement was being played as only "serious" musicians could, *precisely* and with no swing, and she was giving the light comic ditty a full soprano beating, complete with an inappropriate high Bb where it didn't belong. I said, "Sounds great." She snatched the headphones off and said, "Thanks. Get out!" and that was closing day of *Rags*. I found out years later that she was having a huge disagreement with Nonesuch producer Bob Hurwitz about the inclusion of the song on the new record. My suggestion would have been to record all those Kurt Weill songs with theatre musicians and some beat-up cabaret broad with a sense of rhythm and humor, but no one asked me. Side note: Bebe Neuwirth eventually did such a recording/cabaret show but she was certainly not the right kind of "beat-up cabaret broad."

We were closed. Thank God. The original cast album of *Rags* was recorded. The orchestra tracks were laid down in England with British musicians. Thank you, Charles Strouse! Save that nickel! The cast gathered to put down the vocal tracks in New York. The one missing cast member was... (drum roll) Teresa Stratas! Which was too bad. She made a valiant effort and showed up a lot more than was ever expected. And after reflecting back a couple of decades, I frankly wouldn't trade her for a Charles Strouse or a Stephen Schwartz any day.

The library at Lincoln Center filmed one of the last performances and scheduled a screening for the company a few weeks later. Amazingly, I was impressed with some of the show, as was everyone. I have a wonderful audio recording of the *sitzprobe* from Boston (including Stratas) as a souvenir. Betty Corwin, who ran the video section of the library, accepted my request to have a private screening for me and my mother, who didn't have a chance to see it. My mom loved it and couldn't understand why it was such a traumatic experience. Ah, show business. It all looks so easy from the outside. It was still somewhat of an impressive performance.

But I now weighed 250 pounds and could still feel those bony fingers on my throat. I also believed I would never do a good Broadway show again. And I still wasn't drinking. Ah, but around the corner, another fabulous consolation prize awaited me. Two more dazzling professional years with a new show. Simultaneously, my personal life completely fell apart.

23. Into the Woods

After *Rags*, I went begging to Paul Gemignani for a job on the next Sondheim show, *Into the Woods*. I had missed the first couple of readings. Some of the music I heard on the tapes he gave me consisted of the Opening sequence, the title song, "Hello Little Girl," and a short early version of "Giants in the Sky." When Paul agreed to give me a job, the show was set to go to the Old Globe Theatre in San Diego for six weeks. I started to play auditions for director James Lapine at Playwrights Horizons. Some memorable people who showed up for these auditions were Gregory Jbara, Edward Clements (the redheaded kid from the film *Metropolitan*), S. Epatha Merkerson, Alice Playten, and Lord have mercy, Ms Susan Anton, a Hollywood celebrity not known for any special talents. Ms Anton was in for the character of the Witch, complete with orange pantsuit and a deep, deep California tan, offset by hot-pink lip goo, capped teeth, and absolutely not one page or fragment of music anywhere near her person (this would be a regular occurrence with the Hollywood types). She "ducked" her way into the theatre space and announced to Lapine that she wished to sing George Gershwin's "IT'S

Wonderful." Okay, I thought, I know *that*, and I gave her a B♭7 arpeggio. She began. "IT'S Wonderful, IT'S Marvelous... wait, could you make this lower please? Thanks." I played an A♭7 arpeggio. "IT'S Wonderful... Lower please!" F7 arpeggio... "IT'S Won... could you make it just a little lower, please." E♭7 arpeggio... And finally, we got a version of "IT'S Wonderful" further down in the vocal basement than even Lauren Bacall could dream of achieving.

Patti LuPone showed up at this early point, naturally, for the Witch, but she was determined to play Cinderella and learned the early Cinderella song, "Back to the Palace" (a cut song which doesn't seem to have surfaced yet in the rare Sondheim songbooks). She came over to my place, learned it, and performed it as only she can, letter perfect.

"Great," said Lapine! "We want you for the Witch."

Patti said, "But I want to do Cinderella!"

End of story.

Eventually we moved auditions to the Eugene O'Neill Theatre on the set of *Big River*. The first person to sing that day was on a suggestion from Paul Gemignani. "We need a rocker to play the Witch, someone like Debbie Harry," he opined. So, I worked briefly with... Debbie Harry (why not?) the night before she was to audition singing the "Witch's Rap" and a new song, "Boom Crunch." The lyrics to "Boom Crunch" began, "Told your little lie, did you? Naughty, naughty now, BOOM CRUNCH!" At the audition, Debbie got that phrase out and an explosion literally rocked the theatre. They were blasting for the new Holiday Inn Crowne Plaza next door! It was 10 AM. Right on cue! "Boom Crunch" BLAST!! Lapine didn't seem to notice and cut her off saying, "Thanks, Debbie, that's all!" Kind of sad, but unmiked there was just no voice there… or personality. Finally, semi-rocker Ellen Foley was chosen to play the Witch. Ken Marshall (Tony in the 1980 Broadway revival of *West Side Story*) played the Cinderella Prince, John Cunningham played the Narrator, George Coe (from *Company*) played the Mysterious Man, and LuAnne Ponce played Little Red Riding Hood. The rest of the cast pretty much ended up in the Broadway cast.

We began rehearsals at the Westbank rehearsal space in the village, a dark, gloomy, windowless hall with an old, rotten baby grand piano. At last I was back to playing a show with REAL music, composed and written-out professionally. Thank you, Stephen Sondheim! Things seemed to be going along well, but Ellen Foley later told me that James Lapine came to her the first week and said, "Don't get any idea you're ever going to Broadway with this."

At this point there was no "No One Is Alone," a longer "No More," a longer "He's a Very Nice Prince," "Back to the Palace," a new "Giants in the

Sky," no "Stay With Me," no "Children Will Listen," a long, long, long "Maybe They're Magic," "I Know Things Now," both "Agony"s, "Your Fault" was hot off the press, a song for the Narrator called "Interesting Questions" to be interrupted by the cast as they toss him off to be killed by the Giant, the song "I'm So Happy" was at the end of Act One, and the duet "It Takes Two." Plenty to work with, but some big gaping holes in the score, especially in the second act. We worked in near darkness with James (such a darkly funny director with a great eye for casting). This is also when I met Joanna Merlin, the casting director—probably one of the nicest, warmest, most generous, funny people to ever be in show business. I loved Joanna Merlin. She was the original Tzietel (in the south, we pronounced it "Tit-zel") in *Fiddler on the Roof* and was one of the dancing girls in Cecil B. DeMille's *The Ten Commandments!* (Her comment on that was, "All I remember is a lot of sand.") What credentials!

This will be a long chapter since there were many colorful characters and interesting events. It was also the longest Broadway job I ever had, all in all about two-and-a-half years.

And now my brief lecture on long runs of Broadway shows...

Prior to *A Chorus Line* and the excrescent *Grease*, very few shows ran more than five to seven years. Most musicals ran for one or two years, toured and then released the stock rights. With the British invasion of *Cats*, *Les Miz*, *Phantom of the Opera*, *Miss Saigon*, the Disney children's fest—*Beauty and the Beast*, *Lion King*, *Mary Poppins*, and *Aladdin*—the grunge factor with *Rent*, the jukebox travesties *Jersey Boys* and *Mamma Mia*, and the worst offender of all, the rip-off of rip-offs, the bare stage revival version of *Chicago*, going at top Broadway prices of $150.00 a ticket, more Broadway shows have run for decades just taking up space. Yes, they make money for SOME people. (I know, I know, it's show BUSINESS! But we've forgotten about the SHOW part.) For almost 30 years, developing new composer/lyricist teams and nurturing new starring personalities slowed way down in favor of attempts to repeat the blockbuster successes mentioned above. Many theatres now sit with the same show on the marquee for 20 - 30 years. During the first part of the 21st century, I was hearing people complain about what I've been saying for decades—there are no new shows. A couple of generations of talent were neglected while corporate America took over Broadway, and all its old master artists retired or, worse, died. Just enough time for absolutely every bit of the history of the American musical theatre to escape the nation's memory banks. I believe, if only for the health of the art and the encouragement of new talent, that producers need to make the turnover more frequent. There seems to be a slight lean back in that direction lately, but the 30-year gap from 1980 to 2010 has caused a huge reduction in the creation of new Broadway musicals. For quite a while, tourists and locals only came for repeated viewings of *Phantom*, *Lion King*, and *Wicked*. I mean, really, how many times can you come to New York and go back to see *Phantom*? Two generations from now, parents will be taking their kids to see... *Phantom*, *Lion King*, and *Wicked*. I haven't set foot in the Winter Garden Theatre since 1982 or the Majestic since 1987. And during one recent season, two Tony nominations for Best Score went to incidental music for two non-musical plays!

So, I have been grateful for the short runs that have kept me hopping from show to show, otherwise, boredom and creative anorexia would set in...

Let's go back to the woods.

On the last day of rehearsal before San Diego, I ran into Barbara Bryne, who was playing Jack's mother, near the Westbank space. She was standing on the corner in a daze. I asked her if there was something wrong and she said, "I think I broke my ankle." She had! But she continued and did the entire run with her foot in a cast and a crutch. What a trooper the way she worked that crutch, especially in the second act Giant scene.

We flew to San Diego and began rehearsals on the stage of the Old Globe. We were living in an apartment building and the Denny's restaurant nearby became my hiding place. The Old Globe was a delightful place to work with its beautiful setting. At this point, Eric Stern came in to sub for Paul Gemignani for a few weeks, including the *sitzprobe* and first previews. Paul had a scheduling conflict. The sets were sparse, the costumes nice, and we had a big special effect of a giant's hand that dipped down and knocked people over. It was a large, flat, two-dimensional puppet, but like most special effects onstage, the mechanics were too slow and couldn't keep up with our expectations or how quickly our eyes and mind travel. (In the recent debacle, *Spider-Man*, every time one of those silly gymnasts jumped off a balcony or a ledge to fly, my eyes beat him to his landing spot. As Madame Rose said "You're behind, honey! Catch up! Catch up!") I find special effects in theatre not very special even with today's high tech.

We had a wonderful batch of local musicians, delightful to play with. Paul Gemignani loved them. But there was a lot of exposed piano. I always thought the orchestration for *Into the Woods* should have been bigger and more magical, but after seeing a recent production, it was clear that NOTHING should ever get in the way of those lyrics.

Performances began, and the editing started. After a couple of weeks, Sondheim came back to rehearsal with the encompassing *pull it all together* song for the end of Act Two, "No One Is Alone." We sat around in a circle backstage at the theatre and he played and sang it for us. After many oohs and aahs, a break was called. For the next ten minutes, the cast all meandered around humming to each other, "Who can take a sunrise… the Candy Man can!)" Oops! But nothing was ever said. This song addition was the major change we made for the San Diego production. The reviews were medium, but we had a lovely time.

At the opening night party, I decided that after four years of "dryness" (not drinking), I deserved to celebrate and have a glass of wine. I had six glasses of wine and was off to the races. I drank alcoholically every day for the next eight years and my weight shot up even further. I'm sorry… did I say, "my weight shot up?" No, rigorous honesty makes me admit that I ate like a pig for eight years, hence I was slowly becoming obese. So, it was back to fighting the hangover every morning and during every performance (as with *Hollywood/Ukraine* and *Annie* on the road). One particularly sad day, I took a train from San Diego to Placentia, California to see an old roommate who was at his parents' home dying of AIDS. He was in bad shape and asked me to rub his back. I was glad to see him, but a week later he was dead. The plague had been around for a few years, but now it was getting close to home. People today always discuss *Into the Woods* as being an AIDS play. It is not. All through this entire experience I never heard AIDS mentioned in reference to this story. It's a story about personal responsibility. The giant in the story was a "consequence," NOT AIDS.

Streisand came to see the show. I strained my neck to watch her throughout the show. She was sitting in the back row with Baskin-Robbins heir, Richard Baskin, all decked out in black, with a big black hat and veil and big black sunglasses.

Back in New York, we waited to start rehearsals again. I filled in the time with a short detour to the York Theatre to do *The Apple Tree*. I had gained considerable weight and was drinking heavily.

Finally, the call came to start gearing up for the Broadway run. James Lapine wanted to do more work on the show, so a two-week workshop was scheduled. Most of the eventual original cast was assembled with one big exception. Betty Buckley would be playing the Witch. We were at 890 Broadway this time and most of rehearsal was spent reviewing. There were no new songs yet, so Lapine wrote and rehearsed three versions of the ending of Act Two—the one we currently had, another where absolutely everyone in the show dies a horrible death, and finally, one where everyone magically comes back to life for a completely happy ending. We would do three run-throughs for a tiny audience, using each of the second act rewrites. My only memory of the reading is trying to teach "Boom Crunch" to Betty Buckley who, after hearing the piece played, simply said, "I don't feel it that way." And... awaaaaay we go. Wheeeeeeeee! She was late to rehearsal a lot and made the stage manager walk her dog.

After the reading was over, a little time passed, and I got a phone call from Sondheim. "Don't tell anyone but... (first, there was no Internet, Twitter, Facebook or whatever yet in 1986, just old-fashioned landline telephones, so who was I going to tell? Maybe my mother?) ...meet me at Bernadette's apartment and bring the Witch songs. But don't tell anyone!" I showed up at Bernadette's and Steve was pitching the show to her. We played, sang, and taught Bernadette the Rap and "Boom Crunch." He promised to write more for the Witch if she would please do a quick read-through. This read-through was with everyone from the original cast, gathered in someone's fabulous townhouse. The piano was in the stair hall! So, we crowded into the hall in a tight circle. The surprise mystery guest, of course, was Bernadette and we began the read-through. Bernadette, as usual, was completely prepared and nailed it, with big applause after her two numbers. She was in! Whew!

At last we knew that the theatre we would be in was the Martin Beck on 45th Street right across the street from my apartment. Believe me when I say, if you drank as much as I did at this point, it was hard getting my ass across the street to go to work. Sometimes on a light day I would sleep till 7:30 PM and trudge across the street bleary-eyed. But nothing was going to get between me and my vodka and wine, unless it was a big show business emergency... like doing a Broadway musical eight times a week.

Rehearsals began at 890 Broadway with Bernadette Peters as the Witch, Robert Westenberg as the Wolf/Cinderella Prince, Tom Aldredge as the Narrator/Mysterious Man (the roles being combined at this point. Lapine had hoped for Vincent Price, but he was too old to do it. Then I recommended Christopher Lee but Lapine had never heard of him, and Walter Cronkite, another possibility, was not interested), Danielle Ferland as Little Red Riding Hood, and a few other new folk/understudies including Marin Mazzie, Carolyn Marlow, Jonathan Dokuchitz, Jeff Blumenkrantz, Suzanne Douglas, and Cindy Robinson, all of whom have continued on their own interesting paths.

At this point I had come up with theme songs for everyone. The theme of my favorite person in the show (Joanna Gleason) was the vamp of the song

"Monica" from *I Love My Wife*, a Cy Coleman show that she was in. She would always strut around to this music. I hope she had fun, because I did. Other theme songs were "Yoo Hoo" (the cut *Sunday in the Park with George* song) for Danielle Ferland, and practically any tune from any show for Merle Louise who had been in so many great shows. Barbara Bryne's was an old English song, "Waitin' at the Church," which she actually performed for us during tech rehearsals, a funny, spontaneous moment. For Tom Aldredge, I played the opening vamp to his 1959 flop beatnik musical *The Nervous Set* and he would drop everything and do his first few lines from the show: "Man, we're beat... too hung up to care... nothin's cool in front... everything is square... etc." Lots of songs for Lauren Mitchell from *Annie* and *Back On the Town* (since she was cast in the show that never was, I thought she would like to hear some of the songs we never did). For Joy Franz, an audition number of hers, "Do I Hear a Waltz," but in 4/4 time (Joy was rhythm challenged), and for others I generally used their audition numbers. We never had a bad time on this show, just steady work to figure it all out. It was a festive affair. Even with a hangover.

New material finally came in—a new Cinderella song, "On the Steps of the Palace" for Kim Crosby (challenging and fun), a huge production number, "Second Midnight" for the entire cast in Act One, and a new song and reprise for Bernadette, "Stay With Me." Very exciting.

We rehearsed "Second Midnight" every morning for weeks and performed it on press day (which I recorded). It was a montage with all new music including various themes about "children listening." But we were to lose (gasp) "I'm So Happy" from the end of the first act and Joanna Gleason's "Maybe They're Magic" was cut down to one chorus. We also lost the "garden" music and lyrics from "No More." "Boom Crunch" remained. (I always wanted to hear Streisand sing this song in her bluesiest style. I think Streisand impersonator Stephen Brinberg, in his show *Simply Barbra*, may have already done it.)

We basically decided on the original second act ending from San Diego, where some characters die, some don't. I casually said in passing to Joanna Gleason, "Oh... this is a Tony award for you." And she said "Ohnononononono!"

My partner in crime on the piano was, again, Scott Frankel. The Martin Beck Theatre was graced with a giant's leg and boot on the roof hanging down over the front of the theatre—really unattractive and kind of dumb. There was really terrible poster/marquee art that was finally replaced with the classic Heidi Ettinger Landesman work.

As we moved into the theatre and the sets by Tony Straiges appeared, we marveled over the forest of trees, the Cinderella castle in the distance, and the magical Rapunzel's tower that rose out of the floor. Not so much over some of the backdrops or the tree panels that kept slipping off their tracks and almost killing Chip Zien on several occasions. (The Rapunzel tower got stuck many times during performances and wouldn't rise, causing the show to stop.)

Speaking of Chip Zien, I loved him as much as I loved Joanna Gleason. I love Chip's voice and he made me smile and laugh and sigh with relief every time we worked together. Even when he was complaining and putting on his curmudgeon act, he was hilarious and lovable.

The time came for the gypsy run-through (or the "invited dress" as it is now called). Nothing broke down, but we went very long. The dress rehearsal the night before this gypsy run-through ran so long they had to let the orchestra go and I played from "No One is Alone" to the end of the show on solo piano. Sondheim's voice rang through the house, "Be the orchestra, Paul, be the orchestra!"

We now had a new solo for Bernadette in the finale, "Children Will Listen," culled from "Second Midnight." But alas, in the historical tradition, the song we had spent so many hours singing and dancing and rehearsing and marveling over, "Second Midnight," never made it past the invited dress rehearsal. One audience saw it, but what remained was "Children Will Listen," which was also inserted into Bernadette's second act reprise of "Stay With Me."

Audiences were loving Act One and, as with *Sunday in the Park with George*, were wondering why bother with a second act? There was no longer a giant puppet hand, but instead a giant's head fell on the stage at the end of the show. Work was still being done and the top of the second act needed something special. Finally, we were gathered in the mezzanine lounge with Steve and James being told that "I'm So Happy" was being resurrected with adjusted lyrics as the new Act Two opening number. Hooray! (I'd thought about this a week or so earlier and I told Steve I thought it was a good idea and had imagined it myself. He good-naturedly said, "Well, why the hell didn't you say so sooner?" Now I know to open my mouth more.) Odd musical remainders: the "Interesting Questions" song for the Narrator was long gone but the vamp from it remains as underscoring, as does the "garden" music from "No More" and bits of material from "Second Midnight."

The final challenge was to do something about "Boom Crunch." Throughout the four weeks of previews an unusual thing happened with this song. Steve came in first with a coda for "Boom Crunch" that picked up tempo for a more dramatic finish. Jonathan Tunick orchestrated it and we tacked it on to the end of the song. A few days later, Steve came in with more music. This was to replace the last chorus of "Boom Crunch." Jonathan orchestrated it and we surgically removed the last third of "Boom Crunch" and attached it. Bernadette was now singing about "last midnights" after spending the first two-thirds singing about "booming and crunching." The new section was a quick jazz waltz with a sweeping melody. A week later Steve came in again with a whole new song, "Last Midnight," a wild, dark, jazz waltz with fantastic harmonies. This would play much better and show off Bernadette's voice.

Now the show was ready for opening night. But Lapine had one more thought to try. He believed the first act was dragging during what he called the "passerelle" numbers. These were "I Know Things Now," "Giants in the Sky," and "On the Steps of the Palace." He thought we should try the show without them! Thank God it never happened. The show received good if not rave reviews and it became the longest-running show I ever did.

The time came to record the original cast album. RCA was the company and Jay David Saks was the producer. We recorded in the wonderful RCA studios on West 44th Street (now an internal revenue office). The recording went smoothly, and the only real glitch is that Bob Ayers, our percussionist, got off in the opening number under Jack's Mother's lyrics "There are bugs on her dugs..." and his accents are a measure off. I was replaced by a real harpist on the "Agony" songs, "Any Moment," "Children Will Listen" and a few other spots. The resulting album, in my humble opinion, sounded echo-y and far away and anemic. And the edits and ins and outs of numbers were not planned well. Songs started and stopped abruptly. However, compared to the next recording of the score from the original London cast, ours really showed what a wonderful collection of voices we had in that original cast. Paul Gemignani always felt that there had to be variety in ranges and timbres so that it didn't sound like the same person on every song. On the London recording all the men sound alike and all the women sound alike. British. Other than that, the London recording has a better, closer sound, allowing the orchestrations to be heard. All in all, a score I would not take with me to the desert island. There are bonuses on the original cast though—the longer, complete version of "A Very Nice Prince" and the longer, uncut version of Bob Westerberg's "Any Moment."

What felt like minutes after we opened, Bernadette announced she was leaving at the end of three months. I was so depressed and believed that we would close very quickly, but auditions were scheduled for her replacement. The powers that be went to Los Angeles to see many people and came back to start the New York search. This is when the fun really began for me. Of all the people we saw, my two favorites were Petula Clark and Eartha Kitt. The list went on to include Gretchen Wyler, Lainie Kazan, Nancy Dussault, Karen Morrow, and (holy moly!) Suzanne Somers.

Gretchen Wyler, the sassy '50s Broadway dancer and singer from Cole Porter's *Silk Stockings*, gave a very funny, excellent audition on the Witch's rap number, but after she was through, James Lapine asked if she could be clearer on her diction. Since Wyler was a child of 1950s unmiked Broadway singing, the one thing she had no problem with was projection and being understood. She glared at Lapine, drew her shoulders back and said "But dahhhhling, diction is what I'm knooooown for." Bye-bye, Gretchen. Karen Morrow did a wonderful rendition of "It's a Perfect Relationship" from *Bells Are Ringing* (completely inappropriate for the Witch), but Lapine, having no sense of theatrical history, had no clue who she was and dismissed her immediately.

Eartha Kitt was a nervous wreck and had not worked on the material, but that VOICE! That PERSONALITY! I mean it was EARTHA KITT! The role was meant for her. Who else could capture the weirdness and grotesqueness of Act One and the glamorous transition in Act Two? She missed all the lyrics on the Rap and could only manage the word "last" on "Last Midnight." "It's the laaaaaaaaaast midnight, lah lah laaaaaaaaaast lah. It's the laaaaaaaaaast midnight, dah dah dah dah laaaaaaaast dah!" But that VOICE! She would have been spectacular, better than anyone. James Lapine said, "I'm afraid of her."

I had the great pleasure of escorting the fabulous, wonderful, professional, musically talented Petula Clark into my living room one day and after she perfectly read down the Rap number and "Last Midnight," I mentally said "thank you" for one of the most thrilling moments I would ever have in my home. She was perfect in her audition the next day and I was hoping and praying and hoping, but she explained to Lapine that she was in the midst of writing her own musical, a civil war epic, in England! and wouldn't be available. Damndamndamndamn! All of these auditions were held on the Martin Beck stage and were very exciting, but occasionally we would be at 890 rehearsal studios.

The most enjoyable, scary, mind-boggling, baffling, insulting, hilarious, and just plain BAD audition I ever played—bar none—was when Suzanne Somers "thigh-mastered" her way into the room in a cloud of stinky California perfume. James, Steve, Joanna Merlin, and Paul Gemignani were all there. Suzanne Somers announced that, "I'm not really a Broadway belter, I'm a jazzzzzzzzzz singer." Hooboy! That's when I noticed that she came into the room empty-handed, not even a purse. So I broke out in a sweat. "Oh, am I now going to be jammin' with Suzanne?" What's with these Hollywood dames that show up with no music? It's a professional theatre audition, not piano bar night at the Hollywood Roosevelt

Hotel. She said to them, "I can sing a little bit of "It Had to Be You." And I thought, well I can start it, but I wasn't sure of the bridge of the song. Before that thought even went through my brain, she gestured to me, no eye contact or acknowledgment, and said, "FIND ME!" and began to sing *a capella*. "It had to be youuuuuu, it had to be yooooouuuu..." Gesturing wildly for me to "find" her, I found her in the cracks of the keys, somewhere between E Major and F Major. So we "found" each other in F and when we ended, we were requested to try the song once more. I was mortified. Afterward, as a mean joke (I was positive of this), Paul Gemignani slyly asked her, "Do you have anything ELSE?" WHAT? She came in empty-handed, whaddya mean "anything else?" And she said, "I can sing a little bit of a character song for you, 'Adelaide's Lament' from *Guys*..." at which point I gave her a loud Db7 arpeggio clearly suggesting "Find THIS, lady!" Fortunately, all she sang was the last chorus from "In other words..." to the end. End of audition. A few years after this event, my friend Don Oliver wrote a little book on "How NOT to Audition" and included this story, no names attached. A few years after that, Don and I found ourselves sitting next to each other at the opening night of *Victor/Victoria*. We were a few seats away from Joan Collins, who while waiting in line to go up the escalator to the opening night party, said to her escort, "Oh Dahhhling, must we wait heah with all these... all these... all these PEOPLE?" Don and I got on the escalator to go up to the party and who should be standing in front of us with her date but "The Girl in the White Thunderbird" herself, Suzanne Somers. Don and I exchanged private glances and I finally said LOUDLY to Don, "If we get separated at the party, just come FIND ME! Do you think you can do that, Don? Just FIND ME!" I said this directly into the back of her hair, but she didn't bat an eyelash. Don however was choking back tears. Ah well, every day a little death...

So, after all this, Phylicia Ayers-Allen Rashad, straight from *The Cosby Show* was hired. WHAT?!?! Thoroughly professional and musically capable, she gave an uninteresting performance for six months. She was in the cast by the time the Tony Awards rolled around and was on the telecast. That year, my partner Charlie and I took advantage of the Tony Award tickets offered to the company and went, excited by the showdown between *Into the Woods* and *Phantom of the Opera* (even though I disapprove of competition, it's unhealthy).

We were in the balcony of the Lunt-Fontanne Theatre and cheered with our section as Joanna Gleason stepped up for her Tony Award. Bernadette presented it to her. So satisfying and wonderful. Soon Mandy Patinkin and Lee Remick came out to present the Best Score award. Looking adult and glamorous, they read the nominees. And the Tony award went to... Stephen Sondheim! We screamed in our section and cheered him. He made his acceptance speech, mentioning the cast, James Lapine, the producers, the musical direction of Paul Gemignani, the orchestrations of Jonathan Tunick, "and also Paul Ford, the world's most tireless rehearsal pianist and a walking memory bank of every song that has ever been written for any musical on any continent."

Charlie let out a very loud yelp next to me (which can be heard on the broadcast). And that, folks, was my 15 seconds of fame. Unbelievable. I will not say that I wasn't completely and utterly blown away.

The show went on to win best book for James and we had our three Tonys for the evening. Afterwards, Charlie and I decided to crash the *Into the Woods* party at the Sherry-Netherlands Hotel given by our producers, the Dodgers. We had no problem getting in and went up the elevator to the suite. The door opened and lo and behold greeting us was this snooty, albeit gorgeous old drug dealer from my old Atlanta cabaret days. "Oh... hello" he said to me, as if he smelled something bad. "Hi, Danny, are you working this party?" and I grandly swept past him. We only stayed for twenty minutes to congratulate everybody, but I really had to thank Stephen Sondheim for his wonderful words. He was in great spirits and said, "I was going to say it on *Sunday in the Park with George,* but I didn't win!" Wottanight!

A funny Paul Ford-Stephen Sondheim moment happened a couple of weeks earlier... We were prerecording the *Into the Woods* three-minute montage to be partly filmed and partly performed live on the Tony broadcast. I arrived early, as usual, before anyone, except Steve who was sitting with a newspaper in the tiny green room off the recording studio. We said good morning and I sat and waited while he continued to read the paper. Then I noticed that the intercom from the recording studio was up loud and we could hear everything going on in the studio. What was going on was the prerecording of "Music of the Night" from *Phantom of the Opera.* Michael Crawford was finishing the last section. At the end, Crawford said politely, "Could we try it from the beginning again... perhaps a bit slower?" I looked at Steve and he immediately put the newspaper up in front of his face. The "Muzak of the Night" began again... slower. At the end, Crawford said politely, "Once more please... a tad slower, if you don't mind." Steve started to slump in his chair with the newspaper still covering his face. By the end of the third take of "Mucinex of the Night," the newspaper started to shake, either from frustration or laughter or both. But let me tell you, "Mueslix of the Night" was reeeally slooooww that day. The more to hear those (gulp) hideous lyrics, my dear!

Bernadette left the show, but then at the end of six months (horrors!), Joanna Gleason decided to leave. No, please no, not Joanna! By this time the wondrous "can do ANYTHING" Betsy Joslyn was standing by, but not for the Baker's Wife, just the Witch. And neither understudy Lauren Mitchell nor Kay McClelland was being considered. The Baker's Wife is a huge role and James Lapine decided to give the role to Cynthia Sikes. Who? Cynthia Sikes, you know, the judge from *L.A. Law*. Oh... Who?? When I met her in the lobby to start teaching her the score, she had two weeks to learn this enormously difficult role. I casually asked her what kind of background she had. What musicals, if any? Could she read music? Had she been onstage? The answer I got back was no, no and no. She had never sung onstage or been in a musical. I took in a deep breath and mentally said, "Thank you, James Lapine." She never was in tune or with the orchestra and lost every single laugh in the show. Chip Zien was having a stroke. Three months to go with a cypher as the Baker's Wife. She was then replaced by Mary Gordon Murray, a better singer but, again, no laughs. Finally, Kay McClelland was given the chance to finish out the run, and we got the laughs back. Kay is an expert comedienne. But unless you have that skill or are a uniquely true urbane Jewish goddess like the divine Ms Gleason, the role just doesn't work.

After Ayres-Allen Rashad left the show, happily Betsy Joslyn played the Witch for three months, doing her usual magical chameleon act. This woman from Staten 'Oiland' with the unglamorous moniker nailed those songs, got the laughs, acted the shit out of it and wiped up the stage, looking beautiful to boot. I love Betsy Joslyn. The best story she told me during this period was about her experience at Linda Hart's New Year's Eve party. Betsy and Ellen Foley connected at the party and were all glammed up, Betsy in a floor-length red dress. They were leaning against a table chatting and the table collapsed... with all the champagne bottles and glasses on it! There was Betsy in her red dress on the floor drenched in champagne. Someone helped her get away with as little embarrassment as possible. The next day she called Linda Hart to give her deepest apologies. Ms Hart was cool about it, except for the fact that Betsy's champagne-drenched red dress had tracked red dye all over her new white shag carpet. Betsy paid to have the carpet cleaned. I was crying with laughter listening to this story. I loved hearing her stories, but I wish Betsy had had a better time of it.

Then the powers-that-be decided we needed a more box office name in the cast. So, flipping through the files they settled on the box office magnet (oy!) and nice person, Nancy Dussault. She was outfitted in Bernadette's wigs and capes, but Nancy doesn't have the physical presence of her predecessor, so she tended to remind me of Carol Burnett playing "Nora" Desmond on her TV show. She was a wonderful person who was not really given much help with the role.

PBS decided to film the show for broadcast, so all of the original cast came back for two weeks. Hallelujah. After the filming, James Lapine brought back LuAnne Ponce from San Diego as Red Riding Hood and, at last, Ellen Foley finished the run as the Witch.

I actually left around this time to play for Mandy Patinkin at the Helen Hayes Theatre, but I continued to do rehearsals and sat in the pit for the last performance. The closing night party was an intimate gathering and a very warm goodbye. Paul Gemignani left the run in the middle to work on *Jerome Robbins' Broadway*. I played some dance rehearsals/auditions for that show, as did every other pianist in New York. In fact, the days I was there, four pianists were rotating, Eric Stern, Pam Drews, Scott Frankel, and me. Paul offered me the second pianist job, to work with Scott Frankel. His pitch was this. "You can play rehearsals for this new show but since it will be time consuming, you had better give your notice to *Into the Woods*. Oh, and you're going to have to take your 'abuse pill' every day." I immediately flashed back on the *Rags* experience and without batting an eye, and for the first time, I said... "No, I don't think so. I'm happy where I am right now." (And I was not going to take any "abuse pills" either, thank you very much.) I never regretted that decision because, in my humble opinion, *Jerome Robbins' Broadway* was a dud. I thought we would see some never before resurrected sequences, unseen since the original productions. All we got was a half hour of *West Side Story*, a half hour of *Fiddler on the Roof*, and many numbers that had recently been done better in revivals, from *Peter Pan*, *On the Town*, *Gypsy*, *The King and I*, and *Forum*. And the cast was much too young and inexperienced to play the characters they were assigned. (I never want to see Nancy Hess play Roxie Hart or Tessie Tura or any other prize role again. Not at $100.00 a ticket.) "The Bathing Beauty Ballet" from *High Button Shoes* and the Charleston from *Billion Dollar Baby*, featuring the best member of the company, the overlooked Suzanne Fletcher, were the only two high spots in what looked like a glorified high school production. And people won Tony Awards for this show! No. I was happy to stay with *Into the Woods*. Happy with my Stephen Sondheim-blessed "safe" world.

Toward the end of the run of *Into the Woods*, Charlie Stramiello, my partner of six years was diagnosed HIV positive. I was negative. Still am. At that point it was a death sentence. The next six years would be pure hell.

24. What Can You Lose?

1988 - 1989

An exciting year on the Sondheim front started with my wonderful experience (no kidding) with Lauren Bacall, performing Steve's "The Saga of Lenny" on a gigantic marathon for Leonard Bernstein's 70th birthday, and a new Sondheim show on the horizon for which I was asked yet again to be the "motor" by conductor Paul Gemignani.

Steve gathered a small group together (including Victor Garber and Joanna Gleason) in his townhouse to make a casual demo recording of a big number he was writing for a proposed movie musical called *Singing Out Loud*. The song was called "Lunch" and had a 16th note rhythmic vamp to it. It was a fun, successful session, but I never heard the song again. The project was dropped, and the music ended up years later in the score of *Wise Guys* as "Addison's Trip."

But a second movie venture was far more successful for Sondheim, earning him an Academy Award. He wrote five songs for Warren Beatty's movie version of the comic strip *Dick Tracy* starring Beatty himself and a dead-on-arrival performance by Madonna. What a waste. Steve asked me to come over one afternoon and accompany him, so he could record three songs for Madonna. I would play, he would sing... for Warren Beatty and Madonna! They weren't there, of course, but they would be hearing the recordings. Between shots of vodka (Steve's not mine; I was drinking again, but only hung over that afternoon), we recorded "Sooner or Later," "More," and "What Can You Lose?" He informed me that Mandy Patinkin would be singing the last song with Madonna. Great, a new song for Mandy's growing repertoire! Hot off the presses!

Steve told me that in his conversations with Madonna, he had casually suggested to her that since she was so adept at turning out hit pop records, perhaps she might enjoy learning a little more about music. She just looked at him and blew a big bubble with her bubble gum. (I'm making that part up, but it conveys what Steve said her reaction was to his suggestion.) We chuckled over that. But he wasn't kidding. She didn't know anything. Most of these pop singers don't and they rely on the back-breaking work of submissive *real* musicians to clean up their mess. (Shades of what I would soon realize my own career was all about.) When he asked her over the phone for an idea of her vocal range, she "smacked her gum," and said "I'll have to get back to youse on that..." Later, she contacted him to say she had been informed that she could sing up to a D Minor. Of course, what she meant was that she could sing up to a D♭, an octave above Middle C. This woman made millions off of other people's knowledge and backs. She didn't know that a "D Minor" was a chord, not a note of the scale! He was as astounded as I was. No, not really astounded… not even surprised. Just another pathetically rich uneducated rock star making money off other people's smarts. Her reaction to the songs? "Why do they have to be so hahhhhd?" ("Hard" in English.)

I think "What Can You Lose" is a nice song and perfect for Mandy but, unsurprisingly, in the film we hear Mandy singing the first part over a montage of traffic. When the film cut to Mandy and Madonna at the club, where he plays and she sings, only Madonna is seen picking up the song and finishing it in her inimitable (out-of-tune) fashion. It *was* to be Mandy's moment but, unfortunately, not. By the way, Mandy played Madonna's piano player in the movie, his character's name being "88 Keys." He was completely bald and neurotic, and he told me he based the character on me. I don't believe him, but it was fun to imagine anyway. Ironically, the best song in the movie was only heard on a car radio sung by Mel Tormé—"Live Alone and Like It." Madonna's numbers ended up being washouts, heavily edited and drearily shot and performed.

Later that year, Mandy and I began performing our concerts—bare stage, upright piano, Mandy singing and me at the piano. That was all. Beatty and Madonna came to see us. Backstage, I was breathless about meeting Mr. Beatty, though I couldn't have cared less about Madonna. Beatty had told Mandy that when he and Madonna sat down in the theatre, she had gasped incredulously and said, "A piano?! A PIANO!? Wow. He's one brave mother-fucker!"

Not everybody needs claptrap, honey! Just good music and lyrics.

25. Lauren Bacall

In 1970, on my first school trip to New York, we saw the spirited, trashy show *Applause* (based on the classic film *All About Eve*) starring Lauren Bacall. I had seen her in a few movies on TV, but most memorably I knew of her from the 1946 Warner Bros. cartoon *Bacall to Arms* in which an anthropomorphized wolf character was sitting in a movie theatre watching the Humphrey Bogart-Lauren Bacall film *To Have and Have Not*. The movie in the cartoon was called *To Have... To Have... To Have...* and the stars' names were Bogey Gocart and Laurie Becool. On the screen was a cartoon Humphrey Bogart polishing his pistol when in slinks a cartoon Lauren Bacall. They performed the classic scene, "You know how to whistle don't you? You just pucker up and BLOW!" which drives the wolf in the audience mad with lust and passion. So, it was a treat to see the star of one of my favorite cartoons in a big Broadway musical. I had yet to see the film *All About Eve*, so the whole story was new to me.

The production was very adult (or sophisticated) to me, particularly when three dancers showed off their bare asses in the title song (forget *Hair*, where the lights were too dim to discern anything... these guys' asses were brightly lit!) and there was a great big, fat, gay bar scene. It was a big, ugly, loud show, but I loved it. While everyone else on the school trip went back to the hotel, a friend and I, both just 18 at the time, decided to stay for autographs at the Palace Theatre stage door. It was December and snowing, but we waited... and waited... but no Lauren Bacall. We waited an hour and were the only ones left. Finally, Bacall came out on the arm of her co-star, Len Cariou. She saw us and said "Jeeeeeeesus," while rolling those eyes from the West Side of Manhattan to the East Side.

"Oh, Miss Bacall, could we have an autograph and a picture? Oh, please, please, please?"

"Allllllllllright..." she said with another eye roll.

"Might I be in the picture, too?" said Mr. Cariou (somewhat put out).

"Oh, yes, yes, yes, of course, of course, Mr. Cariou."

So, we thanked them and went off giggling back to the hotel. I never got to see those pictures.

After that, I saw many more films with Ms Bacall, including *Written on the Wind*, *Designing Woman*, and *How to Marry a Millionaire* (courtesy of the Regency revival movie theatre in New York) and, finally, her latest epic, *The Fan* (a must-see for any fans of the Broadway musicals of the early 1980s). She came back to Broadway in 1981 in a new musical, *Woman of the Year*. The less said the better. The only memorable moment—and it was truly memorable—was her duet with Marilyn Cooper, "The Grass is Always Greener." Bacall won another Tony award and if you watch that Tony broadcast, you can actually see her say "Shit!" when they call her name.

Woman of the Year did a tour with Bacall after she left the New York cast and I was hired to play two weeks of rehearsals. I was not to work with Ms Bacall, but with members of the supporting cast including Kathleen Freeman (the vocal coach in *Singin' in the Rain* who tried to get Jean Hagen's Lina Lamont to say, "I cahhhn't stahhhnd him." What a hoot she was!). One morning, I came in early and was sitting by myself in the larger rehearsal room and in walked Ms Bacall. We were face to face, so I waved and said, "Hi. Paul Ford. I'm one of the rehearsal pianists." She was casually spritzing her arms and neck with mist from a small aerosol can. She sauntered over to me saying "Good moooorrrning. Would you care for some 'orange water?'" and sprayed the mist straight into my eyes and face. As I wiped down my face with my hand, I said "Ooooohhh, THANK YOU! That was very refreshing." We had no other contact during those two weeks.

During the run of *Into the Woods* in 1988, Stephen Sondheim called me and asked, "Have you ever worked with Lauren Bacall?" I said I was in a room with her once and she sprayed some orange water mist on my face, but that was my only contact. He asked if I was interested in playing for her at Leonard Bernstein's 70th Birthday celebration at Tanglewood. Steve had written new lyrics to the Weill-Gershwin song "The Saga of Jenny" (my favorite song!) making it "The Saga of Lenny"—eight verses with Bernstein musical quotes between each verse. It was very funny and fun to play. However, he wrote it in C Major, saying it would have to be transposed to maybe F Major, musical quotes and all. (Sheesh! And with no computers then!) By the way, I said YES! He sent the music and I practiced it in more appropriate keys for her and scheduled with Steve to meet her for rehearsal. I arrived early, of course, at his townhouse and waited with him in the second-floor studio for her arrival. The doorbell rang and I heard clomp, clomp, clomp up the stairs. Suddenly a voice boomed out, "I want to meet this guy who says I threw ORANGE JUICE IN HIS FACE!!" (Steve can be a real rascal sometimes.) She entered the room and I greeted her and made the disclaimer that oh no, Ms Bacall, it was just a little orange fragrance you spritzed on me. She cracked a smile and said, "Oh, ooooookay" (rolling those eyes from the East Side to the West Side this time). We proceeded to rehearse and I made an appointment to meet her at her home at the Dakota apartment building (where *Rosemary's Baby* was filmed!).

Her apartment was overwhelming, with 14-foot ceilings, dusty rose walls, beautiful furnishings, photos of famous people and one of Cole Porter's pianos. She was very relaxed and personable with me and we talked about her two Broadway shows and which one she thought was the better show. She expressed her fears about having to memorize such an epic piece of lyric writing and performing it in front of everyone and God, so we came up with the idea of having file cards with each verse and keeping them on the piano, just in case. I asked her if she had a favorite song and she told me "In Love in Vain," the Jerome Kern ballad from the 1946 film *Centennial Summer*. Great! What an unusual choice! We made another appointment to rehearse again. We needed to perform it for Steve at some point, so we decided to go to his place from the Dakota one day. I asked if we should take a taxi and she said, "Hell no! We're walking. Besides, I want to see the windows at Saks." So, I ran after her from Central Park West and 72nd to East 49th and Second Avenue. I could hardly keep up. As we passed Saks, we briefly went from window to window. "Garbage... Trash... Yecch... All junk!" was the assessment.

The day arrived, and I was on the train to Tanglewood alongside her wardrobe/make-up person, who did not want to discuss Ms Bacall. I checked in at the inn provided for me and hit the bar but didn't get drunk. The next morning, I was driven to the amphitheater and we got our schedule and where we were placed in the program—second to last before the grand finale of "Make Our Garden Grow" from *Candide*. And it was a loooong program. We both shuddered to think of the pacing back and forth that we would be doing while the hands of the clock crept ever so slowly. These kinds of programs are the worst when everyone lines up in the wings to take their turns. You're better off being near the top of the list.

Backstage was a large array of opera singers, none of whom I really knew. The friendliest was tenor Jerry Hadley, with whom I would end up working on three CDs before his tragic suicide. The evening came and the performance started. I wandered backstage throughout the day and evening, out front as well, checking in repeatedly with Bacall in an offstage rehearsal room to run the song multiple times. People kept poking their heads into the room and she would yell, "Get out!" and lock the door. One man got the key and unlocked the door, but Ms Bacall threw her body weight against the door, almost severing his arm!

The program was over four hours long, with Bernstein sitting on a throne out front. After several hours had gone by, I was hanging out in the greenroom backstage and spoke to Roddy McDowall, telling him I had a favorite film of his. "Oh yeah?" he said suspiciously. "*The Legend of Hell House*," I said. "Oh, well that was a good movie!" he agreed. Then we noticed Quincy Jones was on the TV monitor speaking about Bernstein. The door to the greenroom opened and in strolled Bernstein. Himself! He had dismounted from his throne and come backstage during Quincy Jones's speech. He looked at the monitor and said, "Who's that asshole?" He threw his head back, cackled, and exited.

The time came for us to go on, at 12:45 AM! Beverly Sills announced us and we walked onstage. The nerves were long gone, replaced by sheer exhaustion. Bacall nailed the little ditty and we were done. (Actually, we had to do an encore at 5 PM the next day at a "songfest" before we were truly through, but the tough one was over.) Even at that late hour, there was a reception at someone's mansion. I went for a short while and chatted with Patricia Routledge, the star of Bernstein's original production of *1600 Pennsylvania Avenue*. I told her I was a friend of David Krane (who had done the dance arrangements for that show) and that he spoke very highly of her. She was charming to me.

I left and went back to the inn. The next day I was invited by Steve to go "antiquing" in the country with him, Ms Bacall, and Phyllis Newman, who drove. What a fun time that was! Walking into shops around the area with that trio was hilarious. Phyllis alone bought something—a rusty wire letter-holder to hang on the wall for $20.00. Then we had a nice lunch outside at an inn and I just enjoyed listening to the famous people talk. At 5 PM, we did our encore performance and it was over. I said goodbye and sighed with relief, but also sighed over what a great experience that had been. Later when the concert was broadcast on PBS, the program was cut down to an hour-and-a-half, and we were juggled to appear early in the program. Ha! If only!

I would run into Bacall occasionally after that and she was always lovely and gracious to me. My mother, of course, was beside herself that I had this experience. She bought Bacall's latest memoir and discovered that I had been mentioned as being her accompanist. She kept that book open to that page resting on a pair of ceramic Jesus hands on her coffee table from that day to the day she died.

In 2004, I was doing the *Assassins* revival at the Roundabout Theatre and my mother was visiting. This was the second to last visit to New York she would make, and she got to sit next to John Weidman, the *Assassins* book writer, during the performance. I wanted her to meet everyone in the company, especially Mario Cantone, so I brought her backstage and we waited. The stage door opened and who should walk in but Ms Lauren Bacall. I was able to introduce my dear sweet mom to Bacall that night. My mother was, for once, speechless! And that closes my chapter on Lauren Bacall. Quite a nice arc from the Warner Bros. cartoon *Bacall to Arms* to the Palace Theatre stage door in 1970 to the Roundabout stage door in 2004! One of the greatest experiences of my life, thanks to Stephen Sondheim.

26. There's Something About A War

After *Into the Woods*, I got wind of Sondheim's next new musical and its subject matter. John Weidman would write the book which dealt with the people who attempted to or succeeded in killing a president of the United States. Why not? Historical, dramatic, a wide range of musical styles. It certainly wouldn't be an ordinary show. John Weidman had been the book writer for Sondheim's *Pacific Overtures*. His father, Jerome Weidman, wrote the books to such musicals as *I Can Get it For You Wholesale* and *Tenderloin*, both under-appreciated, fascinating shows. If casting director Joanna Merlin gets the award for nicest woman in show business in the female category, John Weidman wins hands down in the male category. Always upbeat, personable, and appreciative of anyone's effort.

I frankly can't remember who was in charge of the very first read-through of *Assassins*, but it was held at Playwright's Horizons. The cast included Robert Joy (a remarkable lookalike) as Lee Harvey Oswald, Victor Garber as John Wilkes Booth, Christopher Durang, Amy Wright, John Pankow, Tony Shaloub, Kevin Anderson, Nathan Lane, Paul McCrane, and a handful of other stars. I might be confused on this list but somewhere in the three incarnations (reading/workshop/production) of this show, these people were there!

Steve had written an opening number and "The Ballad of Booth." He was particularly proud of the lyric "C'mere and kill a president." We were told the original idea came from a script Steve had discovered that he thought could be the basis for a terrific musical. The original author had signed an agreement to have his idea adapted, so Sondheim and Weidman were free to do their own version. The script was very funny—it had to be—and almost like a revue, an historical pageant. Each assassin was presented in his own style of music or straight comedy sketch or dramatic monologue. As the evening proceeded, the various assassins would interact with each other until the final scene set in the Dallas, Texas Book Depository where all would appear together. There was a balladeer who sang three numbers, and a small ensemble. The first afternoon reading was closely followed by a two-week workshop with Kevin Anderson (not the opera singer, but the singing actor—there's a difference) playing both the Balladeer and Lee Harvey Oswald. (The roles were combined at this point—the right choice.) Terence Mann, Christine Baranski, Swoosie Kurtz, Michael Jeter, and Jonathan Hadary would assume roles, and we were now directed by Jerry "I know funny and this (*Assassins*) is not funny" Zaks. We did two run-throughs for a small, invited audience which reacted enthusiastically. We now had the two numbers mentioned before, plus "How I Shot Roosevelt," "The Ballad of Czolsgosz," "Unworthy of Your Love," "The Ballad of Guiteau," and the "Gun Song" (which included an unsingable barbershop quartet). As with the reading, the cast had a blast with the material and laughs came fast and furiously onstage and off. The most dramatic showbiz event of this time occurred when, during one of the run-throughs,

Mandy Patinkin was in the audience, sitting front row center. After a bit, he took out a piece of paper and began innocently jotting down moments and lyrics that he liked so he could remember them. The actors were so close to the audience, in their laps in fact, that starting with Victor Garber, word spread that Mandy was out front "taking notes" on their performances! Panic ensued. They all ran to Papa Sondheim complaining that Mandy was writing notes all through the performance. Steve later called Mandy and chewed him out saying, "How would you like it if someone was writing about YOU during a show?" He made Mandy send a note of apology to everyone in the company, which he did without hesitation. Ah the thea-tuh, the thea-tuh. Such drama! Show Business Emergency! Show Business Emergency! (I coined this phrase.)

A production date was set for a limited off-Broadway run at Playwrights Horizons. Debra Monk and Annie Golden joined us, with Jace Alexander as Lee Harvey Oswald. The Balladeer was Patrick Cassidy (the roles were now split— bad choice). D.J. Gianni (son of choreographer Danny Daniels) was hired as choreographer and the orchestra would consist of me on the piano, Paul Gemignani on drums and Michael Starobin on synthesizer. It is an understatement to say how this cast bonded and laughed for the next few weeks, despite director Jerry ("I still don't think it's funny") Zaks's lack of enthusiasm for the material. He kept gasping and shaking his head at every joke or outrageous politically incorrect moment in the script. I say "keep 'em coming!"

The show did not go through radical changes, but we did lose one character and an actor after a couple of days. Reluctantly Zaks and Weidman chose to discard one assassin and with him went Chris Durang. He was regrettably sent home one afternoon. We were all sad, but that's show biz. One of my favorite people in the world, Patrick Cassidy, had the difficult Balladeer role, difficult because Zaks decided to remove the payoff by making Lee Harvey Oswald a separate actor. We tried to have him play the banjo during his numbers, but Sondheim, Cassidy, and the banjo didn't really gel. Then Cassidy was subjected to a series of personas and costume changes ranging from cowboy to railroad engineer, with a series of hats and caps. We had fun teasing Patrick about his daily fashion parade, but he was a good sport.

Jerry Zaks kept agonizing, especially over the opening number, "C'mere and kill a president," and the whole idea of a carnival shooting gallery. He begged Sondheim and Weidman to come up with an alternative. I truly believe Sondheim wrote the worst, most innocuous alternate opening song he could think of in order to keep the original. The new song, "The Flag Song" was a simple march for the ensemble about the excitement of having the president in a parade in "our home town," which would be abruptly interrupted by gunshots (an assassination) leading into "The Ballad of Booth." The ditty was staged but after a couple of days everyone was going to mutiny until the original was reinstated. "The Flag Song" tune would be used in a new song, "Another National Anthem," fully developed for the assassins. The tune would again re-emerge years later as Papa Mizner's deathbed anthem in *Wise Guys/Gold/Bounce/Road Show*.

Most of the songs remained largely intact during rehearsals with only "Another National Anthem" being a late entry.

The night before the reviews came out at the opening night party (which was fun—Shirley Jones was there, *kvelling* over her son Patrick Cassidy) a thoroughly disgusting thing took place. I will speak for myself, but I was extremely worried about the reception the show would get and whether it would ever move to Broadway. At the party, a group of people were gathered in a corner and suddenly a big cheer went up from them. I ran over asking, "Was it the reviews? Did we get a good *Times* review?" (I can be such an *idiot*.) Oh, no, I was told. Such-and-such team won the game!!!!!!! Ha! The GAME! It's always the GAME! I hate sports with a passion. I was so pissed and disheartened at the priorities of the people in that room. I was seething the rest of the night. I had gone into musical theatre, at the very least, to get away from this idiot country's obsession with fucking children's games! I was appalled that anyone in that room that night would have their minds on that nonsense! Where were their priorities?? I'm a silly, deluded, hopeless, old queen sometimes.

Coinciding with the opening of *Assassins* was a lovely little thing called the Gulf War which everyone was watching in the dressing rooms. Suddenly, killing the president was not such a funny idea, and the silence in the audiences clearly indicated that. Even Shirley MacLaine, after a performance, said there was something wrong with the show (in a metaphysical sense, probably). She scrunched up her nose and shook her head and said, "Nope, something's not right." My mother, who had come from Atlanta for opening night, LOVED it! But all of the reviews were terrible, and any idea of a Broadway transfer was out of the question.

I read the reviews of the show while having breakfast with my mom. They were all depressingly bad. Clearly, it was a case of wrong time, wrong place. The reason I say wrong place is that my mother made an interesting observation. We were at the tiny Playwrights Horizons Theatre on West 42nd Street. She loved the show but felt there needed to be much more distance between the gunshots and the audience. It unnerved her in the wrong way.

We finally got that distance at the Roundabout's Studio 54 space for the 2004 revival. But I agreed with my mother. The show needed more space, more production values (we had slides)... and more musicians. Even though *The New York Times* critic, Frank Rich, was complimentary to the orchestra of three "august" (which I cynically took to mean "fat") musicians, the *Assassins* score needed an Aaron Copland/John Philip Sousa type of orchestration.

Halfway through the run, I went to the performance one night with my left hand feeling very warm and sweaty. As the show went on, my arm and hand began to swell up to elephant size and Paul Gemignani dropped me off at the emergency room at Roosevelt hospital. I waited and waited and finally was seen. I filled out all my forms stating, as I always did, that I was allergic to just one thing—penicillin. The doctor on hand judged that it was an infection and gave me an injection of some antibiotics and told me to wait there. Soon my face bloated to Elephant Man proportions and I alerted the doctor. I asked if there was penicillin in the shot and he blithely said, "Oh... a form of it." So, I was kept on a slab in a hallway for observation until 9 AM the next morning. I was released after I made an appointment with my MD for 10 AM. I made my way to my doctor on the Eastside with people shunning me as they cowered at the sight of me. My doctor took one look at me and said, "Cancel my appointments!" and he ran, not walked, with me to Lenox Hill Hospital where I was immediately put in a room and hooked up to an IV. I stayed there for a week, happily high on Percodan, feeling really good as the swelling subsided. It was decided that I had a staph infection in my elbow. I figured it came from my lying on my (then) filthy old carpet, propped up on my elbow for four hours while I did my taxes. I had rubbed my elbow raw and infected it. My partner, Charlie, came to see me the first day in the hospital and said "Oh, get up, you're fine," and then never came back. He didn't pick up the phone or return my calls for a week. We had some relationship! I had two other hospital visitors, Victor Garber and Davis Gaines from the cast. I was horrified at my appearance and wanted to hide under the covers as these two handsome matinee idols entered the room. Finally, the doctors drained my elbow of about a pint of yellowish liquid and sent me home on antibiotics. Musical legend, Eddie Strauss, subbed for me on the show, thank God, and then I went back to finish the run. One note on the fabulously handsome cast member, Davis Gaines. When he came in to audition for *Assassins*, I simply did not recognize him. He had had his face and eyes done and looked like a cross between an upper Eastside matron and a deer caught in the headlights. I guess it was ironic that, shortly after the surgery, he began a very long run playing the title role in *Phantom of the Opera* in which his face was covered by a mask!

The consolation prize for the failure of *Assassins* was that RCA Records recorded the show with a 26-piece orchestra, arrangements by Michael Starobin. Not bad. In fact, absolutely fabulous.

27. Putting It Together

SONDHEIM: A CELEBRATION AT CARNEGIE HALL

Even with my perpetual hangover, this 1992 concert was a thrilling event. The DVD has some wonderful moments. Dorothy Loudon and Peter Howard's medley of "Losing My Mind" and "You Could Drive a Person Crazy" was the top and perfection. Patti LuPone first sang "Being Alive" at this concert and knocked it out of the ballpark. Daisy Eagan did a sweet, funny, sincere "Broadway Baby," far superior to Julia McKenzie's calculatedly earnest version in the oh-so-British *Side By Side By Sondheim*, and Daisy was only 12! Bill Irwin conducted the orchestra in a brilliantly goofy arrangement of "Comedy Tonight" by Don Sebesky, and even *Sweeney Todd* came off well with Sebesky's symphonic suite, probably the best way to experience *Sweeney Todd*—no singing, no lyrics, no story.

And Looza Minnoolli (Charlie's nickname for her) provided us with more fodder for the gossip machine, with her over-enthusiastic tap dancing (choreographed by Susan Stroman) atop Billy Stritch's manically played piano in one of the *Dick Tracy* dead-on-arrival tunes, "Back in Business." During a rehearsal, I sat out in the Carnegie auditorium and watched the Minnelli number, because (Thank God!) I didn't have to play it. After it was over, I felt a presence hovering over me. It was Sondheim, sneaking up behind me. He whispered in my ear, "You look horrified! Are you horrified? You look horrified!" I said "Nope." I WAS horrified, but I lied. Actually, Liza still scares the bejesus out of me. After Billy Stritch did his bossa nova jazz rendition of "Anyone Can Whistle" (which of course I was jealous of), Steve again sneaked up behind me and whispered, "Why don't you play like that? All I ever get from you is triads!" and he raced up the aisle. Of course, he meant every word, but I didn't let it worry me... much. Other highlights were Victor Garber and Patrick Cassidy reprising "The Ballad of Booth," this time with full orchestra. I loved Victor Garber's comment, "Oh great! I get to go on public television and sing 'nigger lover' for the whole world to see." That made me laugh. And it was here that we first did "Sunday" as the finale of a Sondheim tribute. Watch the DVD and see and hear Eddie Korbich singing A♭s at the climax of the number while everybody else onstage is singing Gs. God bless Eddie's enthusiasm.

This was all a lot of fun even though many of the selections were experiments... in terror! Betty (a Lesbian vocal group—don't ask) and their arrangement of "I Never Do Anything Twice" will never be matched for weirdness. The Tonics, a close-harmony group, sang "Good Thing Going," arranged by the soon to be super composer Jason Robert Brown (he finished my synthesizer part 30 seconds before we performed it and I'm not kidding!). David Loud did a nice arrangement of "Our Time" and "Children Will Listen," performed by the intense Betty Buckley and the not-so-intense Boys Choir of Harlem (who thought up these ideas?), and the two absolute pre-requisites for any evening such as this, (1) the standard Susan Stroman-choreographed "woman vamps man/woman chases man/woman eats man alive/woman must destroy all men, sexy, song and dance" to the sizzle-less "Sooner or Later" performed by Karen Ziemba, and (2) the "opera singers do Broadway" routine with Jerry Hadley and Carolann Page in opera singer tux and gown ensembles screaming their lungs out on the meant-to-be-caressed and underplayed "With So Little To Be Sure Of." Ah, opera singers and the English language. Opera singers and Sondheim. Although Harolyn Blackwell *did* get quite an ovation for her high C at the end of "Greenfinch and Linnet Bird." (The high C was *my* idea.)

This was a well-received endeavor, extremely well organized, and well paid—one of the last of these for me. With later PBS shows, such as the two *My Favorite Broadway* evenings and the *Sondheim 80th Birthday Concert*, the enthusiasm, inspiration, organization, and pay began to diminish.

Oh, and last and least, Glenn Close coldly portrayed Desiree Armfeldt singing "Send in the Clowns." During rehearsal at my apartment, she never spoke to me or looked at me and asked the typical question to Paul Gemignani, "Should I sing this song or speak it?" I don't know Glenn, what do you think? At least she remembered the words, which is a miracle in itself, since nobody knows the lyrics. It's right up there with the National Anthem.

This was a very successful concert with CDs (double and single) and DVDs. And ANY show with Dorothy Loudon was worth all the time and effort. It was also my Carnegie Hall debut. I felt calm and serene there. And Charlie and my mom were in the audience. Soon he would be dead, and mom wouldn't be able to travel much more. My support group (this was all I had) was disappearing.

In 1993, Scott Ellis directed the first major revival of *Company* in New York for the Roundabout Theatre which was then in the converted Bond Department Store at Broadway and West 45th Street. I played all of the auditions, which was a treat, but the production seemed to be cast too young and felt like a cruise ship show to me. I truly believe that, for the stage, there used to be a perhaps unconscious tradition of casting "older" to make performances more believable. I go by the fact that Mary Martin was 47 when she played 20-year-old Maria von Trapp in the original *The Sound of Music* and made that believable because of her experience as an actress. When I saw the original *Company*, I may have been only 17, but those people looked OLD on that stage, and I BELIEVED them as hard, lived-in New Yorkers. Even Debra Monk in the Elaine Stritch role in the revival came off as slightly playing "dress up." In the original production, Elaine Stritch made me think "60 years old," but Elaine Stritch always made me think 60, even in her early days. Watch her on the *Ed Sullivan Show* from 1954 perform her number from the *On Your Toes* revival, and she looks 60. There are so many seasoned performers today who should be playing leads, but lately the directors and producers are hiring right out of college. It takes a 35-year-old to play a 20-year-old masterfully on the stage, in my not so humble opinion.

28. Passion

At the Public Theatre, a one-day reading of a show called *Muscle* by James Lapine and Stephen Sondheim was held. *Muscle* was to be Act Two of two new one-act musicals. Act One was to be something called *Passion*. *Muscle* was based on a book about a young man who becomes obsessed with bodybuilding to the point where it almost kills him. Stephen Lang played the steroid-ruined gym-rat trainer. Michael Hayden played the protagonist and a young actor named Jere Shea was in it as well. Madeline Kahn played the mother. John Cunningham played the father. Sondheim wrote one big long opening number similar to the opening of *Into the Woods*. Musically it was supposed to be very *Company/Merrily We Roll Along* in style (contemporary, for 1993). But it was not. I still have the music somewhere. It was hardly a song... it was more a series of snippets with underscoring. It was morphing into an actual song at the end with the leading man singing about his frustrations with his life at his office, but I don't believe Sondheim ever finished it.

We read through the *Muscle* script. The bodybuilders were all going to be wearing prosthetics as the play went along to make them get bigger, and there was to be a love scene between the leading man and his girlfriend where they couldn't make love because their bodies were so overblown. It was supposed to be really sick and funny. That was *Muscle*. Eventually, James Lapine directed it with a score by William Finn in a workshop at the Public (or somewhere). A disaster.

During this, I asked Sondheim what *Passion* was about. We had one of our few private moments. He said, "Oh, well let me tell you about that. I went to 'such and such' movie theatre one day and saw this movie called *Passione d'amore*. I'm sitting there watching and it's rolling along. Set on a remote military base, the characters keep talking about this woman named Fosca. The handsome leading man, Giorgio, is anticipating meeting this woman. Agreeing to meet him, she comes down the stairs in the dark and steps into the light, and we see that she is grotesquely, hideously UGLY! I just threw my head back and howled because of the expression on the leading man's face. And the story goes crazy after that." Then Steve added, "I had to write this as a musical!" I said, "That sounds really fun." Steve continued, "She begins to torture him, and stalk him, and make his life miserable." And I thought, "Sounds great!"

At Lincoln Center, we were scheduled to do a three-week workshop of *Passion*. We were in the black box on the seventh floor of the Rose building at Julliard. We had our auditions, and Donna Murphy and Marin Mazzie were pretty much cast immediately on sight. Then, I think, they just handpicked Peter Gallagher as Giorgio.

I first met Donna Murphy in a little rehearsal room at 890 Studios during the first week of *Rags*. She was hired to understudy the opera diva Teresa Stratas and we were plunking through the music. She told me then and there that she might not be with us for long. Sure enough, she left to go back to *The Mystery of Edwin Drood* to replace Betty Buckley. Smart move! A year later, Donna called me to ask about the *Into the Woods* auditions. She was being called in for the Witch. These were very early auditions and James Lapine and Paul Gemignani had thought about such ideas as "rock singer" and "scary," and "frightening." So I told Donna they wanted a rock singer-type and to be scary and frightening. Donna meticulously planned her auditions during those days with her faithful pianist and she prepared some piece of music that built slowly into a roar of anger and rage. It was *rock*-y and scary and frightening alright. This was my first real taste of just how far Donna Murphy would go. It was truly impressive, and scary and frightening and she has always been the first one to recall this audition with humor. Perhaps it was too much! Four years later, I was honored and privileged to be in a rehearsal room in the bowels of Lincoln Center with Donna, looking at a piece of music by Stephen Sondheim. There was no title yet to the song, but it was certainly long and intricate. One thing I've noticed about the four Sondheim shows I've been involved with, is that the first two or three numbers he writes are always very complicated, but as we get closer to the opening, the newer material becomes sparser and simpler. *Sunday in the Park with George* had the title song (a bitch to play) and "Color and Light" (utterly fantastic, but hard as shit) in contrast to the last two songs written—"Children and Art" and "Lesson #8." *Into the Woods* had the opening number and "Hello Little Girl" and ended with "No One Is Alone" and "Children Will Listen." The first two numbers of *Assassins*, "Everybody's Got the Right" ("C'mere and Kill a President") and the "Ballad of Booth" contrast with the far less complicated remainder of the score (although one last-minute piece, "Another National Anthem," was pretty brutal), and now *Passion*. *Passion* begins with "Happiness" and "I Read" and graduates through the "Send in the Clown"-ish "I Wish I Could Forget You" to the simplicity of "Loving You" and the quiet version of "No One Has Ever Loved Me."

The piece of material which would eventually be titled "I Read" was staring back at Donna and me. This was still in the days of the copyists and the ink printer, so no instant computer transpositions were possible. Steve had written it in three flats, C Minor for the main statement. Donna needed it in F Minor, F# Minor, G Minor, or perhaps Ab Minor. Jesus Christ! She would make up her mind right before the audition. So we had fun laughing over the discoveries we were finding as we went along, the intervals and the harmonies—"oh gawd," we would say. We went in the next day and Donna auditioned for Fosca in *Passion*. In the show we ended up in G Minor. I'm not sure what we did it in that day! Donna always took her time with this number, which I frankly loved. I believed Steve had it in mind to be a little more schizophrenic and jerky, but the music is so beautiful and I love her hypnotic, dreamy interpretation. And we were being very careful and taking our time in front of the composer! That's the problem with having actors audition with material from the show. It's hard if not impossible to change the original "take" an actor comes up with. But it was obvious that day that Donna and Fosca were made for each other.

I had a wonderful conversation with Sondheim during this about film composer Bernard Herrmann (*Psycho*, *Marnie*, *Vertigo*). One of Sondheim's earliest influences was the film, *Hangover Square*, a psycho thriller from the

1940s Twentieth Century Fox studio. The star was the tragically short-lived Laird Cregar, and the score featured a piano concerto by Herrmann. Sondheim loved this concerto and it's jarring opening chords and said he was frankly centering the whole *Passion* score around those chords. I, of course, knew exactly what the music and film were and considered myself extremely fortunate to be playing this "homage." The score for *Passion* may have had no jazzy swing music, but a Bernard Herrmann homage was the next best thing!

The auditions for the beautiful voluptuous Clara began. On the list was Marin Mazzie. I remembered Marin chiefly from her understudy duties on *Into the Woods*. She was very impressive in rehearsal and successfully pulled off Rapunzel and Cinderella—very musically secure and dependable. And she even tackled the Witch in rehearsal and was terrific. But if anyone remembers Melanie Griffith in the first half of her movie *Working Girl*, that is how I recall Marin during this period. A little clunky and big, big hair. At the auditions, her name was called and in walked a vision! Waist-length white Jean Harlow hair, slim, fabulous body, dressed to the nines, almost unrecognizable. Everyone was blown away. What a transformation. She was hired on the spot. She admitted to giving herself a major makeover and it certainly paid off with many Broadway leading roles and Tony Award nominations. Oh... and nudity was no problem! (Since the opening number of *Passion* was to be in the nude.)

I had to teach Peter Gallagher some of the music and get him going on it before we started the workshop. He came over to my apartment with his wife who was about 27 months pregnant—she was HUGE—and I thought, "if you get anything on my couch..." She was about ready to drop that baby, she was so big. We started going through the song "Happiness" and the first four "letter" songs, leading up to Fosca's entrance. They were very long. Some of them were written in straight 3/4 waltz tempo, but Peter was having a really hard time wrapping his brain around them. I kept telling him "They're waltzes!" He turned to his wife... and I don't know if he was kidding—he was a real kidder—and asked, "What's a waltz?" And I thought, "Great! Another Cynthia Sykes!" Much of this music was cut. I don't know why, but it got cut. I won't blame Peter. Whatever he could learn he did fine, and then we just cut the rest of it! But I just loved me some Peter Gallagher. He is the funniest person in the world and a terrific actor.

We began rehearsing, and we didn't have much time. For me, it was hell, because my partner Charlie went into the hospital for the first time. It was horrible, but I had the show and had to go on.

We had "I Read," several songs with no titles except Letter #1, #2, #3, "Happiness," the garden scene which had lyrics all the way through (most of the lyrics would be cut, and it became one long underscored scene). We did not have "Loving You" or "No One Has Ever Loved Me" yet. We did have "I Wish I Could Forget You" (which for me is the hit song), but not much after that. There was no music in the second half. We dummied up a finale out of "I Wish I Could Forget You." There were a couple of Gossip sequences with the soldiers. I believe the finale that ended up in the show is the same as what we dummied up in that workshop.

James Lapine wanted us to use the soldiers to shift scenes, so Paul made me ad-lib and riff on Sondheim's Gossip music as marches. Ad-lib Sondheim, ha! But a piece of special material that James wanted for the workshop was a musical nightmare sequence for when Giorgio goes nuts and wakes up sick in bed. Paul sat the soldiers down during rehearsal one day, and without letting me in on it said, "Play 'em the nightmare." "The nightmare?" "Yeah... you know... play 'em the nightmare." The nightmare, eh? Stammering, I said, "Well... I guess they could sing a little bit of Giorgio's song from the garden scene ('How can I describe her, the wretchedness,' etc.)." Out of my ass I pulled all of this. He didn't even give me a night or a morning to think about it. He said, "Play the nightmare." So, I said, "Let's start with that." They learned the whole page of Giorgio's music. Then he started doing it as a round, and we added a couple of adjustments and voila! the *nightmare*! AND IT'S IN THE FUCKING PUBLISHED VOCAL SCORE OF THE SHOW! Exactly as I pulled it out of my ass that day. It went in the show—not a word was said by James or Steve, and not a note was changed.

Tony-winner Katie Finneran was in the workshop as the "mistress." I said, "I know you from somewhere. What do I know you from?" And she said, "Well, I've done a movie or two." "Oh really, what movies?" She said, "Well, I did the remake of *Night of the Living Dead*." "THAT'S IT! Wow you are some screamer!" She said, "I know, I can scream." Lapine wanted to have Donna as Fosca scream offstage a few times and Donna didn't want to do it, so I said, "Katie can scream!" Katie did all of Donna's screaming. I mean, blood curdling screams. This is all on the videotape, because it was filmed for the Lincoln Center Library. It's there for everybody to see. A future two-time Tony Award winner screaming offstage for a future two-time Tony Award winner onstage.

We did three performances. It went very smoothly. We had costumes, lights, props, no sets but beds, chairs, and tables. I remember one chaotic moment right before the first performance. Donna was putting on a wig and putting on her moles and I said, "I thought this was a reading." And she just looked at me and rolled her eyes as if to say, "No. We're putting on a full production."

There was one awful thing I had to do. It was supposed to rain during the scene when Giorgio and Fosca are up on the hillside. She faints and he has to pick her up and carry her off, and we needed the sound of rain. We didn't have any sound equipment. I had to stand up at that point and hold up two 8-foot long "rain sticks" with granules in them and tilt them back and forth simulating the sound of rain. I did it, but I was right in full view of the audience, standing there tilting these things back and forth. EVERY EYE was on me, as if to say, "What the fuck are you doing? Put those things down! SHHHHH!" But it was all Paul Gemignani and his love for little percussion toys. "Oh, yeah, I can get you some rain sticks. I can make it rain! Ford'll do it." Thanks.

We also had Simon Jones playing Fosca's cousin. I forget who played the doctor. We had some of the same soldiers as on Broadway. There just wasn't a lot of music yet. I was miserable because Charlie was in the hospital for two weeks during this. I was going right from Lincoln Center to Roosevelt Hospital every day. And then trying to learn this music... and transpose it... and REMEMBER AND WRITE DOWN THE NIGHTMARE SEQUENCE!! I'm a piano player, not a composer.

After the workshop was done, we were immediately headed for Broadway... because it was Tony Award time... so whether or not we were ready, we were heading for Broadway. Peter Gallagher dropped out. I kept running into him saying, "Please don't drop out...what's the matter?" and he said, "I... I... don't get that show. I don't understand why Giorgio falls apart at the end... I don't know what the scream is about at the end of the duel... I just don't get it." And he was so funny during the workshop, because he couldn't remember one line, and he was cracking jokes all the way through the rehearsals, and we were laughing SO hard, even James Lapine was laughing. But I thought, "Geez, Peter's gonna have to be on book." But he nailed the workshop. He nailed every single line for three performances. Still he said, "I just don't get it... I don't get what that character is about."

I don't think there were any auditions. If there were, I wasn't called to play them. I saw actor Jere Shea in a restaurant. He had been in *Muscle*, and I recognized him. He said that he was going to play Giorgio!

We rehearsed at 890 Studios. It all went so smoothly. We had *naked day*, where the whole cast was dismissed for the day and all the blinds were pulled in the studio. The lights were turned out, and Jere and Marin got naked. Paul Gemignani and I were at the piano, and we ran through the song "Happiness" two or three times so they could rehearse... naked. Oh... yes... the show opened with Giorgio and Clara at the height of orgasm, naked in bed. Wheeeeeeeee!

The character of the doctor was played by an actor whose name I can't remember right now, but he was fired in previews, and Tom Aldredge came in. Then said first actor died shortly thereafter. Very sad. But he was one of the reasons that the audiences were laughing so much in previews because he was a big old southern queen. Here we were in Italy, and he was someone out of *Cat on a Hot Tin Roof*... it was just... wrong.

But the thing that was really troublesome (as was typical with every James Lapine show I worked on) was the choreography. For *Sunday in the Park with George*, we had Randolyn Zinn. For *Into the Woods*, we had Lar Lubovich. For *Passion*, we had Jane Comfort. These were all supposedly legitimate dance people. Lar was famous. Later he was hired for *High Society* and was fired after the first preview. (That show would be an entire book about how NOT to do a Broadway musical, DOA, Dead On Arrival.) Jane Comfort was brought in to do the marching for the soldiers and any other kind of movement that was needed. First of all, every day of rehearsal this woman wore a jester's hat. A jester's hat but without the little bells on it. She couldn't count the music. A choreographer! She'd say, "How do you count this stuff?!? (Jester hat bobbing) One... two... three... and a half?... and... one... two... and a half? One...two?" She had these poor character actors playing the soldiers marching in one and a half beats, or one and three quarters beats. "A kick a step a step a skip a step." And when we got to the nightmare sequence, she had them skipping and hopping in circles around Giorgio's bed. Watch the DVD. Look at what they're doing...if you can see it... it may be too dark. But when we were in tech rehearsals on stage, the late great Francis Ruivivar, Cris Groenendaal, and Bill Parry, were up there hopping and skipping around that bed singing, "How can I describe her, the wretchedness?" (Skip step step skip step skip, then do half a step, now do a little half hop, then do a little half skip.) In rehearsal the "boys" would look out at me and Gemignani and mouth, "HELP!!" Then she'd come out and ask, "Paul, what was that count again?" and Paul would say, "ONE TWO THREE FOUR FIVE SIX SEVEN EIGHT, a ONE TWO THREE..." She couldn't count to 8, and these were military marches. All she had to do was have them march across the stage in counts of 8. So, if you check the published score and look at the vocal arrangement, it's all off by a half measure, or there's a 5/4 bar or something, but no counts of eight. Watch those things sometime and try to figure out what she was doing. We spent more time on those marches! Oy! And she got a great big credit... AND royalties!

Randolyn Zinn on *Sunday in the Park with George* did "I'd be in the Follies..." in the "Color and Light" number and "Well, if you want bread or respect or attention..." in the title number. Then she helped move people around during the first act finale, and that was just about it. Lar Lubovitch did the loopy choreography at the end of Act One of *Into the Woods*, which was "Into the woods, hop skip a skip..." What is it with these people that they can't just go: "skip skip skip hop. Skip skip skip hop." It's gotta be: "Skip hopty scopty skipatee scopty skip skip hopatee skip." AGAINST THE MUSIC. And poor Barbara Bryne with her broken ankle and her crutch... crazy. But James didn't like choreography or choreographers... obviously.

We will now go to the previews of *Passion*. We were housed in the Plymouth Theatre (now the Schoenfeld) and the orchestra dress rehearsal went fine. Petula Clark was there! Good old Jonathan Tunick and his beautiful orchestrations, everything fell into place. Easy to play. My keyboard gave me not only a beautiful piano sound, but harp and harpsichord as well, and Nick Archer, my co-keyboardist got to play all the string patches, and everything just fell into place with Tunick. Unlike the late Bill Brohn, the worst orchestrator in the history of musical theatre. *Wicked* sounds like a bunch of garbage can lids being beat together.

The first preview. The show started and the audience started to laugh. Early on. And they laughed, and they laughed, and they laughed, and they laughed. And they laughed on cue when Fosca stepped into the train right before where the song "Loving You" eventually would be. They really howled at that, but we kept *that* laugh in... it was like Mama Rose's "I'm gonna make you a star" laugh in *Gypsy*, which was a GOOD laugh. At the end of the show, when Giorgio is sitting in the asylum, going through the box of letters that was brought to him with Fosca's belongings, out of the box he pulls her braids and the audience just screamed with laughter. Is he going to pull out her moles next!?? As Fosca, Donna was wearing great big moles on her face. Next day, after the preview, the moles were cut. The braids were cut. Every weird sounding line of dialogue was cut. There was a line where Giorgio is up in the hills and he's singing about a letter from Clara, and Fosca interrupts him. The audience laughed at her sudden interruption. Giorgio said, "Your hand's bleeding." And she said, "Uh... oh... I must have fallen on some of those Acacia spines and cut myself." The audience HOWLED. What the hell is an Acacia spine? Well, that went. Anything that sounded like that was cut. And we went through the whole script the very next day, and Lapine was going cut, cut, cut, cut, cut, cut, cut, cut, cut. Then it started getting better.

The other sticking point, the number we spent the most time on was a flashback scene. It was different musically and really fun to do... eventually. James Lapine kept saying, "I think we ought to cut it." Then we would have been left with an hour-long show with no musical variety whatsoever. He wanted to cut all the passerelle numbers in *Into the Woods*. He wanted to cut "I Know Things Now" and "Giants in the Sky" and "On the Steps of the Palace." He thought they held up the show. People want to hear songs. They don't want to hear underscoring for three hours. But we kept the flashback scene, and Steve must have rewritten the Count Ludovic section five or six times. The lyrics always stayed the same, but he would change the music. Matt Poretta (son of '60s opera singer Frank Poretta) as Count Ludovic was terrific, a great singer, but up until the very last preview before the critics came, he was having to learn a new version of his music. Every three nights it was different. Two performances before the critic previews began, he started his segment beginning with "Ah well, at last you know the truth, Signorina..." and... he went blank. We had two pages of music to play, but he stopped singing. He had no idea where he was. He just tipped his hat to Donna and Paul Gemignani conducted faster. We raced through all the music, as Matt turned and walked a few steps, turned, tipped his hat, turned, walked a few steps and tipped his hat again, and exited the stage. It was a lot of music. But he was brain fried, couldn't remember a word or a note. This happened two nights in a row. He was crying in the wings after both shows. He couldn't remember any of it, because it had been changed so many times. Finally, he surmounted it, but it was really painful for him. We had to rehearse and rehearse it before every performance. He was down in the pit saying, "I can't do this. I can't do this. He has to stop re-writing this." If you look at that music or listen to it... it's HARD. Matt left the show pretty early on, and James hired some non-musical talent to replace him... but George Dvorsky was the only one who could actually sing it after Matt, and he was the understudy and was bypassed! Go figure. We had this actor who was a Chris in *Miss Saigon*. He couldn't count to one. He was impossible, and terrible. I don't know where they got him, and he quit the business after this show. I tried to help him and tried to help him and tried to help him. I understand Paul Gemignani's complete and utter frustration, because no one EVER consults the musical director when hiring. Does *anybody* consult the musical director when doing a musical? Ask me about Jenna Elfman in the *Nine* revival someday. THAT's a real story! Not to be included here.

We ran for nine months and won the Tony Award, beating out the horrible *Beauty and the Beast*. We were afraid we were going to get lousy reviews, but we got decent ones. But no business. One evening I came upstairs from the pit after the show and came face to face with a woman. I gasped—it was a good gasp from me, but I don't know how the woman perceived it. I extended my hand and introduced myself. The woman was Valeria D'Obici, the actress who portrayed Fosca in the film *Passione d'amore*! She was very lovely and stylish. Our press rep took her around to meet everyone, and the next day he told me that as they were standing outside the theatre looking at the photo of Donna, she jabbed herself in the chest stating grandly, "I am Fosca!" True, she was!

Donna Murphy was so much fun on this show. We had a good time, and in tech rehearsals Donna would be sitting there with her moles and her wig and her makeup, with her sewing on her little settee waiting for the lights to be set. She made the mistake of telling me that she had done *Flower Drum Song* (of all things) as her senior high school musical. The explanation for doing *Flower Drum Song* was that she (with all humility) was the most talented girl in her class, and the most talented boy was an African-American. They didn't quite know what musical to do, so they chose *FLOWER DRUM SONG*! She said everybody was in yellow makeup. She played the Pat Suzuki part— "Grant Avenue" and "I Enjoy Being A Girl." And I'm loving this because this was my favorite musical for a long, long time. They did only one performance and she was doing the big strip-tease number at the end of the first act with her ponytail hanging down her back. As she was flipping her head around doing *hair*ography, the braid flew right off into the audience. She said they had yellow makeup ALL OVER their costumes. During the *Passion* tech, she would be sitting in her somber Fosca pose, and I would play the two-bar intro to "Grant Avenue." She would drop her knitting, stand up and sing, "Grant Avenue, San Francisco..." in her Fosca drag. That was our theme song. Fifteen years later, I played it for her a few times when we did my last ever Broadway musical, *The People in the Picture* (see Chapter 42) and she smiled from across the room and wearily nodded... I don't know if I'll ever see Donna again, because I quit show business during *The People in the Picture*.

Giorgio's song "No One Has Ever Loved Me" was a big high energy tango at first. It was in a strict tempo, "No one will ever love me bah dah dap bah dum!" It was a big, grand number that he sang as he was running through the hallways to Fosca. Paul asked me to ad-lib in rehearsal... play a chord... Jere sang the first line, then Paul said play another chord. We invented the present accompaniment on the spot, and out went the tango! I've got the original music somewhere and it's probably published too. It's a really big dramatic arrangement, and it really does sound like a tango. I kept thinking, "They're going to buy this song, and use it as a commercial when they revive Fresca: "Good and delicious, good for you too, dah dah dap dah.. that's Fresca! Dah dah dah dah dat dah."

Also, we needed a Christmas carol for the party scene where Fosca freaks out and exposes Giorgio. So, before Paul could say, "Play the Christmas carol," I went home and I thought... ok... a Christmas carol that sounds right for that period, and I picked "God Rest Ye Merry Gentlemen." I suggested that they translate it into Italian. Then I had to put an accompaniment to it that sounded like Fosca, who was to be miming playing the piano onstage. I wanted it to sound as if she couldn't make up her mind whether to be in major or minor mode. Frances Ruvivar sang it in Italian, and did a sort of showy ending, because as one of the soldiers he was characterized as a big ham. Donna mimed playing the piano for him. As Frances sang the last phrase he did his hammy ending. I don't know who started it, but Donna came to me and said laughing, "You're starting to get a little showy on that piano down there (in the pit)." "Oh, you want SHOWY!?" So I really got showy. People would tell me she would be looking in the pit and at her hands as if to say, "WHAT AM I DOING!?" When I went to see *Passion* in London, the ONE THING they did besides putting in an intermission (big mistake), was to write an entire big Italian chorale of their own making for that moment. I thought WELL! But the New York version was mine—my idea and my arrangement. As was "the nightmare," as are those little marches all the way through, as are many of the underscoring cues too. And all are in the published vocal score.

About halfway through the run, Charlie died, and I took three weeks off. When I came back, one of our musicians had been replaced. He had been having a lot of trouble. He had been dropping his instrument and hitting a lot of wrong notes. I was thinking, get it together! I may be hung over, but you are really fucked up! After the show closed, five months rolled around and I went to an AA meeting. May 3rd on West 73rd Street. My next AA meeting was at 7:30 AM the next morning on 96th Street between Broadway and Amsterdam. I walked in and who was ringing the bell and leading the meeting? My absent musician friend. He had been bottoming out during *Passion*, six months before I bottomed out, and the reason he disappeared was he had to go get sober. I went to him and said, "Now I know what happened, and now I know this is where I need to be. I'm so happy to see you!" At that moment, it was one of the greatest moments of my life. Maybe.

The show never sold tickets. We made the album. I can't listen to it because all my piano work is buried under extra strings. I was basically faded out in the mix and it is simply not a good recording. We also made the videotape (problems there, as well, with music editing). The TV commercial (on YouTube) made it look like a murder mystery, a totally different show. It had gun shots in it, as if Donna was going to shoot somebody. I didn't do the 10th Anniversary Concert. I was doing something else, but I really loved doing *Passion*. It was a pleasure to play. It was one act and it was never boring, and my friend Nick Archer was my happy-go-lucky obscenity-spewing co-keyboardist. I was unhappy all the way through, but it was never boring or unhappy in the pit for me.

Opening night was a big sign of my out-of-control alcoholism. I didn't go to the opening night party, because my invitation AGAIN said, "Third floor of Sardi's" and I thought I should have been on the first floor with everybody. So, one of our Fosca understudies peered into the pit and said, "Will I see you at the party tonight?" and I said "No, I'm not going because I've been relegated to the third floor with the musicians." She said, "Oh." I had forgotten that there were some musicians in the pit that were two feet away from me and one of them said, "Well, we're sorry about that, too!" Then I kind of realized... maybe, just maybe, I was being an asshole, by saying that, or expecting anything more than an invitation. And maybe I am nothing more than a pit pianist. I started really having grave doubts about who I was and what my part was in the scheme of things. I was lucky to even be invited. Opening night of *Into the Woods*, the musicians weren't even invited.

Oh, and Sondheim won the Tony for best score again. In his acceptance speech, he once again singled me out: "And Paul Ford, the same indefatigable master of the musical theatre who knows every song ever written... and plays them the same way," which is either high praise or a very subtle dig, depending on your viewpoint. Charlie was too sick to attend, so I watched the show at home, drunk. *Passion* closed in January of 1995. Charlie was dead, and I was a 300-pound, miserable, sloppy alcoholic.

29. Everyday A Little Death

1995 - 2006 *WISE GUYS*

Post *Passion*, I played the first three readings of Stephen Sondheim's last fully original musical, *Wise Guys*, made a demo recording of the score with Sondheim singing, played a private reading with Hal Prince reading the script in his office (Sondheim sang) and played for the final reading at the Public Theatre under the title *Bounce* before the property became *Road Show*.

To make a very long story short, the first reading had little music and a wild farcical script. Sam Mendes joined the team and created a whole new opening scene. I saw the first workshop when Ted Sperling took over the musical direction. It had disaster written all over it. Time passed and Sondheim invited me to his home to make a full demo recording with old songs, new songs, and new old songs. The next morning the Hal Prince reading took place and there was a discussion between Hal, Steve, book writer John Weidman, and Judy Prince who suggested *Gold* for a new title. It was opined that audiences would mistake *Wise Guys* for gangsters. More time passed and a full production was scheduled for Washington and Chicago under a new title, *Bounce*. The musical direction was now by Andrew Lloyd Webber conductor David Caddick with orchestrations by Jonathan Tunick. A full original cast recording was made, complete with sluggish tempos. More time passed and I was asked by new musical director David Loud to play a reading at the Public Theatre, this time directed by Eric Schaeffer, with Bernadette Peters as the mother. Next, I heard charlatan British director John Doyle and his musical director Mary Mitchell Campbell were helming it for a limited run at the Public, under yet a new title, *Road Show*. A new original cast album was recorded. I have yet to buy or listen to this recording. And I never saw either production.

Enough was enough. To continue to make a very long story short, the show was based on a book about the "fabulous" Mizner brothers, an epic biographical telling of the escapades of two rascally businessmen. Irving Berlin held the rights for a long time and Bob Hope was also interested. Sondheim waited a long time before the property became available.

The first reading starred Victor Garber and Patrick Quinn. There was a lengthy title song, "Wise Guys," which Paul Gemignani immediately suggested Sondheim "adjust" because it was a direct lift from the "Pineapple" song from *Cabaret*. He changed a couple of notes, but it still sounded like the "Pineapple" song. This was a fun, full-out vaudeville number in several tempos and many sections setting the tone for what was supposed to be a bona-fide, raucous musical comedy. Following the opening number came a funny scene around a song called "Benicia," followed by a long farcical sequence set in the Klondike. All of this was fascinating, but we were 30 minutes into the reading and the story hadn't even begun. It was long but crammed full of interesting and funny scenes.

When Sam Mendes held his reading, Nathan Lane joined the cast. Mendes and book writer John Weidman came up with a prologue before the opening song. It would be an old-time historical pageant detailing events of the first half of the 20th Century with possible film clips and live tableaux accompanied by booming narration. At the point in the historical timeline when the title characters, Addison and Wilson Mizner, should have been included (but are not), a ruckus was to occur in the two opposite box seats. The two brothers would appear and start razzing the pageant, then come down to the stage and begin the opening number. I liked this idea and had to improvise on American patriotic songs for this new prologue. What followed was a heavily edited (in score and script) version of the show from the first reading. A lot of material was already gone, including "Benicia" and much of the lengthy Addison's Trip sequence. Paul Gemignani and I were now out of the picture. I'm not sure why.

I went to the next Sam Mendes staged workshop, but only Act One was staged. Gone were the opening, the title song, and much of the farcical element. And the fun. What was left was what the British do best. Dull and earnest, but with one new true gem in the score, "A Little House for Mama" sung by Nathan Lane. As far as I know, this song has never been published and just might possibly be restricted for Nathan Lane's own private use. I haven't heard it since, and it was dropped from the score. I'm not sure it's ever been published. Too bad.

When, much to my surprise, Steve asked me to his house to record the next demo for the show—always an honor and a privilege—there was much new music right off the press. Both of us rehearsed each song a few times and then recorded. None of it was in Steve's keys but we left it that way since so much was new. Before every take of every song, Sondheim knocked back a shot of vodka. I tried not to take it personally about my piano playing! The next day, in his office, Hal Prince read the script, I played, and Steve sang. From then on it was Hal Prince's show. Victor Garber and Nathan Lane were gone, and Howard McGillin and Richard Kind were in. I was also gone. Jane Powell was cast as the mother, but "A Little House for Mama" was gone. I did not travel to see the show but did sit down to listen to the new CD. Following a lackluster Overture, which reminded me of Jerry Herman's *The Grand Tour*, came a series of watered down, even more edited versions of the songs from the Prince office reading. I've never listened to it since.

Time passed. David Loud called me. What, again? It was exciting to be in a rehearsal room at the Public Theatre again in 2006, with Bernadette, Richard

Kind, and new (or sub) "Wilson" Marc Kudisch and even more new material. We hung on by a thread because it was a very quick process with a lot of new people. We did only one read-through, simply staged. The show was now absolutely devoid of humor with songs such as "Talent," and "Get Out of My Life" seemingly out of place in what was once a raucous show. The original script had such complicated montage sections—"Addison's Trip," the Klondike scene with a polar bear on stage (already cut), the New York montage scene about boxing and theatre producing, the Boca Raton scandal scene. I felt the show was let down by the limits of the stage and how they planned to pull off some of these elaborate sequences. Actions such as Addison collecting the huge bag of souvenirs from his trips, and his proposed fall down a gang plank, with the bag bursting open and antiques going everywhere, giving Addison the idea of "rearranging" them and going into interior design, could be effective in a film, or even an animated cartoon. The polar bear fight scene, and all of Addison's mansion planning and building could have been magical with imaginative animation. But the stage was too slow and too small for this stuff. There never seemed to be a payoff for these lengthy sequences. I could see the two brothers almost as a Popeye and a Bluto getting into whirling fist fights and the pace going at lightning speed. I left the Public Theatre that day feeling like we did as good a job as we could, but I was never called again. I never saw *Road Show*, but since it was done in one act, it must have been a mere shell of what had been originally imagined. I also missed the original title.

Reflecting back a couple of decades since the first reading, I fondly remember the title song ("Wise Guys"), the Benicia scene, "A Little House for Mama," "The Best Thing That Ever Has Happened to Me," and the original "Addison's Trip" and Boca Raton scenes. But most of this stuff never really saw the light of day. The show is never discussed anywhere.

30. Anyone Can Whistle
Carnegie Hall 1995

During *Passion*, on October 14th, 1994, I called my partner of 12 years Charlie Stramiello at home and his dad picked up the phone. Charlie had not called for a few days but told me he was going to spend time with his dad that week. I asked his dad how Charlie was and hesitantly he said, "Not good... not good." I was in a cab in two seconds heading to the Schwab House on West

73rd and West End Avenue. When I got there, his dad let me in and I found Charlie gasping for air, rolling around on his bed and flailing his arms. "How long has this been going on?" I asked. His father shrugged, and I called 911. I tried to ask Charlie if he knew what was happening to him. He couldn't speak but seemed to be desperate to say something. The paramedics arrived and we were off to Roosevelt Hospital. Charlie was unconscious and never regained consciousness. He was also blind. His brother and his mother quickly came and we waited overnight.

The next day, the 15th, Charlie's doctor asked his dad if he wanted to keep him on life support and he said, "NO! TURN IT OFF!" I shared his feelings. I couldn't stand to see him suffering one more second. I kept talking to him and crying and holding his hand and stepping aside to let his family do the same. The doctor explained to us what the procedure was. It would take three hours for his death to occur, so we waited. Charlie's brother started to panic about his car not having enough money in the meter and begged me to go put money in the meter! He wasn't sure what street it was on and even though he told me the color and make of the car, I wouldn't know one stupid car from another! So I spent 20 minutes trying to find his fucking car! I went back to the hospital room unsuccessful and... Charlie had died. His brother apologized profusely. Well. What the hell...

Several of Charlie's friends had shown up and we were discussing plans for the next few days. I walked passed Charlie's cubicle for a second. The curtains were drawn but I saw something in the crack of the curtain that made me gasp and freeze. I didn't know that when someone dies, I guess they immediately wrap the body from head to toe in sheets and there he was, lying wrapped up like a cocoon. It shocked me and it made me start to cry again.

Charlie's funeral was a few days later, open casket. I cried a lot and sat in the front row with his parents. I called all of his friends, including his pot dealer, with whom he was very close. Some of his friends were appalled but, hey, hypocrites are we? There were times when I thought Charlie was more concerned about the welfare of his pot dealer than he was about me. His pot meant EVERYTHING to him. The pot dealer thanked me for including him. The service was run by a generic minister at a chapel in a community center close to his parents' home in the Bronx. The reverend was really long-winded, as they always are, and talked in florid terms about *Charles* Stramiello, and people were starting to titter (as well they should have). I had to laugh myself when the service was over, when Charlie's dad did something that Charlie had done with me every time we saw a show or a movie over the preceding

12 years. He got up from his chair muttering "Jesus Christ! Well, that was... alright... but it went on 15 minutes too loooonga!" That made me laugh.

That night I put my mother to bed and I went to Cleo's Saloon around the corner until four in the morning and got wasted. I did that very same thing every night for the next seven months.

In December, I was still playing *Passion* and was numb. The only thing I felt was the hangover I had every day. For some idiotic reason I recalled that Charlie and our friend Brenda had been to a psychic she knew, and both had enjoyed the experience, so I asked Brenda for his information. In no uncertain terms did I believe any of this bunk, but I was grasping at anything. I went to this guy's apartment after giving him very basic info on the phone. He had done some charts and prepared some information for me. The first thing he said of any significance was that I was at the end of a long ten year plus period. Well, duh! But nevertheless, it triggered me to burst into tears for a half-hour, much to his dismay. After I calmed down, he said, "Well, I can see you in the spring, in a classroom setting of some kind. *Lots of classrooms, chairs, tables, people at the tables speaking.*" I had started playing a three-week summer class at Manhattan School of Music, but it wasn't a regular gig yet, so I dismissed what he was saying as being nothing significant to me. I taped the session to listen to later, but still nothing came up that was really significant.

In the winter I got a call from a Peter Bogyo about doing a concert version of *Anyone Can Whistle* benefitting God's Love We Deliver, one of Stephen Sondheim's charities. I said he should be talking to Paul Gemignani. *Passion* had closed and I was bottoming out alcoholically and emotionally, though glad to not be working at the moment. This concert would be wonderful, especially since the plan was to star Bernadette Peters, Scott Bakula and Madeline Kahn, and have Angela Lansbury, herself, as host and narrator at Carnegie Hall on April 15th, 1995. It was also what I consider one of Sondheim's greatest shows. I started working with the great, though chronically worried, Madeline Kahn on the score. Not for one minute was she ever comfortable with the entire process, and I begged her to give herself a break and enjoy the great songs, for we would take care of her. I loved her talent and I loved her fragility, but as often happens, it got tiresome and her reticence came through in her performance. She did manage to get some "hot" laughs. Scott Bakula was never seen until three days before the concert, but he was completely prepared and fit right in, quite a feat considering the difficulty of his music. And I had the great pleasure of Bernadette coming to my house and rehearsing the songs, including the cut song "There's Always a Woman."

I told her about Charlie's death and she was genuinely sad. She didn't know I had a partner. Nobody did. But she had some good news. She was getting married! I was thrilled for her. She told me how she had been waiting for a car service in front of her building to take her to a function. She was all dolled up (when is she not!) and this handsome man was strolling down the street in a tux. They looked at each other and laughed, he held his arm out, she took it and they started parading down the sidewalk. A year later, they were engaged. The marriage would last for ten years, ending with his death in a helicopter crash somewhere in Europe.

I had some fun times at Sondheim's house during this show with Paul Gemignani and Arthur Laurents (who was actually in a good mood). I loved this show and wanted to do a great job on it. I had planned to stay sober for the whole two weeks of rehearsals and the performance. I was a 100% complete failure. I was out drinking every night till 4 AM.

In the published script of *Anyone Can Whistle*, there was a large section of lyrics in the Interrogation Scene that is not in the score or on the original cast recording, which is very complete. I noticed it and asked Paul Gemignani if we should have the stage manager remove this section from the casts' scripts. "No! We're doing it." End of discussion. Okay... where is the music? What is the music that goes with these lyrics? And are there any orchestrations? Steve had no information. So, with no answers forthcoming except "No! We're doing it," I sat down and read the extra lyrics to see how they matched a similar section of lyrics earlier in the number. With a couple of slight edits, I figured we could make do with repeating a section and inserting it. The alternative was to just do the score as is and leave out the missing section. But "No! We're doing it!" Guess which section Scott Bakula completely screwed up in performance and on the recording?

The cast was huge. A great chorus filled with future Broadway luminaries, most of whom could read music, thank God. And we had two of the original ensemble men from 1964, Sterling Clark, the handsome veteran dancer who danced right behind Fred Astaire in *Finian's Rainbow*, behind Streisand in the "Hello, Dolly" number, and behind Tammy Grimes in the original cast of *The Unsinkable Molly Brown*, and the ever beautiful, delicious Broadway and movie baby of all time, Harvey Evans. I think I was more awestruck over these two than anyone. As Madeline Kahn's three "stooges," we had the lovely Chip Zien, the lovely Ken Page and the incredibly lucky Walter Bobbie (who never learned his music and couldn't even read from the script during the performance and had Arthur Laurents screaming at him from the wings, as well he should).

Herbert Ross, who did a good job on the Lincoln Center *Follies* concert, was back again. This was a plus since he was the choreographer of the original production of *Anyone Can Whistle*. He staged all the showbiz numbers but turned the Cookie Ballet (what little we were doing of it) over to Robert LaFosse. It was a chaotic rehearsal period, but exciting, and things were getting done.

When we got to Carnegie Hall and tech rehearsals, Herb Ross got a microphone in his hand. Oy! People who love to talk in *non sequiturs* and stream-of-consciousness and to just plain hear themselves talk, do not need a live microphone in their hand. Pretty soon everyone had their fingers in their ears screaming for it to stop. But the show still got done and was lots of fun.

The night of the performance, Angela Lansbury hosted and narrated. Fine, but her props (such as the miniature "miracle rock" next to her) never worked. Madeline did fine, Bernadette switched some lyrics on "There Won't Be Trumpets," which was fixed for the recording, and Scott made a late entrance in the Interrogation Scene that caused a train wreck for 32 bars which is on the recording! There is a great in-house Carnegie Hall archival video tape which has made the rounds and is great fun to watch, but the audio CD released on RCA is very piano heavy (not that I'm complaining) and what pray tell is that tempo of the Overture?!?!

My mother came up to see it and had a wonderful time, but after it was over, I was mad at the messiness and didn't want to go to the reception, not that I believe I was even invited. *Anyone Can Whistle* is in my top five favorite shows, and I was thrilled to be a part of this.

So... my plan to stay sober for two weeks and one performance failed. I was at Cleo's Saloon every single night till 4 AM and up for rehearsal at 9 AM with three hours sleep. And after the big show, I put my mom to bed and went to Cleo's Saloon and got smashed. This show was one of the first times I had ever snapped back at Paul Gemignani in rehearsal and it scared me, but I let it all hang out at Cleo's to anyone and everyone who would listen. Ranting and raving about Paul, Scott Bakula, Walter Bobbie, and even Bernadette. No, not Bernadette! Never Bernadette! For the next two weeks, I was the mad grumbler walking around with a hangover muttering "how could she go up on 'There Won't Be Trumpets?' Why did Paul have to miss that cue? Why is Walter Bobbie rich and famous, why, why, why?" Frankly, the performance was a joyous occasion, warts and all, but at the moment I was just a little bit pissed off at God and the world. I went to my therapist on Monday the 1st of May at 5 PM and started in on my weekly rant. Same dialogue, same characters, same complaints, same Cleo's resentments, same... "IF YOU DON'T GET TO AN AA MEETING AND STOP DRINKING, YOU'RE GOING TO DIE. YOU'RE DYING, PAUL." Excuse me? My therapist had just cut me off in mid showbiz rant when I was delivering it with such style and panache. He cut me off! I was stunned, and the next thing out of my mouth was, "Okay, I'll go...if you go with me." "Wednesday night, 6 PM, 73rd and Broadway, Rutgers Church, Lambda Meeting (a gay meeting, oh the horror!) of Alcoholics Anonymous, 5th floor. I'll meet you downstairs." On May 3rd, I started sitting in *classrooms and church rooms in folding chairs and at tables, listening to people at the head of rooms sitting behind tables and speaking*. Since May 3, 1995, I have been a sober member of Alcoholics Anonymous. What did that psychic know?! Obviously, a lot!

31. Booze and Broadway Part 2

During the tryout of *Into the Woods* in San Diego, I ended a four-year bout of dryness from alcohol by picking up a glass of red wine. I was hung over for *every* performance of *Into the Woods*. I was hung over for *every* performance of *Assassins*. I was hung over for *every* performance of *Passion*. I was even hung over for Bernstein's 70th birthday performance at Tanglewood with Lauren Bacall.

In December of 1994, two months after my partner Charlie's death, I played piano on the *Inside the Actor's Studio* TV show with James Lipton. It was his second interview of the series. The first was with Al Pacino, the second with Stephen Sondheim. Steve didn't know they were videotaping us and put up a fuss and almost didn't go on with the interview. I was playing the piano for Jim Walton and Liz Callaway. We had learned about 20 songs. They read the music off music stands. We refused to learn "Someone in a Tree" because it was impossible for the three of us to do it. I actually said "No" to James Lipton. James was going to pick excerpts of songs and then play it by ear during the whole interview. It went fairly well. Then it was shown 6,000 times on the Bravo Channel, as were all of those shows. We were the first televised one. I got a total of $1,200 for that job, and it was on every time I turned on the Bravo Channel. There I was... hung over on television. That's the whole point of *that* story.

I was at Cleo's Saloon, my neighborhood hole-in-the-wall gay bar, every night. One night I was sitting at the bar just drinking and chattering away to anybody who would listen about how fucked up Broadway was and how terrible everybody was and how terrible my life was when I felt a tap on my shoulder. It was a neighbor from my building, Ralph, a bodybuilder. He was accompanied by none other than... Stephen Sondheim. And Sondheim said,

"Hi, Paul." Ralph said, "You know, Paul, we've seen each other in here before, and I was having dinner with Steve around the corner. I told him that I see Paul Ford at this bar all the time... let's go see him." So, they walked into the bar and there I was, drunk, yakking it up with some other nasty drunk queens. I had to introduce Sondheim to the people I was yakking with (I didn't even know them!) who were completely freaked out and drunk and didn't know what to say. *I* didn't know what to say. *Steve* didn't know what to say. And it was ten minutes of the most uncomfortable HORRIBLE instance of being caught in my element, "caught in my cups..." by Stephen Sondheim.

Somewhere around this time I was starting to think that selling my apartment, moving back to Atlanta, shacking up in the rear bedroom of my mother's apartment, and drinking myself to death was a good idea.

My dismal failure to stay sober over the course of the *Anyone Can Whistle* concert led me to my first AA meetings.

But here is the weirdest, ghostliest, strangest, most unbelievable part of this story... and of my whole life...

THE HAUNTING

My parents took me to see Robert Wise's film *The Haunting* in 1963 when I was ten years old, an event that has influenced my life to this very day. Mom showed me a photo layout in *Life Magazine* about "a new cinema ghost story" with a black-and-white photograph of the scariest place I had ever seen or have seen since. A huge, grim, shadowy, gothic castle shot at a distorted angle. This photo was burned into my imagination for the rest of my life, and I've never found a more ideal place where I would want to live if I won the lottery.

I couldn't wait to see the movie. I read that it was based on a novel by Shirley Jackson. I discovered this title accidentally while looking through a neighbor's books. I begged to borrow the book and curled up to get more of this story from a different angle. It was my *Peter Pan*, my *Cinderella*, my *A Christmas Carol*, my *Catcher in the Rye*, my *Red Badge of Courage*, and even though I was a huge Lewis Carroll fan, it replaced *Alice in Wonderland* in my heart.

But what kind of heart are we talking about? Well, in a nutshell, the story of *The Haunting (of Hill House)* centers on a neurotic... did I say neurotic?... no, a super-duper-neurotic, narcissistic woman, completely ill-equipped to function in the world, who is invited to participate in a paranormal study in a New England mansion. She thinks of it as a vacation where she's going to meet her lover! "Journey's end in lovers meeting!" she keeps saying. She's already somewhat demented and when she sets foot in the mansion, it practically pushes her over the edge. In the movie, through multiple interior monologues, we hear actress Julie Harris as Eleanor describing her paranoia, fear, and growing obsession with wanting to stay in the house long after the experiment is over. She gets her wish!

Talk about identification. Julie Harris's character spoke right to this lonely, odd, 10-year-old boy. The mansion (the art direction and set direction) was a fantasy dream playground to me, and I became obsessed in re-creating it in drawings and making floor plans and 3-dimensional Lego block re-creations with interiors and staircases and the infamous tower. I would build it, tear it down, and build it again. Remember, this was long before computers, video tapes and DVDs, and all I had to go on was one *Life Magazine* photo and my memory of the one-time screening of the movie. My parents had no intention of letting me sit through that again! But it was too late! I was poisoned, obsessed, and wanted my own haunted house to disappear into forever. I never got to see the movie again till college when I finally caught it on TV.

Ten years later, in 1973, I worked at a dinner theatre in downtown Atlanta. It was a shockingly terrible production of *George M*, but nothing shocked me more than the star. What the heck had happened to Tom Thumb, and Riff, the leader of the Jets? Who was this grizzled tired-looking man? Where was Luke Sanderson, one of the quartet of characters in *The Haunting*, my favorite movie of all time?

Here was Russ Tamblyn walking through *George M*. He turned out to be a really nice guy, and I had a private talk with him about *The Haunting*. I didn't care about *West Side Story*. I didn't care about *Tom Thumb* or *Seven Brides for Seven Brothers*. The first question out of my mouth was "WHERE WAS THAT

HOUSE IN *THE HAUNTING*???" He looked surprised and said, "Oh, that was a terrific old mansion that was being operated as an inn, outside of Stratford-upon-Avon. That was a great place! There was a cave that went under the nearby cemetery and we were given a tour of it, although it was off limits. You know, of course, the interiors were all studio sets, but we were there doing exteriors. That was some place!"

A clue! He couldn't remember the name of it though, but that was okay. I never thought I would be going to London or anywhere anytime soon. I was only 20, and at the rate I was drinking I thought I would be dead by 30, and I was not the least bit adventurous.

In New York in 1978, the wondrous, spectacular, *necessary for my sanity* Regency movie revival house on the corner of 67th and Broadway (now the site of a soul-killing Apple Store) showed *The Haunting*, and I got to see it on a big screen again for the first time since 1963. I took a friend. He jumped out of his seat at the last big scare when Mrs. Markway opens the trap door in the tower, and he walked away from me, either traumatized or pissed off or bored, I never found out which. It's a very negative, depressing, sad movie.

The Haunting rates as the all-time Number One "personally made for me" motion picture experience of my life. Eleanor is who I am—isolated, neurotic, paranoid, unable to have a relationship with another human being, with a death wish and a desire to become a ghost. Yep, folks, that's me. That was me at 10 and that's me at 68. Don't know why this movie touched my soul, my imagination, at 10. Where was little league, softball, play dates, summer camp?

In 1983, I bought my first VCR and bought the first video release of *The Haunting*. I was a happy camper and screened it for many friends. They just looked at me curiously—good movie, but why the obsession? Charlie couldn't have cared less.

In 1990, I was spending a lot of time in Coliseum Books at 57th and Broadway, looking through architecture books and travel guides. Charlie and I had no immediate plans, but my mother wanted to go to London and wanted me to go with her. As I was checking out travel books, something drew me to a book on England. I turned to Stratford-upon-Avon and looked up inns/hotels. There was still no Internet or Google, so this was the only way. There were tiny black-and-white pictures of some of the places listed, and only one seemed to be the right size and architectural style. But it had no resemblance to my *Haunting* house. I was about to close the book when I noticed a tiny logo for the place in the facts-and-figures section. It was a half-inch drawing of what must have been the front of the inn and... THERE IT

WAS! The distinctive design of a gothic mansion with a tower on each side. This was it! Ettington Park Hotel, near Stratford-upon-Avon. I was choking with... I don't know what... but I was going!!! I made a rare international phone call and found that indeed it was the house used in *The Haunting* and rooms were very much available at a reasonable price! A month or two later, after my mother and I had seen *Me and My Girl* (great!), the Brighton Pavilion (also great), Windsor Castle, (yawn), Winchester Cathedral, Parliament, and Big Ben, we were on a train to Stratford. After a lovely two-hour train ride, we arrived on time with beautiful weather. In fact, there was a rainbow over the station. Definitely a good sign. We hired a taxi—he knew the place well—and we were off. Six miles out we turned onto a road marked Ettington Park Hotel and drove down a long tree-lined drive. Up ahead, in glorious, real live Technicolor, was my very own Hill House. So, there was no question, it was real, and meticulously restored in a beautiful setting. Additional cabins and rooms had been added tastefully in the back. It was a dream come true. In the film, the house is approached from the far right as seen from Eleanor's car, but the actual drive came from the extreme left. There was a dirt road leading directly from the center front through a bank of trees and across a short bridge (the Stour River runs about 300 feet in front of the house) that dead ends in a field stretching out in front. There were sheep and cows. There was an ancient chapel off to the right and the cemetery with the cave! All pictures on the current Google image search usually only show the house from the back which has a big garden, but it is not the classic recognizable view used in the film.

We went inside and a bit of disappointment set in, but that was okay. I was actually standing in my dream house, my very own *haunted* house.

The whole interior was a clash of beautiful old woodwork (good), delicate plaster molding painted light colors (not so good) and Laura Ashley-style wallpaper everywhere (a disaster). Nothing ghostly or threatening here. Just cozy old Laura Ashley. Absolutely none of the interiors were used in the film, but for color glimpses of the place, including the entrance hall and stairs, check out the Disney film *Watcher in the Woods*. It makes a brief, startling appearance.

My room was on the second floor on the right if you're facing the house. In the film it is the creepiest darkest aspect of its appearance. The hallways were tiny and went in many directions, which was good and atmospheric, but the Stour Room (my room) was bright and sunny with a fireplace, modern bathroom, and great cable TV. Outside of my door, however, was another door marked "Exit." I opened it to take a peek and found myself in the main tower. At this point, I was adjusted to the fact that this place was about one-third the size of how it was made to appear in the film. The tower in the film was supposed to house a five or six floor library with an ominous, iron spiral-staircase going up into the rafters. A huge room. The actual tower was only big enough to hold a wooden staircase filling the entire tower. It still was fascinating. The other tower on the opposite end of the house had a circular stone staircase. Both gave access to all the floors and had exits in the conservatory-like entrance hall on the ground floor. I saw that the stairs in *my* tower continued up, so I went up and through the door at the top. It opened into a large vaulted ballroom with gothic wood carvings and stained-glass windows. It was very atmospheric and exciting, even though Laura Ashley had crept in there, as well. The whole place was a hotel for big conferences and weddings, but there was certainly enough authenticity hanging around. My mom and I started exploring the place. Nothing spectacular, but definitely *old*. Back in the rear left of the house was a very nice, heated indoor pool. We went outside and took a thousand pictures. We checked out the chapel and hung around the various rooms, asking about the history. This was probably the most wonderful vacation of my life. We made reservations for the big gourmet meal in the large dining room and went and rested. This is when I figured it out. It was off season, the middle of the week, and we were the ONLY people staying there. I was up late walking the halls and opening every door that wasn't locked. What a trip! The next day was beautiful, and after breakfast, our stay came to an end. We were picked up by a tour guide who gave us a tour of the Cotswolds, but nothing came close to exploring the glorious Ettington Park Hotel. The pictures came out great and some are really funny. And now there is a pristine letterboxed Blu-ray DVD of the movie.

Charlie wanted to go to London to visit all the places where he went to school. He was a brainy type who finished high school early in the Bronx and went to college for a couple of years in London, and then backpacked all over Europe. This was something way beyond my scope of imagination. I still needed my mommy at that age. So I insisted we go to my new favorite place. He sighed, because I had taken him to so many old movies at the Regency that he hated. He had put a "block" on me. But he agreed to it. It was a perfect trip all around. Our one day there, with our third-floor attic room, our private swim in the pool, and our luscious private dinner, ALONE again in the dining room, ended with Charlie actually turning to me and saying, "This was nice." That was the *nicest* thing he ever said to me in twelve years. There was even a pianist in the parlor playing a little cocktail music as we sat alone, holding hands. I turned to Charlie and said, "Guess what that music is he's playing?" And, rolling his eyes, he asked, "What's that music he's playing?" "It's a suite from *Lady in the Dark*!" How did that pianist know that it was one of my favorite musicals? Charlie just covered his face and moaned, but for me it was magic.

I went back one more time on a weekend London trip courtesy of Mandy Patinkin in the 2000s. The trip was gratis, but the extras were not. I was really broke and I couldn't afford to stay overnight, so I ate lunch and videotaped with my archaic video camera every inch of the building. Fortunately, as the day wore on, the weather went from sunny to dark threatening thunderclouds, so I got a lot of fun footage and once again, not a soul in sight. My own private haunted house. End of the Ettington Park Hotel.

We now go back to May 1, 1995 in my therapist's office. He had just said that I was dying and needed to go to an AA meeting. My response? Miraculously, I said "Yes... if you go with me." He said, "Wednesday night, Rutgers Church, 6 PM!" The next day, Tuesday May 2, I didn't have to work, so I decided to go into Cleo's Saloon EARLY. I went in around 8 o'clock and was sitting there, basically alone, getting trashed. 10 PM rolled around, and one of the bartenders who was off that night came in the door of the Saloon. He was with a small group of people and I said "Hey." He said, "We went to the theatre tonight." There was a short woman with them. I noticed that one of the people was a stage manager with whom I had worked at one time. He came over to me, reintroduced himself, and said, "Maestro! (God, I hate that. I'm a fucking piano player!) Good to see you! You know what? I remember us talking during that show we did, and I have a surprise for you. Do you remember how much you said you loved that movie *The Haunting*?" and I said, "Yes." "Well, I've got Julie Harris over here, I'm sure you would like to meet her." He walked away and brought over the short woman... and it was JULIE HARRIS! AT CLEO'S SALOON! The trashiest bar in Hell's Kitchen. She happened to be friends with these people and they all went to a play together and stopped by to have a cocktail.

The place was empty, and I found myself sitting there at the bar saying, "My name is Paul Ford. I have loved you for years, and I've loved the movie of *The Haunting* for 30 years, since it came out." She was very polite and pleasant and told me stories about the day that they had to travel to the Ettington Park Hotel. She said that for the whole trip from London to Stratford, there was a thick black fog they had to drive through, and after they pulled up in front of the house, it just lingered over the whole place for a couple of days. She said it was quite an experience. I was thinking, "I can't believe I'm sitting here talking to 'Eleanor' at CLEO'S SALOON!" Fortunately, I wasn't so trashed that I couldn't put words together, though she did most of the talking. I trudged home in wonderment.

The next day, May 3, I got up with "the hangover," still in wonderment that I had met Julie Harris the night before AT CLEO'S SALOON! It was not a hallucination, it was REAL! At 6 PM, I met my therapist at Rutgers Church and we sat through my first official AA meeting. And I haven't had a drink since. I believe Julie Harris was my guardian angel. She was sent that night to Cleo's Saloon expressly to say to me, "It's time for you to get the fuck out of this stupid bar and stop drinking." The end of my own ghost story.

32. Mandy Patinkin

But what of my work with Stephen Sondheim? You might think that it was over by now. Four big shows, some concerts and special events. Not quite over, but a new career path was ahead. One that included an abundance of Sondheim's songs.

Towards the end of the run of *Into the Woods*, I started down a new path — a long lucrative path. It began with a new recording of *South Pacific*. I suspiciously bought this new 1986 recording starring (gulp) Kiri Te Kanawa, Franco Corelli, Sarah Vaughn and Mandy Patinkin (at least HE was appropriate). At last, here was a recording of the complete *South Pacific* Overture, but why did conductor Jonathan Tunick keep those damn snare drum rolls in the Bali Ha'i section? They were probably meant to sound like waves crashing but they made it sound like a high school marching band. Corelli's keys were raised, so Te Kanawa sounded more masculine than he and Mary Martin put together. She of course was impossible. And Sarah Vaughn was doing jazzzzzzzz! Mandy was the only appropriate voice in the bunch. So it was appropriate that Columbia/Sony offered him a chance to make his own record. He said yes and went to work.

THE FIRST ALBUM - *MANDY PATINKIN*

Mandy turned to his friends Ted Chapin, Jonathan Schwartz, and his conductor of choice Paul Gemignani for assistance. Paul called me and told me to grab some music and meet Mandy at his apartment on 90th and Amsterdam. The one song Paul and I discussed for Mandy was "I Don't Remember Christmas," the Maltby-Shire "mambo" with lyrics urging the singer to "forget her! Forget HER! FORGET HEEEEEEEEER!" I hated this song, but then... who am I? So, Mandy and I started with that song and immediately he said, "Oh... I don't want to sing angry songs, I want to sing happy, joyous, celebration songs. Fun songs." (THANK... GOD) And we have never sung that song in 23 years. Oh, we've done some sad songs, but never any "I hate me, therefore I hate you" songs. Maybe an angry song if it is genuinely funny, and certainly songs of regret and nostalgia.

Mandy's first song pick came from his Al Jolson songbook, "Rock-a-bye Your Baby with a Dixie Melody." Being from Atlanta and loving Atlanta does not mean that I have ever appreciated grits, *Designing Women*, Reba McIntyre, drag queens, RuPaul, Ray Charles, "Georgia On My Mind," or taking the "Midnight Train to Georgia." But even Judy Garland couldn't make this song work for me. Mandy and I have performed it for 23 years. Oy! I like our arrangement—partly Judy Garland, partly Luther Henderson (who wrote the dance arrangements for—get this—*FLOWER DRUM SONG!*), and partly me and Mandy. It never fails with the audience. Beats me. I hate it. Out of the Jolson songbook also came "Sonny Boy" (or "Sonny Oy!" as I like to call it), which Mandy had sung at the memorial of his architect friend, Alan Buchsbaum, "Me and My Shadow," "Pennies from Heaven," "Swanee," "Mammy," and "There's a Rainbow Round My Shoulder," which would begin a medley we called the "Happy Medley."

Mandy's pal Jonathan Schwartz had suggested an old song, "And the Band Played On," and Ted Chapin had exposed him to Sondheim's "scrabble" tribute album when they were long ago roommates, so the song "Anyone Can Whistle" was on the list. I was playing *Into the Woods* at the time and I brought in "No More" and "No One Is Alone." Paul Gemignani suggested "Over the Rainbow" and "Soliloquy" from *Carousel* which, though I didn't know it at the time, Mandy had sung at age 15 in a Jewish Community Center production in Chicago. Mandy also had an affinity for Randy Newman, since Newman wrote the beautiful "Tateh's Theme" for Mandy's character in the movie *Ragtime* (which frankly was a complete rip-off of Kander and Ebb's "If You Could See Her Through My Eyes" from *Cabaret*, but who's paying attention?) Mandy also expressed an interest in Newman's song "Marie." Add to all this, a whole batch of Irving Berlin songs.

Very quickly we had a song list—a long one—so Paul, Mandy and I thought a couple of medleys were in order. First was how to treat "And the Band Played On." This began and *patented* our "medleys made easy" machine for the rest of our music collaboration. This is the routine of how we put medleys together. What is another song that sort of just... sits there? Well...

Randy Newman's "Marie," for one. Okay... Mandy sings "The Band Played On," one chorus *a capella*, then segues to "Marie," with light ethereal accompaniment, then "The Band Played On" interrupts "Marie" in a big-band shell flourish. Mandy finishes the second chorus of "The Band Played On" and... Well, the lyric he is singing is "and the band played..." So, what was the band playing? Another beautiful showtune we had gone over was the Strouse and Adams standard, "Once Upon a Time," so I started playing that song in waltz time and Mandy started to sing it. The first phrase ends with the lyric "very long ago" and musically I went back to the original 4/4 accompaniment of "Once Upon a Time" and... boom! we are now in the present and the memory portion of the medley was over. Mandy finishes "Once Upon a Time," but can't resist one more go at "The Band Played On" *a capella* before fading away... INSTANT MEDLEY! Its creation happened as quickly as I wrote this description! Our first medley.

Our second medley came from "What the hell do we do with all these Jolson and Irving Berlin ditties?" It was time for a manic singalong building to some kind of climax, what, I didn't know. "There's a Rainbow Round My Shoulder" followed by what...? "Top Hat, White Tie and Tails" followed by what...? "Puttin' on the Ritz" followed by... (we were getting more manic musically now; was this medley getting too long? Not if you keep going faster!) "Alexander's Ragtime Band" followed by a double-time tempo "Swanee" followed by an over-the-top chorus of "My Mmmmmmmmammy!!!" and... is that the end? No, now there has to be a real showpiece to end this marathon. What? I suggested Fats Waller's "A Handful of Keys" from *Ain't Misbehavin'* (at this point I should have said to myself, "Shut up, Paul! Who the hell do you think is going to have to PLAY it?") I described it and sampled it for Mandy and it sounded like a good idea. A second medley was born! We performed these medleys for 23 years... successfully. However, we replaced "A Handful of Keys" with "Buddy's Blues" from *Follies* and eventually let go of "My Mmmmmmmmmmammy!" (I miss it.)

While we were putting all this music together, I was extremely alcoholic, extremely fat, extremely unhappy, and suffering from severe back pain. Mandy's apartment was being completely overhauled and was in a state of chaos. His little Yamaha upright piano was in one of the most bombed-out rooms. Life was sad.

We were running through the *Carousel* "Soliloquy" one day and were up to the lyric, "dozens of boys pursue her, many a likely lad does what he can to woo her from her faithful dad." when the combination of my intense bad feelings, the music, and Mandy singing "faithful dad" softly in my ear, caused me to break into tears, sobbing away. I think I was just now mourning my dad's death from seven years prior, and the dire situation with Charlie. Mandy thought this was good, and just let me have my moment. One of my favorite Mandy moments.

Mandy and I rehearsed. The record company wanted him to present the material to a small group in the great RCA Studios on 44th Street. We arrived, got set up, and Mandy, looking a little green around the gills, came into the room. We started. There was the expected distraction and forgotten lyric, but what was already happening was the magical, funny way Mandy handled and dealt with an audience. A born comedian. What a relief. What a miracle and a gift right there—the ability to be spontaneous and funny and true and *himself* and make everything okay for everybody. But mostly, to make people laugh. I fell in such "like" that afternoon that I forgot my sad life and my own crushing nerves for a minute.

The recording went fine. Orchestrator Luther Henderson had a long pow-wow with Mandy about whether or not he really wanted to sing "Rock-a-bye" and "Mammy" (supposedly racist songs). I got to be present for this nonsense. I have no patience with the so-called political correctness. These were songs.

We went ahead anyway, and NO ONE DIED! Henderson wrote charts that fell together without any musician breaking a sweat. Bill Brohn wrote his usual upside-down go around the world to get to the same place gobble-de-gook. Horrible orchestrator! His version of *Anyone Can Whistle* has never left the disc—we reverted back to Steve's perfect original arrangement in our concerts. Brohn crucified all the other Sondheim on the recording. For the big "happy" medley, Tom Fay and I played a two-piano arrangement on "A Handful of Keys." The first recorded take was spectacular. Then Mandy wanted to do it one more time. It was going well until, all of a sudden, I heard my name called. We were wearing headphones (a ghastly condition for recording music), so I stopped for a split second, then continued on. It sounded as if someone was telling me to stop. It turned out Mandy was improvising and screamed out, "PAUL FORD ON RAGTIME PIANO!" It fucking ruined the take. Guess which take ended up on the record?

The one bizarre moment I had alone with Mandy while working on this recording, which sums up many years of learning how to communicate with him, happened with "Over the Rainbow." We were running through it, half committed, and he said, "Stop. I want you to pound on the piano with your arms first and keep it up during the verse while I'm singing." I started sweating, I can't do that. It's against my ordered world, how will I know what actual notes

I pounded!!!! It must be exact! I must be able to repeat it! "Just pound!" "I can't." "Just pound up high on the keys." "Mandy, I can't!... I... won't." "Sure you can. Pound in the middle and then go up high and then come CRASHING down to the bass!" I closed my eyes and pounded. "That's it! (singing) 'When all the world is a hopeless jumble'..." I was sick to my stomach. "Great, do it again!" "Mandy, I don't know what I did..." "Come on, but this time start high and make lightening noises and then BIG BOOMS in the bass!" I closed my eyes and did the *Psycho* shower scene violins and then BIG BOOMS in the bass praying "oh God, oh God." Mandy sang, "When all the world is a hopeless jumble..." We did this routine several times. I wanted to quit and go home. Then he said, "Now just play what you would normally play..." "What?" "Just play what you want to play." "Really?" "Whatever you feel like." So, I wearily put my hands on the keys and played a more reasonable intro and we ran the song. "Great!" "But what about the storm clouds?" "Oh, I just wanted to hear that in my head, but you can play the normal music." Thank you, Jesus God. Thank you, Jesus!

It was much easier after that and our shorthand whittled down to practically nothing but telepathy.

MANDY PATINKIN: DRESS CASUAL

When Mandy decided to sing publicly, we needed more songs, so we started looking. This is where my dad's old book, *30 Years 30 Hits*, really came into service. We needed an opening number. One of my dad's favorites was a ditty called "Doodle-Doo-Doo," so historically it had a large *cringe factor* for me... BUT... the first lyrics *were* perfect to start a concert with.

> I'VE JUST HEARD A MELODY
> THAT IS ALWAYS HAUNTING ME...
> FUNNY LITTLE STRAIN
> RUNNING THROUGH MY BRAIN...
> IT'S AS SWEET AS CAN BE...

It turned out to be a great opening number that we have gone back to over and over. In my head, not necessarily Mandy's, I thought it would be fun to capitalize on his budding reputation of being slightly "over the top" by starting simply and friendly with "Doodle-Doo-Doo," then moving into another song from the *30 Years 30 Hits* book, "When the Red-Red-Robin Comes Bob-Bob-Bobbin' Along" and getting a little crazier and gathering steam, and then slipping into the little known verse of one of my favorites from *Lady in the Dark*, the patter song "Tchaikovsky." The medley would build into great intensity with "Tchaikovsky," eliciting a burst of applause from the audience... but we weren't done yet. In order to recover and pull the audience (and Mandy) back to earth, he would sing one final sweaty desperate little bit of "Doodle-Doo-Doo." Just to get back on track. It has never failed to get a huge laugh and applause. Then he had the audience sing with him on the last phrase. We put this together in five minutes.

Another hit from the *30 Hits* book was "On the Atchison, Topeka and the Santa Fe." I didn't know at the time that Mandy was obsessed with Lionel trains and we created a wonderful fantasy arrangement. Mandy had seen *Pal Joey* in Chicago, choreographed by Ann Reinking, so what the heck, let's do *Pal Joey* in seven minutes, and hell, bring Reinking along. So, she staged it and coached him. Being from Chicago, Mandy reached way back in his early days and pulled a couple of songs an old high school friend wrote (the less said the better), and our program really started to fill up. We also wanted some quick comedy numbers, so we chose Sondheim's "You Could Drive a Person Crazy," "A Tisket-A Tasket" (in a Stan Freberg-style parody), and "Sam, You Made the Pants Too Long" coupled with Mandy's buried Irving Berlin treasure, "Cohen Owes Me Ninety-Seven Dollars."

With all of these songs, plus a few more, our second record was ready to go and he named it after his concerts, *Mandy Patinkin: Dress Casual*. We also included a "Hollywood Dance Medley," but that has never translated to our piano-only concerts. Paul Gemignani conducted once again, and we had some of the same expert orchestrators (and the same lame one).

Oh, and I forgot! To add to this already overflowing array of music, we did the premiere recording of the four songs from Stephen Sondheim's *Evening Primrose* (a TV musical) with the beautiful Bernadette Peters singing more in her glorious soprano than usual, backed by Michael Starobin's imaginative and ethereal orchestrations. This and the songs from the first record would culminate in a big New Year's Eve concert at Avery Fisher Hall with Paul Gemignani conducting his handpicked orchestra. This was our first time doing all this material in public under Paul with his big orchestra... and the last time.

DRESS CASUAL - THE SHOW

In 1989, Mandy and I did our first piano-only concerts, performing for six Monday nights at the Public Theatre. Shortly thereafter we moved to the Helen Hayes Theatre for a two-month run. Our little show (now called *Dress Casual*) was heavy with Sondheim and eventually Steve came to a matinee. That afternoon, some thugs accepted from someone on the street, three complimentary front row tickets and the minute Mandy started to sing "Please play for me that sweet melody called Doodle-Doo-Doo..." in his falsetto, they began to snicker and harass him. He asked them to leave, which they did, but he was so distracted, we ended up doing an entirely different song list. Steve came backstage and we were ever so slightly freaked out that he witnessed our train wreck, but he said he loved what the incident brought out in Mandy and enjoyed the concert. He's always a good audience.

EXPERIMENT

Mandy was then courted and signed by Bob Hurwitz of Nonesuch Records to do seven recordings. We have done six. The first was called *Experiment*, inspired by the song by Cole Porter which had been suggested by Jonathan Schwartz. Mandy had always loved the Harry Nilsson record *A Little Touch of Schmilsson in the Night* and wanted to fashion something along those lines. Romantic, heavily nostalgic, heavy on the reverb. The list of songs went back and forth from ancient Irving Berlin to up-to-date *Les Miserables* to, of course, a generous helping of Sondheim. My Sondheim suggestions consisted of "Something's Coming," "Someone is Waiting," "Multitudes of Amys," "So Many People," "Good Thing Going," and (maybe my third favorite song of all time) "The Road You Didn't Take." I also suggested Fats Waller's "The Jitterbug Waltz," Jerome Kern's "I'm Old Fashioned," and the old Dick Haymes '40s hit "I Wish I Knew." It was all to be a stream-of-consciousness, almost non-stop suite. One song recorded but not used was "Surrey With the Fringe on Top" which would have been the second song after "As Time Goes By." We performed *Experiment* as a second act in our concerts for a year. It was 45 minutes long. This was the only time we had an intermission until the Patti-Mandy show in the 21st Century.

We had Eric Stern conducting now. Paul Gemignani was out for reasons only I know. Eric is brilliantly meticulous and can play piano beautifully as well. He suggested we try something different this time by having the same orchestrator do all of the songs instead of several different styles. And since Mandy wanted a lush romantic sound, Eric suggested Danny Troob, who had been working on many Disney films as of late. We performed all of the songs for Danny. And I gave him my pencil sketches—yep, still no computer for me! He went off and did his work. When he was done, he asked me to come over and actually coached me on the keyboard parts. I was surprised and a little taken aback, but of course he was right. I needed coaching badly. I had many bad habits and I was still afraid of my own shadow. (I love that expression, it really says it all.)

The day to record arrived. My phone rang early, early, early and it was Mandy. I still had not yet tuned in to all of Mandy's idiosyncrasies, and I was very surprised when he said he was going to his son Isaac's soccer game that morning and did I want to go with him. I laughed and said, "No, I'm going to the recording studio at 9 to get ready to record your next record, *Experiment!* I'm hoping to see you there!" "Oh, yeah, yeah. Just wanted to know if you wanted to join me. See you there." (Hmmm.)

At the studio, we started and things were moving along, but Mandy was having concerns and seemed dissatisfied with what he was hearing. After an hour, he stopped Eric in the middle of a read-through and said, "Okay I want everyone in the orchestra to be very quiet and Bob (Hurwitz), I want to do this record with piano only. Everybody (meaning the orchestra) sit back and relax. Turn the tape on and we'll start at the top. Hit it, Paul."

Hey, I do what I'm told! By the time we got past the verse and into the chorus of the first song "As Time Goes By," Hurwitz came out and escorted Mandy into the sound booth. After a short break we had a meeting in the booth, and Mandy expressed his feelings that the orchestrations were a little too much and could they be toned down or thinned out. Danny and Eric were a little panicked because the clock was ticking. This was an enormous job considering that Mandy was not really being specific. We chose to single out the song "Taxi" by Harry Chapin, which can be quite a long drone, and Danny had filled it up with what Mandy found distracting ornamentation. Danny said, "Well it's seven minutes with nothing going on!" (I agreed with that. I hated the song.) And... that was the last time Danny Troob was seen anywhere near Mandy or the recording studio. Eric and I did the best we could "thinning out" the orchestrations. It is not the clean, spectacular collection the next record would be (*Oscar and Steve*), but it sold well, and we got a lot of mileage out of those songs over the years.

Recently I went to a wonderful Thanksgiving dinner at someone's sprawling Upper Westside home. The host purposely put the *Experiment* CD on (quietly) through dinner which at first was giving me agita. I don't like music at dinner or any other inappropriate times. I can't help but have one ear out to listen. But it was fucking gorgeous, every second. Absolutely beautiful. That was a happy Thanksgiving.

OSCAR AND STEVE

This was a happy recording. I loved finding Oscar Hammerstein songs and pairing them (though not in medley form) with Sondheim's. The recording sessions under Eric Stern's baton were wonderful. We used a few of Jonathan Tunick's original Sondheim show orchestrations, but most were new and not a single one by Bill Brohn! My favorites on this one were "Poems" from *Pacific Overtures*, which he sang with his brother-in-law, Michael-Yukon-Grody, "You Are Beautiful" from *Flower Drum Song*, "Beat Out Dat Rhythm on a Drum" from *Carmen Jones*, "Bali Ha'i," "Not a Day Goes By," and "I Have the Room Above Her" from the 1936 film of *Show Boat*. We also had a guest star in Judy Blazer singing "Pleasant Little Kingdom" and "Too Many Mornings."

We have used these songs often in our concerts, pairing "You Are Beautiful" with "Not a Day Goes By," and for a year or two opened the concerts with the *Carmen Jones*.

I think this one made some money, as did the first three. We never did a show based on this CD, but we could have, very easily.

I love Sondheim's "Poems" (from *Pacific Overtures*). It's a song that has been completely ignored in tributes and retrospectives for decades. Sondheim concerts come and go with barely a nod toward *Pacific Overtures*. How is this possible? I first noticed it in the York Theatre revival. It blew me away and is my favorite from the score now. Also, why is "Bali Ha'i" ignored? Men, women, children singing this song, how beautiful this would be. Mandy and I performed the *Carmen Jones* and "Something's Coming" respectively on two separate *David Letterman Shows*. Both times the camera shot the crowd out on the street, listening to the broadcast. I thought it was hilarious watching the Jerry Springer generation trying to move and groove and snap their fingers to the two songs. They had never heard a song in 3/4 time and were scratching their heads trying to get with the beat. Rock/pop, the infernal "beat" and the lugubrious 4/4 time signature have ruined music forever.

MAMALOSHEN

Wow! This was a hard one. And one that paid off like crazy. Not only did it give us a whole show that we could book, but it was a real creation that required so much hard work, paying off in an absolutely beautiful listening experience. I think it's our best CD, but it was a long haul. Of course,

EVERYONE I knew thought it was a laughable exercise and made fun of the title. Ah, well... everyday a little death...

First of all, I don't know how opera singers, or anyone for that matter, wrap their brain around more than one language. I never could. Even Shakespeare, for me, is "in one ear and out the other." And I really get crazy when people sing in the language that I actually know but are still unintelligible. Mandy had to slave to get the Yiddish down, eliciting the help of experts. The recording sessions, once again under Eric Stern, were inspiring. I still remember the satisfaction on Eric's face at how well the arrangement of "Hey Tsigeleh" translated into the orchestration and how we got it in one take. All the orchestrators did beautiful work (and no Bill Brohn) and I loved hearing how Mandy's and my painstaking work on nothing but lead sheets was transformed.

We went through dozens of songs and, to my ear, so many sounded alike. (Like all rock songs.) There were multiple choruses and lyrics in these songs but no "music," just the melodies and simple chord symbols. Mandy set to work with coaches to learn the language, and I tried to familiarize myself (and distinguish between) the choices we had compiled. Mandy explained his take on each lyric to me, since neither of us really had any history with this material, trying to figure out how we should proceed. Or whose toes we might step on. All the experts had different opinions. We didn't know any traditions connected with Yiddish music and since I am so strictly theatre and show-oriented and Mandy is Mandy, we just proceeded as best we could. We started with melodies only and Mandy started telling me the stories he was conjuring and built from there.

We made a decision to throw in a well-known song or two that would require a translation from English to Yiddish. Those songs were "Take Me Out to the Ballgame," "God Bless America," and after some research, Mandy uncovered Paul Simon's "American Tune." He called the composer and got permission (enthusiastically) to have it translated.

We were considering a song, "Der Alter Tzigayner," which was about a gypsy violinist and the "old favorite tune" he loved to play. I'm happy to say it was my brainstorm to suddenly slip into an uptempo "gypsy" version of "White Christmas" in Yiddish, the most unlikely of all "old favorite tunes" to be sung on a Yiddish album. It has always gotten laughs and even a few requests to perhaps NOT sing that section when playing synagogues. (But Mandy would not be censored nor should anyone else for that matter, except for maybe so called "rap" artists! THAT noise can just GO AWAY!) The other fun tune was "Ten Kopeks" about the lengths to which a pocketful of change can affect a boy's life. He dates a girl, he marries her, they have children and a life together, all from the jangling change in his pocket. After rehearsing the first chorus, Mandy started "eye deedle dyeing" all over my vamp and it sounded so much like Julie Andrews and Dick Van Dyke from *Mary Poppins* to this gentile, that I immediately said a chorus of "Supercalifragilistic-expialidocious" IN YIDDISH should go here! Done. Then in chorus two the couple is getting married, so this gentile played the Mendelssohn wedding march which made no sense but got the point across. Then Mandy wanted the sound of the glass stomping and breaking and Mazel Tovs at the wedding, so what should follow that?... the wedding party! And the "Hokey Pokey" IN YIDDISH! With a bad wedding combo playing it. The jokes were over and we did the third and fourth choruses straight ahead with an ending built on "Supercalifragilisticexpialidocious." It took five minutes to build this number. It has opened many concerts for us and Mandy has had the audience on their feet doing the "Hokey Pokey"... OR ELSE! to rousing applause.

We were fortunate to have the brilliant Nadia Salerno Sonnenberg play the violin on the gypsy number and another rouser, "Rebbe Elimeylekh." This CD won a European Grammy equivalent and was the most creative of all our CDs. It also became the basis for a concert fashioned by Mandy and Eric Stern that we booked for years.

KIDULTS

I love this recording. It's full of happiness and joy and show tunes, and Mandy and I created a lot of interesting arrangements. The guest star this time was Kristin Chenoweth. Their duet on "How Could You Believe Me When I Said I Love You When You Know I've Been a Liar All My Life" is perfection—Popeye and Olive Oyl fighting. Hilarious! All of this material has been useful in our concerts over the years and it was great to gather it all together on one disc. My favorites are "Singing in the Bathtub," "Holiday for Strings," "The King's New Clothes," and "Rhode Island Is Famous For You." During the recording, Mandy tried one take of Murray Grand's "April in Fairbanks" (a perfect song) using a nasal Damon Runyon gangster-type voice, a nerdy gangster, and we kept that take. He had never performed it that way, and now it is the basis for our Ann Reinking choreographed ice-skating ballet in the Patti-Mandy show.

"Holiday for Strings" came in handy later as an encore in our Mandy-Nathan Gunn show and we opened that show with "Singing in the Bathtub." Opera meets show tunes!

"Everybody Says Don't" coupled with "The King's New Clothes" brought diverse audience reaction during these politically heightened times, as did "Swinging on a Star." On a few occasions, while singing the lyrics "and all the monkeys aren't in the zoo..." from "Swinging on a Star," he would add the aside, "THEY'RE IN THE WHITE HOUSE!" (This was during the Bush years!) And the audience would laugh. But there would be one old broad out there who would yell back, "Keep yer politics to yerself!" This CD was not a commercial success, but I dare you to listen to it and not laugh. It's our comedy album and the material has pleased many audiences over the years. A real pleasure to work on.

CELEBRATING SONDHEIM

I loved putting this together with Mandy. I always got a rush out of playing the show live and it got a great response, especially during our anniversary Public Theatre marathon concerts in rep that we did in 2009.

We made this live recording in Philadelphia at the Prince Theatre, recording ten performances. In the editing process I felt the need to make sure my piano track was clean. Mandy often likes to use somewhat flawed takes because of the so-called *humanness* in them, but I felt we couldn't *both* be all over the place. Invariably, when Mandy did something *unusual* it would be reflected by something unusual in my part! I felt one of us had to be constant, so I insisted on cleaning up my piano part.

Another favorite Mandy rehearsal moment... We had strung our list of songs together and after settling on "Take the Moment" as our closing "hymn," what should we do after the bows? I struck one of the *Sunday in the Park with George* "arpeggiated chords." He picked it up, saying his lines, "White. A blank page or canvas..." We started to sing "Sunday" from the show. When we got to the first big climax "...forever...," HE burst out crying, sobbing. That turned out to be the right song for our encore! Nothing like letting your emotions dictate your choices. Sometimes it works!

This recording was, unfortunately, a dismal failure financially (many people have told me how much they hate it and some of the reviews made my eyes bleed from reading them), but the concerts got a better reaction.

This is the only recording where I am featured as a solo pianist. When people say, "I want to hear you play!" I guide them towards this recording. I never hear from them again. Often because they won't listen to Mandy. In fact, most of the people I have been friendly with in the last 20 years have never heard me play because they refuse to go see a Mandy Patinkin performance. I have never forgiven them for this.

And out of hundreds of Mandy Patinkin stories I have, here is my favorite... Sondheim-related, of course.

On tour we played our regular *Dress Casual* concert in Indianapolis at Symphony Hall. As we arrived for our sound check at 7 PM for an 8 o'clock concert, Mandy noticed a rack of powder blue, floor-length, sparkly-sequined evening gowns in the hallway. He was always bugging me to find a funny, spontaneous way to start our concert when he wasn't feeling up to snuff. That night in the Indianapolis Symphony Hall, the lights dimmed to black. In the darkness, the voice of our stage manager spoke. "Ladies and Gentlemen, we regret to inform you that due to illness, Mandy Patinkin will not be performing tonight. (Moans, groans, oy veys.) Instead we have a very special guest performer, Miss Barbara Cook!"

In the dark I played the classic Sondheim intro, and a spot hit the face of Mandy, as he started to sing "Losing My Mind." As the spotlight opened up, Mandy was seen wearing one of the light blue evening gowns, hairy chest, pits, and arms everywhere, and he performed the entire song to thunderous laughter and applause. On the blackout, he quickly changed and we did our regular show. And... we have the videotape. Well, at least we have the dressing room rehearsal with Mandy in the dress singing to himself in the makeup mirror! One of my favorite concert nights ever!

Celebrating Sondheim (or *Mandy Patinkin Sings Sondheim*) was the last recording I would make with Mandy Patinkin.

33. Roads I Shouldn't Have Taken

Amidst all this Sondheim activity, I did squeeze in other projects and shows. Tons of stories to be told, but that's for another book. I worked on an awful musical version of one of my favorite childhood stories and films, *The Secret Garden*, played all the auditions for the bad revisals of *Crazy for You* (culled from the early Gershwin musical *Girl Crazy*) and *Kiss Me, Kate*, a dreadful stage version of the dreadful film musical *High Society*, an absolutely ridiculous version of *The Adventures of Tom Sawyer* (great cast, lousy material) and played rehearsals for two other dreary shows, *Falsettos* and *Steel Pier*. And to top it off, an incredible monstrosity called *Kristina*, a four-*hour* opera by, of all people, ABBA!!!! This was a four-week workshop/presentation, followed by a two-and-a-half-hour concert and recording at Carnegie Hall! I only played auditions, rehearsals, and bits of the workshop presentation. Paul Gemignani's new right hand (wo)man, Ann-Britt DuChateau (yep, that's right!) did the yeoman's part of the task. She was up to it, and is the toast of Broadway, associate conducting *Frozen*. I was getting phased out and was frankly exhausted at 53 years old. The stories, the stories! But not for this book.

I had the pleasure of working on three weird, over-the-top "cross-over" CDs for opera tenor Jerry Hadley, two re-recordings of old shows (*Kismet* and *Man of La Mancha*) which gave me funny stories about Buddy Hackett and Dom DeLuise, and the first full-length recording of the legendary ill-fated 1966 musical flop, *Breakfast at Tiffany's*. Some fun was had here, but a lot of this was just messy. Well-paid messy, but messy, and mostly just depressing.

One of the most enjoyable, odd, and utterly messy experiences, was my one moment on prime-time television (which, unbelievably, had a Sondheim connection of the oddest kind)!

34. Chicago Hope

Mandy Patinkin won an Emmy Award for his work on the TV series *Chicago Hope* in 1994. Mandy did the show for two seasons and developed quite a following. He had a fan club of ladies who followed our concerts around the country and gave him stuffed frogs everywhere we went, in reference to his name for Peter MacNicol's character on the show. I don't watch prime time TV much and usually catch up on stuff in reruns when I can watch several episodes in a row. Therefore, I did not watch *Chicago Hope*. (I hate hospital shows, anyway.) But I was hearing snippets about things that were happening on the show. A friend said, "Mandy sang last night on *Chicago Hope*." What? What did he sing? "'I Dreamed a Dream.'" But that's our concert material. What does that have to do with his character on the show? "Oh, Mandy sang some long medley about the band playing on this week." What? But that's my medley from our concerts. Why is he singing our concert material as a surgeon on this TV show? "Oh, Mandy has an elaborate electric train collection in his office on the show." Wait, wait, wait, Mandy has an elaborate electric train layout in his country house. I was a little concerned about his using our material on the show—I never got paid for the use of our arrangements—but our concerts were going through the roof and selling out and any reference to the show brought cheering and applause from enthusiastic audiences. Of course, all concern and dismay on my part disappeared when he called me and asked me to appear on an episode with him! Doing what?! (Months earlier he had hinted around that it might have been fun to have me on as an inmate in the asylum scenes where his character's wife was locked up. Ha! Me in pajamas, drooling! I'd have done it in two seconds.) Mandy's character, Dr. Geiger, would occasionally have nervous breakdowns on the show and would have to *sing* to snap out of them.

This particular episode, called "Full Moon," had Dr. Geiger exploding at his wife at a big dinner party in a restaurant and dramatically running out. The others chase after him to a dark little piano bar, where they find him alone onstage with a piano player, belting out "Rock-a-bye Your Baby with a Dixie Melody." Again, our concert repertoire! I was to play the piano player.

I was just a teeny-weeny bit excited! They flew me out to Los Angeles and I was picked up and driven to a nice hotel. I had a suite with a terrace that looked out over the 20th Century Fox backlot. Thrilling! There on the giant exterior wall of Studio 10 was a gigantic mural of Tom Ewell and Marilyn Monroe from *The Seven Year Itch*. It was as if they were saying welcome to your television drama debut! (By the way, my father went to high school with Tom Ewell in Owensboro, Kentucky. His real name was Ewell Tompkins. His mother generally didn't let him play with the other boys.) I was looking over where the huge "Before the Parade Passes By" scene from *Hello, Dolly!* was filmed. I was on the lot ten years before, taking a private tour with a local "flame," and took pictures when the entire set was still standing. Now there were just remnants of some of the New York tenement buildings. Where the actual paraders marched was now developed into a new studio complex where *Chicago Hope* was being filmed.

I was picked up and taken not to the Fox lot, but to a location site in a covered parking lot where Mandy was filming a short scene. I watched, and then we were taken to the lot. When I saw Mandy, he looked at me and said, "Oh, no, no, no, no, the beard has to come off!" (We hadn't seen each other in a few months and I had a full beard.) "You have a beautiful face and I want it on camera." Okay, you're the boss! I was introduced around and we ate in the commissary with Adam Arkin. Luscious. So was the food. Then we were driven to another location, a little dive in West Hollywood. I went directly to the hair and makeup van and sat in a chair between his costars Roxanne Hart and Diane Venora.

They proceeded to expertly remove the hair from my face. Roxanne Hart asked me, "Why are you letting them do that?" I shrugged my shoulders and said, "Mandy wanted me to." "But why? Why are you letting him do that to you?" She was somewhat exasperated. I just turned my attention to Diane

Venora. Mandy had worked with her before and loved her. I had a burning question, so I introduced myself and asked her if she was any relation to soprano Lee Venora, and she said, indeed she was. Lee Venora was her aunt. I then became the first-class musical comedy queen that I can be and told her what a thrill I used to get listening to her aunt sing "My Lord and Master" as Tuptim on the RCA Lincoln Center revival recording of *The King and I*, and also her "Baubles, Bangles, and Beads" and "And This Is My Beloved" from the same season's *Kismet* revival. She laughed and said that yes, her aunt had been an opera singer and often dipped her toe into musical theatre. Lee Venora's recordings of those songs are definitive, in my not so humble opinion, the way Leontyne Price's *Porgy and Bess* recordings are. Maybe it's that old RCA Dynagroove recording process, or maybe it was just brilliant singing.

Freshly shaved, they took me into the club, which of course was dark with a beat-up piano in the corner. I was on first. We were only doing the second half of the song and they wanted me to record the piano track a few times and then mime it during the takes, while Mandy sang "live" each time. Great. Terrific. I recorded it two or three times and was done. Mandy came in and we started filming. It was 4 PM-ish. Mandy would sing the song and the rest of the actors (Hart, Venora and Arkin) would enter the bar, watch for a minute, and then start yelling at him to stop. He would finish in a pool of sweat, and they would stand looking at him, confused, frustrated, and helpless. Fadeout. First, we filmed Mandy alone from different angles. They stuffed towels in the piano so I could really play but not make sound. Many, many, many, many, many takes later, the other actors were brought in to make their entrance. Then many, many, many, many more takes with them standing in the doorway. After every take the director said "Cut! Let's move on!" Mandy said softly, "I didn't like it." The director immediately shouted, "He didn't like it. Let's do it again!"

Now, are you ready for this little tidbit? The Sondheim connection! On a break I was stretching my legs and the director was standing nearby, not really attending to anything, so I struck up a very casual conversation. He asked me what else I did besides play for Mandy. I said I was playing Broadway shows and had done several Stephen Sondheim musicals as of late. He said, "Oh really? I was in a Stephen Sondheim show once." "Oh? Where? Which one?" (with a hint of sarcasm in my thoughts) and he said, "You may not have heard of it. It was a flop. I was in *Anyone Can Whistle*." "You were in the original Broadway cast of *Anyone Can Whistle*???????" "Yep, all nine performances! On Broadway." Holy shit! Here I was, talking to James Frawley who was Sgt.

Magruder ("Reporting, Sir! Hail! Heil! Hail! Heil...") Thrilling! Un...believable!

10 PM rolled around and Hart, Venora and Arkin were finally filmed yelling for Mandy to shut up. There was absolutely no acting involved! Maybe two takes is what *they* got! And we were done and off in the van to go back to the lot. Mandy rode with James Frawley and I rode with the others. Arkin was up front and I was sitting between Venora and Hart. After a few minutes of silence, Roxanne Hart said, "I still can't believe you let them shave off your beard." I shrugged my shoulders. I didn't know what to say. "But why?" she kept on. I sighed and said what I really thought. "If I had said 'no,' we wouldn't have even made it into the piano bar, let alone finished the scene!" Adam Arkin said, "I know, you're right! But... but... it just shouldn't BE that way!" I guess Mandy staked out his territory on that show, claimed it, and took over calling many shots. That's how you win Emmy Awards!

35. Here We Are Again

INTO THE WOODS REVIVAL

I played many auditions for the first New York City revival of *Into the Woods* in 2002, but never saw it. I couldn't bring myself to see it. (I haven't even seen the movie.) Let me set the scene. Someone said, "Let's have auditions... in a theatre setting!" The Westside Arts Theatre on West 43rd Street was chosen—the long running musical, *I Love You, You're Perfect, Now Change* was occupying the stage. Okay great, where should the singers be? Oh, stage center of course. And the piano? Well, there *is* one, but it's 20 feet above the stage behind a curtain. No problem! So, I hauled my (then) 300-pound body up a ladder for three days to play callbacks for the likes of Malcolm Gets (good), Billy Porter (as the Witch!? gay nonsense) and (gulp) Jennifer Holliday (as the Witch!?). That was entertaining, if not a little disconcerting. After it was cast (with Vanessa Williams as the Witch, yet again a "safe" choice), I made a decision to refrain from seeing it. Because of the casting. I don't like ruining my memories of good experiences with negligible productions. I had suffered enough and could smell a disaster a mile off. It had a brief run, was nominated for Tony Awards, and yet another recording was made.

SONDHEIM 75th BIRTHDAY CONCERTS

Around this time, everything was coming up Sondheim with his 75th birthday celebration in 2005. We did a lovely outdoor concert version of *A Little Night Music* with the Philadelphia Orchestra, and The Kennedy Center in Washington did a series of six revivals plus two special guest concert artists, Barbara Cook and Mandy Patinkin.

Mandy and I were doing our new *Celebrating Sondheim* show. Our week at the Kennedy Center was successful, culminating with Steve seeing one of the final performances. When I saw Steve backstage, he burst into tears (that was a good sign!) and his accompanying friend, Mia Farrow, exclaimed that it was the greatest thing she'd ever seen! Nice! Happy!

Gypsy came to Broadway with Bernadette Peters, a production I sort of enjoyed. I played some Louise auditions where Jamie-Lynn Sigler and Anne Hathaway were robbed of the role by Tammy Blanchard (who was excellent).

I participated in two other 75th birthday concerts, both inspired by an article in *The New York Times* in which Steve presented a long list of "Songs I Wish I'd Written." The concerts were stellar. The first at the Library of Congress in Washington DC garnered very little press, though it was broadcast on the radio. Nathan Lane, Brian Stokes Mitchell and a crack chorus sang the score to Sondheim's *Frogs*, which was terrific music, followed by a second act of "Songs He Wishes He'd Written" with appearances by Debra Monk ("You Can't Get a Man With a Gun"), Audra McDonald ("My Man's Gone Now"), Steven Brinberg (as Barbra Streisand) singing "When in Rome (I Do As the Romans Do)" and Marin Mazzie ("Sad Was the Day" from *Donnybrook*). A very unique evening gone with the wind. (I eventually found a recording of the radio broadcast.) This concert led to a brand-new recording of the *Frogs* score, coupled with a suite from *Evening Primrose*, all of which was delightful and thrilling to be a part of, especially for the choral writing in *Frogs*. The second concert was a Roundabout Theatre benefit around the same theme, with everything from Mario Cantone on the opening number from *Frogs*, and the entire "Color and Light" sequence by Michael Cerveris and Laura Benanti, to numbers from *She Loves Me* and *70, Girls, 70*. A long evening with Mario, Mandy, Bernadette, Cyndi (oy vey) Lauper, Alan Cummings (double oy vey!), Donna Murphy (with the Boys Choir of Harlem), Raúl Esparza, John Kander, Michael Cerveris, Laura Benanti, Sally (great voice) Mayes, Judy Kuhn, and Boyd Gaines. An endless evening... and there is a sound system tape.

Mandy and I then did a few weeks of our *Celebrating Sondheim* show on Broadway, Monday nights only, on the set of *Urinetown*. This run is significant for me because one night, while standing in the wings, I said my AA prayers— the serenity prayer and my own about asking to be of joyful service to Sondheim, Mandy, the audience, and my landlord, and then walked on stage. Suddenly, I was not afraid and breathed regularly from the start of the show to the end, playing with finesse and expression. This felt like the first time... the very first time... EVER! The miracle (that AA promised) had finally happened. I didn't have stage fright, and ever since that night I have been mostly stage fright free.

36. My Favorite Broadway

Over the years, in my association with Sondheim conductor, Paul Gemignani, I have played for many shows and events that were televised, mostly on the PBS network. The original productions of *Sunday in the Park with George*, *Into the Woods*, and *Passion* were preserved for posterity. Two large Stephen Sondheim celebrations, the *Leonard Bernstein 70th Birthday Celebration*, and the James Lipton *Actor's Studio* hour with Sondheim were also aired. Two special events were specifically designed to be aired on PBS: *My Favorite Broadway: The Leading Ladies*, directed by Scott Ellis (choreographed by Susan Stroman), and *My Favorite Broadway: The Love Songs*, directed by Graciela Daniele.

Both were hosted by Julie Andrews. I barely met her on the first one, but she was more involved with the second. The *Leading Ladies* show was all women except for the opening "drag" number. Highlights included "The Beauty That Drives A Man Mad" from *Sugar* (performed by the original stars Tony Roberts and Robert Morse in their Josephine and Daphne outfits!), "Everybody's Girl" knocked out of the ballpark by Debra Monk, "Mean To Me" sung by a heartbreakingly obese Nell Carter accompanied by the legendary Luther Henderson on the piano (my idea, Thank You Very Much!), "Fifty Percent" by the greatest of the great, Dorothy Loudon, "Life Upon The Wicked Stage" sung by burgeoning child-star Anna Kendrick with the Kit Kat Girls from the current hideously over-praised *Cabaret* revival, which ended up being a funny idea (hmmmm, wonder who thought that up?), "I Can Cook Too" by Lea DeLaria, who is just too good to be wasting her time as a preposterous clown, and Audra McDonald's "I Never Said I Love You" from *Dear World* (which didn't make the broadcast, unfortunately, but was perfectly beautiful).

Experiments in terror included "Nowadays/Hot Honey Rag" by Karen Ziemba & Bebe Neuwirth, "Bewitched, Bothered and Bewildered" blasted by Marin Mazzie, "Man of La Mancha" absurdly shrieked by Linda Eder, "Look for the Silver Lining" and (what else) "Tomorrow," without an ounce of feeling or care or connection by Andrea McArdle, "And I Am Telling You I'm Not Going," as painful as ever by the slimmed down but still overwrought Jennifer Holliday, "Some People" croaked by Liza Minnelli, and a ghastly, endless Andrew Lloyd Webber love trio by McDonald, Mazzie, and Judy Kuhn. McDonald also breathed fire and brimstone into the Streisand arrangement of "Down with Love," which Streisand had just tossed off, achieving far more enjoyable results. Susan Stroman created another bring on the girls number with "I Wanna Be a Rockette," featuring Karen Ziemba and her Ziembettes. Several rehashed Faith Prince, Priscilla Lopez, Elaine Stritch, and Rebecca Luker numbers and a "special" appearance by Rosie O'Donnell singing "Lizzzzhha With a Zzzzzhhee" with Lizzzzzhha, rounded out the evening.

These types of shows are rehearsed with spit and sometimes know-how... if not ever care or inspiration.

The *Chicago* number was originally intended for Ziemba and Chita Rivera, but after an hour of rehearsal where Ziemba somewhat bullied Rivera into making a lot of adjustments from the present revival of *Chicago*, Rivera dropped out and Bebe Neuwirth was brought in. It was a better match, as Ziemba was a *foot* taller than Rivera and Rivera's career was a *career* bigger than Ziemba's.

Linda Eder brought her own musical director who was quite a show in himself. He's hilarious to watch on the DVD.

Debra Monk stole the show as usual.

There was a showdown between Jennifer Holiday, Paul Gemignani and Mike Berkowitz, the drummer. She did not want drums keeping time at the beginning of her *Dreamgirls* number, a more "classical" approach, as she very clearly put it, but as usual, no one was listening to anyone and egos got in the way and there was a costly breakdown time-wise in the orchestra rehearsal.

Elaine Stritch took off her blouse at the orchestra rehearsal and stood in her bra slowly putting on her "rehearsal" blouse just to make sure every eye was on her and that there was absolute quiet.

Lea DeLaria was just terrific on her number.

It was my idea to have the *Cabaret* Kit Kat girls do a German version of "Life Upon the Wicked Stage" with cute little Anna Kendrick from *High Society*.

Liza's vocal on "Some People" had to be dubbed over in a studio, and the atrocious Alan Menken Rockette number fell completely apart at the end, orchestra-wise, during performance.

All in all, a fun, varied (if nutty) evening, with a few highlights.

Not so the second one, the *Love Songs*, with the exception of one fabulous moment. This program was even less well thought-out, with two terrible medleys of "Love Is Sweeping the Country," "Till There Was You," "Lover," and "So in Love" sung by Adam Pascal!, Brent Spiner!!, Rebecca Luker (wasted), Peter Gallagher (wasted) & Marin Mazzie, and secondly, "Not a Day Goes By," "Too Late Now," and "Sometimes a Day Goes By." Also on hand was another Linda Eder scream-a-thon including "Come Rain or Come Shine," "I Don't Know How to Love Him," and "What Kind of Fool Am I?" A few of these songs were movie songs but, hey, who cares? These shows are just a matter of who happens to be in town with any musical arrangements they can scrounge up at the moment. There were several numbers that didn't make sense in terms of love songs: "Lullaby of Broadway," "Let the Good Times Roll" (Broadway?!?), and "Brush Up Your Shakespeare." More "movie" songs that didn't belong: "Gigi," and "How Lucky Can You Get," and of course, the intrusively bad pop/show tunes "Music of the Night," "Seasons of Love," "Elaborate Lives," and "Every Single Day" sung by Barry Manilow from a bad musical he concocted. "Smoke Gets in Your Eyes" got a nice ballroom dance staging, but *Fiorello*'s "When Did I Fall in Love," and *Bye, Bye, Birdie*'s "An English Teacher" and "Rosie" were uninspired in choice and performance.

There were two unnerving rehearsal moments. Bebe Neuwirth did *Sweet Charity*'s "I'm a Brass Band" with the original Fosse choreography. Much of the arrangement is a drum-corp-style solo, all of which has been recorded multiple times. I've listened to this since I was 13 years old. However, the conductor and the drummer had never heard it, and Bebe argued herself blue in the face trying to convey what each section was supposed to sound like. Unfortunately, no matter how articulate she was, the men remained stubbornly clueless. (God forbid, anyone should do research or a little homework.)

The other contest on hand was between me and the conductor when Robert Goulet asked to include the "interlude" in his solo, "This Nearly Was Mine." We were using Goulet's orchestra chart which only had the song proper and he wanted to insert the interlude after the first chorus. Gemignani said the interlude wasn't in the chart and then added that there WAS no interlude in "This Nearly Was Mine." Finally, even after I *sang* it to him, he said, "Never heard that. When it comes to the moment, you play what *you* think is the interlude on the piano." Fine. Orchestra rehearsal day came, Goulet finished the first chorus, then he and I continued with the interlude. 16 bars into it, Goulet came over and gave me a friendly slap on the back. When we were done, the orchestra picked up with, "Now, now I'm alone..." I hate being right all the time, but really... *South Pacific?*

Robert Goulet was funny and nice and sweet, and my favorite moment of *My Favorite Broadway: The Love Songs* was overhearing him and Julie Andrews chatting. During rehearsal, Andrews stood next to me at the piano and did her introduction of Goulet. Goulet entered at the top of the huge Ziegfeld-like staircase looking around like Mr. Magoo, peering into the wings and the flies. Andrews said in her stuffiest British, "Down here, dear," and he unsteadily made his way down the stairs. He came to Andrews and said, "So I guess I sing this to you, right?" "Well, dear... there is the audience... Sooooo, why don't you sing to the audience..." "Oh, yeah, yeah..." he muttered. Priceless. They were so sweet. Then we started the orchestra on his intro for "If Ever I Would Leave You." There I was with Lancelot and Guinevere. Heaven. Goulet began to croon, as only he could, the first A section of the song. All of a sudden, the orchestration took all of us on a ride. It was his Vegas orchestration, and we bumped up a half-step into a swingy Latin accompaniment. The look on Paul Gemignani's face was one for the books. We had to laugh. So much for the original Broadway orchestration we were hoping for. We laughed all the way through it.

The one golden moment of this evening came at the end of the show. Michael Crawford came out and sang "I've Grown Accustomed to Her Face." Julie Andrews had had disastrous surgery on her vocal chords and she couldn't and wouldn't sing anymore. It was devastating and widely publicized. During rehearsal, we gently asked her if she thought she could handle anything. She reluctantly agreed to do a chorus of "The Rain in Spain"—down a 6th key-wise from the original. In performance, Michael Crawford instructed Andrews to say, "the rain in Spain," etc. properly, which she did. When he sang "Now once again, where does it rain?" she responded very deeply and quietly, "On the plain... on the plain." The audience leapt to its feet screaming. The first three notes to be heard from her since the operation. Watch the DVD—it's very moving. The audience was still screaming when they finished the short chorus in a back-bending pose which they had to hold forever. One of those magical, mystical, miracle, musical theatre moments.

37. Assassins 2004

Back on the Sondheim wagon, at last! The long-awaited Broadway production of *Assassins* would premiere at the Roundabout Theatre and win five Tony Awards including Best Revival, even though the show had never played Broadway. Since then, many shows have started off-Broadway, closed and then moved to Broadway and were eligible for Best Musical and WON! The Tony Awards Committee changes its rules every year to serve an agenda—such is life with the human race!

Fortunately, when the Millennium arrived (that moment when the calendar moved from 1999 to 2000), all of the computers *didn't* explode, but in my humble belief the memory chip in virtually every human being's brains deleted the entire history of the world—everything from good manners to Judy Garland—in a snap. This was earth-shattering to me. I had no one to talk to. Then someone blew up the World Trade Center and my next project, the "at long last" Broadway production of *Assassins* was temporarily canceled. It was to be directed by Joe Mantello. A reading was held which was easygoing and exciting, with soon to be *Dexter* Michael C. Hall, Lisa Loeb and Mario Cantone, among others. But 9/11 ended this. Done... over. But for only three years. The Roundabout Theatre picked it up again and we would be playing the Studio 54 space.

Let me say right up front, the original cast of *Assassins* at Playwrights Horizons could not be topped, but this cast was equal to it. The Studio 54 space was the greatest theatre I have ever played in. Our orchestra was split in two. At first this seemed problematic, but with audio and TV monitors we quickly adjusted. We were placed on either side of the stage in the box seats and were able to watch the show as we played it—no orchestra pit! Not only were we not buried in a hole in the ground (or worse, in another building piped in), but this allowed the audience to hear the music truly live with no encumbrance. For those who believe that the Broadway musical began with *Les Miserables*, orchestra pits used to be large, roomy, and most of all, elevated and open. The audience could see the orchestra AND hear it without amplification. PLUS the orchestra could often SEE the show they were playing. What a dream. *Assassins* ran 90 minutes with no intermission and had plenty of dialogue scenes (I love dialogue in musicals, it enhances the music and gives the audiences' ears a rest) and laughs abounded. It was the best work experience for me since *Passion*, and the last show I was proud to be a part of.

Our stellar cast was Michael Cerveris, Denis O'Hare, the delectable Marc Kudisch, Jeffrey Kuhn, James Barbour, Becky Baker, Mary Catherine Garrison,

Mario Cantone, and Alex Gemignani. The ensemble was great too. Denis O'Hare kept a video camera running during the whole process with the idea of making an in-home documentary that I have never seen. I would kill to see it, because it had some of my best work on it, ever.

This show was nothing but fun with Steve and the effervescent, cuddly John Weidman. The incredible vertiginous set design by Robert Brill was one of my favorites, a rollercoaster going up into the rafters and out of sight, with the whole thing at a slight (and disturbing) tilt towards the audience right. A beautiful thing to look at every night.

And now I will tell you what really made *Assassins* 2004 the special experience it was for me. One person. Mario Cantone.

I first saw Mario on *Steampipe Alley*. "Who is this loud queen sitting in the middle of all these kids on this Saturday morning TV show? And why am I watching it?" Well, bottom line, he reminded me immensely of my now dead partner, Charlie, and was almost as funny. A few years earlier I went to the York Theatre to see *The Golden Apple* (yes, they did it again, and again it was great) and he was there in the audience. Who was this cute, funny guy? After Charlie died in 1995 and I joined AA, a new "program" friend and I went to a Jamie DeRoy Cabaret benefit at the Laurie Beechman Theatre (the downstairs room of the Westbank Café on West 42nd Street). On the table were little boxes of Godiva chocolates. We woofed those down like they were martinis and got a good sugar rush going before the show started.

First off was Mario Cantone! He did his "Liza Minnelli/Victor Victoria" routine, his "Michael Jackson jackhammers his nose off" routine, and after that I don't remember because we were vomiting up our Godivas from laughing so hard. For the next few years, I religiously followed Mario at Caroline's Comedy Club until I actually got to play an audition for him. Or almost. His partner/accompanist came in the door behind him, so I got to sit out and listen. I believe this was an audition for the revival of *Into the Woods* and Sondheim and Lapine and Gemignani were there. His choice was "Not a Day Goes By" — a good choice for the role of the Baker. But he admitted to them that he was experimenting with the key. The experiment went a little awry. It was pitched too high and Mario sorta kinda crashed and burned. Not an easy song. Think of the song "White Christmas." Start singing it in a high key and when you get to the lyric "Just like the ones I used to know," you will discover you're in trouble! This gives you an idea of what happened. It was actually very funny, though quite unintentionally. But there was a big voice there. Poor Mario was dismayed. Our next time in a room together was the *Assassins* reading pre-9/11 and I finally had an opportunity to tell him that he had saved my post-widowed/post-alcoholic life with his humor. His eyes grew wide and he backed away a few dozen feet and said "Thank you. Thank you."

Mario was hired to play and do the rageful Sam Byck monologues in *Assassins* and if anyone can make rage funny, Mario can. He didn't get to sing much in the show, but he got to lead the assassins in the "Another National Anthem" production number and was surprisingly quick and accurate and reliable on the difficult Sondheim intervals.

Once we moved to the set at the theatre, the show was very well-rehearsed and it now belonged to the prize-winning lighting team of Jules Fisher and Peggy Eisenhauer. In the staging of *Assassins*, there were many moments when the cast was lined up in a row downstage with Mario center stage. Jules Fisher historically was notoriously painstakingly slow in his technical rehearsals, so there was plenty of time for mischief with Mario center stage. He had been talking about doing a big one-man Broadway show and I was all for it. I don't know who started it—probably me—I already had theme songs for everyone: "Something Sort of Grandish" for Denis O'Hare (he had just done a terrible Florida production of *Finian's Rainbow*, Florida being the key word), the *Tommy* Overture for Michael Cerveris, "Keepin' Out of Mischief Now" for Becky Baker, "The Pink Panther Theme" for Paul's son, Alex Gemignani (he used to play it on the piano as a little boy), "Soliloquy" for James Barbour, "See What It Gets You" for Ann Nathan, "I Feel Pretty" for Merwin Foard (cause he is), and on and on. I couldn't decide how to entertain Mario, the choices were so huge.

The eventful day came when the cast was idling on the stage waiting. Mario called out to me "Did you ever see the movie *Torch Song* with Joan Crawford?" I immediately started playing "Tenderly" from the movie. Then Mario started doing the dialogue from the infamous scene where Joan Crawford puts "blind" rehearsal pianist Michael Wilding to the test. (Remember, this was onstage during tech rehearsal in front of everybody in the company.)

Mario Cantone: *(as Joan Crawford)* Are you up on that "Two Faced Woman" routine?

Paul Ford: *(as Michael Wilding)* Yes, Miss Stewart, I think I can handle it.

(I started playing the exact two bar intro from the movie, 'cause you see, I KNOW this movie.)

Mario Cantone: *(singing as Joan Crawford as dubbed by India Adams.)*
 I CAN'T HELP BEING A TWO-FACED WOMAN
 A LITTLE BIT OF BOLDNESS
 A LITTLE BIT OF SWEETNESS
 A LITTLE BIT OF COLDNESS
 A LITTLE BIT OF HEATNESS.
 DON'T FALL IN LOVE WITH A TWO-FACED WOMAN
 GIVIN' YOU A WARNIN'
 I'LL LEAVE YOU IN THE MORNIN'
 GOT ANOTHER LOVER UNDER COVER
 I'M LIKE A WEATHERVANE
(Here I stopped playing the tempo of the music as Michael Wilding does in the movie.)
 THAT GOES WITH THE BREEZE...
 Wait a minute! I thought you knew this arrangement! What happened
 to the tempo?
Paul Ford: Well, Miss Stewart, it seemed a little fast, so my right hand sort of
 slowed down, it has a mind of its own...
Mario Cantone: Then sit on it!
(And on and on and on...)
 (SCENE)

 Mario then launched into dialogue by Bette Davis as Baby Jane Hudson,
brilliantly, so I gave him a big arpeggio and off we went into...
 I'VE WRITTEN A LETTER TO DADDY
 HIS ADDRESS IS HEAVEN ABOVE.
 And then he did the dance from the movie and repeated the last phrase.
Then he said, "Do you know the title song?"
 I started the intro of the terrible title song written for the movie but only
used briefly as an instrumental.
 WHATEVER HAPPENED TO BABY JANE?
 SHE COULD DANCE, SHE COULD SING
 MAKE THE BIGGEST THEATRE RING
 JANE COULD DO MOST ANYTHING
 WHATEVER HAPPENED TO BABY JANE?
 "Do you know Connie Francis's 'Lookin' for Love,' the *jazz* version, not
the *rock and roll* version?"
 I started the vamp from the soundtrack album I bought when I was 15.

Knocked that one out of the ballpark.

"Helen Lawson. Judy Garland as Helen Lawson."

And away we went!

> I'LL PLANT MY OWN TREE AND I'LL MAKE IT GROW
> MY TREE WILL NOT BE JUST ONE IN A ROW

"Now do..."

"I know, I know..."

(Mario did his best Patty Duke in *Valley of the Dolls*.)

> IT'S IMPOSSIBLE, TELL YOU RIGHT NOW.
> IF I TRIED IT, I'D NEVER KNOW HOW.

This went on for days. Joe Mantello was laughing, Jules Fisher and Peggy Eisenhauer were laughing, the crew was laughing, some of the cast were laughing, some were not... but eventually and frankly all through the run if in a casual moment we were all standing around for a brush-up rehearsal, Mario would shout across the room "Do ya think ya got that *Two-Faced Woman* routine?..." and I'd play the intro and he would start and anyone, man, woman, crew guy, and child would back him up with choreographed jazz hands. I was crying with happiness. I never had so much fun in my life.

This was show business to me. Get the job done, but most of all, HAVE FUN!

I loved and felt honored when Joe Mantello said after tech rehearsal finished, "Paul Ford, I am going to kill you!" No problem, blame me. THAT is what I believe we were there for—good times!

On opening night, I never give cards or gifts 'cause why bother? I'm invisible and the lowest man on the totem pole. In fact, I don't even make it on the totem pole. But this opening night I photocopied, gathered extra copies, and ordered from my sheet music pals, a complete set of sheet music for every single song Mario and I touched on that week and wrapped it in a bow. Whether he ever asks me or not, I hope he does a singing act of all those camp classics in one evening. He's the only one who can! Later Mario did his show *Laugh Whore* at the Cort Theatre and although his impersonations and singing were unbeatable, the family stories and personal history really gave him depth. I was happy to play several readings for Dave Solomon's play *Margaret and Craig*, about female impersonator Craig Russell starring Mario, but our paths have not crossed since. I wish the best for him and love and appreciate his talent.

Before moving on, a little more about "this brand of show business," the fun show business, the communal show business. After this show, I never experienced it again except for one dazzling moment. A few years later, same theatre company, same theatre, same director, same setting (tech rehearsal), I was in the house at the piano. Our star was standing patiently waiting to be lit. I had given up on the theme songs now, and there was no "name that tune" at the piano, all was replaced by *texting* and cell phones. Absentmindedly (and sarcastically commenting on the misery of the situation), I plucked out the tune of "Gee, But It's Good To be Here" from the Ethel Merman musical *Happy Hunting*. In the dark, the voice of Stockard Channing shouted out, "Is that *Happy Hunting!*? I saw that when I was a little girl!" She proceeded to sing snippets of the entire score! "Do you know *Goldilocks* (an Elaine Stritch musical)?" and she sang some of those songs, and then started telling show business stories. Everyone else was oblivious, hiding in corners... texting. The show was a "dead-on-arrival" gruesome, fucked-up, revisalobotomy of a once-great show, *Pal Joey*. God bless Stockard Channing for giving me my last brief moment of the "real" show business.

Assassins ran to capacity for twelve weeks with a planned extension that could have continued indefinitely. The reviews were great *all across the board* (funny, it was the same show, except for the added song, "Something Just Broke," that we did 14 years earlier) and we won five Tony Awards including Best Musical Revival. I believe the difference in this production from the original was mainly due to the orchestra (this score has to be played by an orchestra, not two keyboards and a drum) and the enthusiasm of Joe Mantello for the material. What a joyous experience.

My mother loved it again and the way she was feeling about George Dubya Bush, it couldn't have made her happier seeing all those people shooting presidents onstage. (Aside: I sent my mother a video tape of Will Farrell's George Bush show to watch and she watched it and watched it and especially enjoyed the sex dance between Will Farrell as Dubya and the dancer playing Condoleezza Rice. She showed it to every Republican family member and friend that came to see her, but then confided to me one of her biggest fears. When she dies, what if THEY find that video tape in her closet? What will THEY think? I said THEY will think she was one smart dame.)

Mom got to sit next to and be charmed by the cuddly John Weidman during the performance and, as mentioned earlier, met Lauren Bacall backstage.

Paul Gemignani was going to be conducting a concert version of *Anyone Can Whistle* at Ravinia in late August (it was late May now) and he flew me to Chicago on our day off to play auditions for the ensemble. As was traditional for a few summers, Patti LuPone, Audra McDonald and Michael Cerveris would star in a Sondheim show. We were on a break in the auditions and Paul violently snapped his cell phone shut. "Closing in June." What? Paul told me the Roundabout was closing *Assassins* on schedule, no extension and no unlimited run. No reason why, just done, finished, close it, get it out. The whole cast was dismayed, as everyone had negotiated for a longer run and we won so many awards. The only thing said was "no tickets sold." No other explanation. We did hear rumors that a certain person on the Roundabout board loathed the show and single-handedly wanted to close it, and on the final performance, a Sunday matinee, during the Q & A we were still obliged to give after the performance, *she* was walking in front of everyone talking out loud to contractors about the remodeling of the theatre, until finally Becky Baker told her to "SHUT UP" till we were done! I also believe the Roundabout Theatre got pressure from the Republican Convention coming in the fall, but no box office? Come on! Five Tony Awards and Stephen Sondheim and a musical that very few people had ever seen? Close it? Too bad, but I am grateful for every minute of that show. I have a bad videotape, a so-so original cast recording, hundreds of terrific photos, and great memories.

Footnote...

I loved ALMOST every minute of the revival of *Assassins*. The 60 seconds I did not like were during tech rehearsals after Stephen Sondheim asked me to check on the notes of the "Ballad of Booth" and gave me an instruction. As directed, I went to Neil Patrick Harris (oh yeah, *he* was in the show too) while he was lounging in the theatre during a break and said, "Steve asked me if I would check the notes with you on a couple of phrases from 'The Ballad of Booth.' Do you have a minute?"

"What a HORRIBLE thing to say to me! I can't believe you would... Why would you say that to me?... Okay... okay... where? What is it?" he ever so queenly and rudely replied. I walked away. I felt "set up" by Steve. I think he knew this snippy little queen would react this way, so I walked away thinking "figure it out yourself, bub."

This was the last show I did that felt like we were all "Judy and Mickey putting on a show in a barn" before texting took over and everyone stopped communicating. In other words, the 21st Century. It is now BUSINESS, not "show business," just BUSINESS. No heart, no soul, and no fun.

38. Don't Laugh

PACIFIC OVERTURES 2006

A Japanese production (in Japanese) of *Pacific Overtures* that played Lincoln Center briefly was the impetus to do this show again on Broadway. The Roundabout Theatre asked director Amon Miyamoto (Paul Gemignani always called him Armand) to re-stage his production in English at the Studio 54 Theatre. By the time it was up and running, the show had about as much resemblance to the Japanese production as B.D. Wong's participation had to an authentic performance. The only thing of significance left was the use of a gigantic American flag covering the ceiling of the theatre at the end of Act One to symbolize the big bad Americans' invasion of Japan. Alas! This spectacle remained unseen by half of the audience as the Studio 54 balcony came so close to the stage, most of the audience in orchestra seating couldn't even see the flag.

The cast was delightful and strong (with the exception of the one who wouldn't memorize his lines), and there was fun to be had. The only theme song I played during rehearsals that really got any attention was the *Dragnet* theme I played whenever director Miyamoto would enter the room. He was certainly abreast of American television culture because he immediately picked up on it, laughing with a certain bit of confusion. After the 500th time I played it, he finally (laughingly) said "Why do you play that when I walk into the room? Am I Godzilla or something?" He was a great guy. I asked him if he had ever seen the Ethel Merman show, *I Got Merman* in Japan with the three ladies doing all of Merman's songs in Japanese (I have the DVD). "Seen it?" he responded. "I directed it! That was my show!" Definitely my kind of guy.

Show business nightmare! Opening night, I went up to the pit to warm up and found my score missing from my keyboard. I looked around and marched right downstairs to Paul Gemignani. "Okay, where is it? Where did you put it?' He had pulled this trick on me when I came back from my (enforced) vacation during *Sunday in the Park with George*, just to watch the panic ensue. He refused to admit to playing a joke this time and finally I had to go up and get my rehearsal book ready which was far different from my official keyboard part. It was already past half hour and the opening night audience was filing in. The balcony of the theatre was on the level of the box seat area where the orchestra was set up. I looked out and saw Kathy Edmonds from the Emily Grishman office (our music copyists) and her husband getting comfortable in their seats. I waved her down and in a loud stage whisper, told her my score was missing and I would need a new copy for the next day. Kathy jumped 20 feet into the air saying, "It's in our office! I was making corrections and forgot to bring it back!" and she vanished in a Road Runner cartoon dust cloud. The opening night performance started and we were up to Number 3 ("There Is No Other Way") when I heard heels slamming up the iron spiral-staircase leading to our "pit" and she threw the score at me and returned to her seat. She had run ten blocks to their office and back! This was the most exciting, spontaneous moment of the entire three-month experience.

We recorded the show. Why? We had two synthesizers, percussion, and a violin. Why bother? I don't need to hear an hour of me on a plastic keyboard and neither do you!

And little did I know that this was the last time I would be hired to play the run of a Broadway musical...

FOLLIES AUDITIONS
ROUNDABOUT THEATRE 2006

The three most interesting people who auditioned for this threadbare, useless revival were the amazing, talented Sandy Duncan singing "In Buddy's Eyes" (unfortunately, the vocal chops weren't there but the character was), Leslie Uggams singing "I'm Still Here" (always a pro), and in for the always challenging, always thankless, and always miscast role of Solange LaFitte ("Ah, Paris"), Barbara Feldon (99 from *Get Smart),* who was all wrong but thoroughly charming.

GYPSY 2006

In 2006, I finally got to do a real *Gypsy.* I had played rehearsals for the Darien Dinner Theatre production in 1978, but that was it. The Rose for that production was singer Denise Lor. The director was Morton DaCosta, whom I treasured every second I was in the room with and for whom I played the *Auntie Mame* theme music, to his utter delight. (He had directed the original stage and film versions of *Auntie Mame.)*

I disapproved of the casting of Tyne Daly in the 1989 revival, but then saw it twelve times, because I needed my *Gypsy* fix. I didn't care for the summer stock shtick that director/writer Arthur Laurents put in, or the revamped "Let Me Entertain You" routine, but it was a solid production. In 2003, I enjoyed the Sam Mendes-directed version with Bernadette Peters, but

I still didn't like the added shtick, the re-revamped "Let Me Entertain You" number or Jerry Mitchell's fiddling with the Jerome Robbins choreography, but again a solid production. Oh, and let us not forget the piss poor Bette Midler television version with its Laura Ashley-ish sets and costumes and above all, the discovery that Bette Midler has no voice. I figured that after all these, my chances of ever doing a first-rate production of *Gypsy* were nil.

But three of the most exciting and fulfilling nights of my life were in store for me in the summer of 2006. The Ravinia Music Festival outside of Chicago had hosted concert versions of much of the Sondheim repertoire during the preceding decade, and after productions of *Sweeney Todd*, *A Little Night Music*, *Passion*, *Anyone Can Whistle*, and *Sunday in the Park with George*, all starring in various combinations, Patti LuPone, Michael Cerveris, Audra McDonald and George Hearn, it was decided to produce *Gypsy* for Patti LuPone. Paul Gemignani had the festival bring me out for the first time, even though I had played rehearsals for many of these shows in New York. I was, needless to say, ecstatic. The cast included several New Yorkers along with a group of great Chicago performers.

I started early in New York, working on the music with Patti and on her staging with *Gypsy* "caretaker" Bonnie Walker. The show would be directed by Lonny Price, who had done the previous long list of shows. The choreography would be the original Robbins, and Price planned to be faithful to the libretto and musical arrangements. All of this came true, just to say that there was a happy ending to the first part of this story. This was (for me) a completely joyous experience and provided some dramatic theatre "doin's" and "show business emergencies" to recount.

First, I want to award the prize for the best Tulsa I've ever seen (other than the original, Paul Wallace) to Leo Ash Evans. Blond, curly-headed and muscular, he was right out of *The Little Rascals* and *The Bowery Boys*. His look was the most authentically 1920s of all Tulsas. And he sang and danced perfectly. A real *boy*!

Jessica Boevers was a striking Louise, and Patti's own choice for Herbie, Jack Willis, was a true Willy Loman-esque down-and-out "sad sack." There was an exciting "putting on a show in a barn" feeling to this group that felt reckless and a little less careful and reverent toward the show than with previous casts. The only fiddling with the show was of course a re-re-revamping of the "Let Me Entertain You" number and a two-minute prologue added between the Overture and the opening Uncle Jocko scene.

During the Overture, a large theatrical touring trunk was rolled onstage and turned on its side to become a doorway through which all the characters in the opening scene spilled out. Standing observing this was a tall figure in a beautiful black gown and an extra-large black picture hat (Jessica Boevers as an older Gypsy Rose Lee). She disappeared, and the scene burst into action. Underscoring this prologue, we used the music from the "mirror" scene when Louise does her "I'm a pretty girl, Mama." bit. It was a nice touch (my idea). When I saw Jessica in her costume, I whispered to Paul Gemignani, "There's your Fannie Brice for *Funny Girl* if they ever do it." They won't.

But then came the fiddling with the "Let Me Entertain You" strip routine. Conductor Gemignani was not familiar with the original routine from 1959 or the revamped versions since, and he was determined to stick to the original score version, which was a series of short crossovers to ever increasing snazzier versions of "Let Me Entertain You," but no dialogue to the audience. Originally it was simply an elegant costume parade montage ending in a giant spectacle of a Christmas salute, followed by Gypsy's final chorus of the song. Starting with the Angela Lansbury 1974 revival, Arthur Laurents insisted on giving Gypsy Rose Lee a monologue during this montage. A HUGE mistake. A big, tangled mess cropped up over this as none of the new revisions had ever been "officially" added to the rental materials for the show. I was completely on the conductor's side (this time). In other words, what had never been broken *never* needed to be fixed. I always found the new versions somewhat embarrassing and never performed well. And in a long show, it always dragged out the last part of the show. But Lonny wanted the long, revamped version, so we needed to find it. No recording up to that point had the complete version. I had a cassette tape of the Angela Lansbury production, but Bonnie Walker said that it was not the "updated" updated version. Michael Rafter, the conductor of the Tyne Daly version, offered the orchestra score from his version, but for some reason our conductor wasn't interested and snapped at me for even suggesting we at least explore it. We ended up with a patchwork culled from the original orchestrations and a lot of drum solo vamps, a bad band-aid. In other words... shit. But that was the one fly in the ointment with this *Gypsy*. And we had a *real* lamb for "Little Lamb!"

Rehearsals in New York were smooth, as was the first week in Ravinia. We had a full three weeks to stage it, plenty of time. Until one day, as we were segueing into the Chinese restaurant scene for the "You'll Never Get Away from Me" number, Patti noticed that the scene had not been set properly with the table, chairs and props. This was the day when our director and star discovered that our stage management team had totally different ideas of what we were doing. Our stage management team was under the impression that we were doing a "concert" with scripts, and *our* team was doing a full-out *staged* (sets, lights, props, costumes) version, and OFF BOOK! We came to a screeching halt. Patti made herself very clear that everyone needed to be on the same show, including organization of sets, costumes, memorization of lines by the cast, and props, down to the need for real flatware on the table, washed preferably, and real food including mustard and sweet-and-sour sauce packs as in *real* Chinese restaurants. Quite an argument arose with the director finally bellowing, "Shame! Shame on you!" to the stage management team.

The very next day I was to ride with Patti from the hotel to the rehearsal space. At quarter of 11, Patti was nowhere to be found in the lobby. I called the stage management and inquired, and they told me to hop in a cab, which took forever because we were in the far suburbs of Chicago. I arrived 20 minutes late. Unfortunately, my first duty was to run music with Patti from 11 to 11:30. When I got there, everyone was quiet and... no Patti. She had arrived... and left. Uh oh. She had never been informed that she was to give me a lift that morning. That afternoon, with a curtain tacked up on the glass doors leading into the smaller studio, a secret meeting was going on for an hour or so. When everyone came out, we resumed rehearsal, but not before the director made a speech that in a few days we would have an entirely new stage management team. A week before our first performance. Wheeeeee! Things got back to normal and we continued. From then, it was a great experience. The orchestra was onstage, and I was front and center on the piano right in front of Paul, and when Patti did "Rose's Turn," she was ten feet away from me. We had a huge Chicago Symphony-based orchestra with our own Paul Pizzuti doing the elaborate drum part. Patti got every laugh, every moment, and it was a huge love-in with the audience. A big, energized everybody-on-the-tightrope kind of weekend. I was a happy piano player!

Jack Viertel of the City Center Encores! series came to see it, and it seemed a shoo-in for its inclusion in their season. Onward and upward.

Several months passed and I was sitting in a hotel restaurant in L.A. with Paul Gemignani who had just gotten off the phone. Patti had a decades-long standoff with Arthur Laurents over a choice Patti had made concerning a reading of a play of his and a solid production contract that conflicted. His show business-style revenge would be to *never* let her do *Gypsy* in New York! So they had to settle the matter, and after a meeting with Arthur Laurents, he gave her permission to do the role... under one condition. He would be directing. The next thing out of Patti's mouth was along the lines of "But of course, darling!" Of course, she would say yes! What other choice would she have? Paul Gemignani was outraged, and in support of Lonny Price, stepped down from the job. I'm sure Lonny's disappointment was monumental, but he would get over it. I've talked to Patti about this, and she pointed out that if Paul had not quit, he would have been working for three years. Because *Gypsy* moved to Broadway from Encores! for ten months and then Arthur Laurents turned right around and started up a new revival of *West Side Story* that ran for almost two years. I would not necessarily have had a job in any of this because I don't conduct, and I don't know if Paul would ever trust me with *West Side Story* (I don't know if I would trust myself), but 25 of his loyal musicians lost all of that work too!

But when I saw it, I was so unhappy with Arthur Laurents's changes, from cutting the "Mr. Goldstone" scene in half, to having a *puppet*!!! for "Little Lamb" (Jesus Christ, it's Broadway!), to having the kids spoil their act by getting into staged squabbles during their military routine, to the cutting of Rose's heartbreaking "Small World" reprise, to even cutting (sacrilegious!) 16 bars of music out of "Rose's Turn" because it was too long. Its only three minutes! But, thankfully, the 16 bars were restored. Then there was the unnecessary sight of Patti jumping and grabbing for the lighted *Rose* sign at the final curtain. Talk about trying to fix something that wasn't broken!!!! There was little humor or joy in this production (not to mention sets and costumes) and the whole show was played for "realism" and "grit." Didn't these characters ever have fun in their lives? Even the thrilling "All I Need is the Girl" was heavy with subtext and played like Tulsa and Louise were planning a suicide pact instead of having a showbiz dream. "Keep it simple, Arthur, keep it simple!" is what I wanted to scream from the balcony. That is why I preferred our knockabout loose Ravinia concert. It didn't take itself sooooo seriously.

One good thing! This Broadway revival was recorded, and they happily included some wonderful outtakes, including "Smile, Girls," "Momma's Talkin' Soft" and "Nice She Ain't" with orchestrations by Jonathan Tunick. But for me, I will always treasure those three nights at Ravinia.

SWEENEY TODD - THE MOVIE

Paul Gemignani may not have been the conductor on the latest Sondheim revivals, but he was handed the plum role of musical director for Tim Burton's planned film version of *Sweeney Todd* starring Johnny Depp. (Eventually he would do the dreary film version of *Into the Woods* as his swan song.) I never even dreamed I would have a job on this operation, but a call came through to show up at a recording studio to play (on video) some Mrs. Lovett auditions. Attending these along with Gemignani would be director Tim Burton himself, his casting director, and producer David Zanuck. The auditionees were to be Geena Davis, Bernadette Peters, Cyndi Lauper (Oy!), Toni Collette, and Reese Witherspoon. This should have been (and it was) a fun afternoon. They were given a choice of songs and all chose "The Worst Pies in London" except Davis who sang "Wait," and Lauper who also sang "Poor Thing" (double-oy!). Davis was the shakiest, Collette hugged me, as did Witherspoon. Bernadette and Lauper brought their own accompanists. Therefore, I was obliged to stand in as "The Customer" in their videos. It was a relaxed day, just schmoozing with Burton and Zanuck. The closest I'll ever get to working on a movie! Although things were looking up.

Next, I was to fly to L.A. with Paul to meet and work with Johnny Depp. This was too good to be true. Courtesy of the production, we checked into the Chateau Marmont, the old Hollywood landmark where John Belushi croaked, and one of my favorite '60s William Castle horror movies, *The Night Walker*, was filmed. We expected to be there three to four days depending on Depp's schedule. He was filming one of the *Pirates* movies, but the plan was to wait by the phone and then run around the corner and up North Sweetzer Avenue off Sunset Blvd. to his gargantuan castle/compound overlooking West Hollywood. I couldn't breathe, I was so excited. If anything, I wanted to see this house which I had photographed years before he had bought and restored it. Two days passed, and Paul finally called saying, "Tonight is the night!" I waited and waited... and waited. 8 PM and the phone rang. "Bad news. I'm going up there right now... but only I'm invited..." No problem! I waited some more and he called back to tell me that they had chatted and that Depp was still in his Pirate drag and, yes, the house was colorful and right out of a Dracula movie. But that was it. As early as possible the next morning we were tumbled out of the Chateau Marmont and sent home. A possible second trip was mentioned, but I wasn't holding my breath. Sure enough, a few weeks later, the call came and out we went again. This time the money people put us in a hotel off the freeway. Again, I was told to wait by the phone. I waited and waited... and Paul called and said, "I'm being taken to a studio now to meet Depp... but only I'm invited..." No problem! I love Los Angeles, anyway. So I waited and he returned later that night with his story. At dinner, Paul said that they went to the recording studio of a high school friend of Depp's who had put down synthesized accompaniments and already recorded Depp on his songs. Paul was being asked simply to listen. He did. They were fine. And... the end! Back to the hotel.

We were to vacate L.A. as fast as possible so the movie people wouldn't go broke on our hotel room. But there was a consolation prize. The next morning, we had a session in the hotel boardroom with *Borat* star Sacha Baron Cohen to check out his singing for the role of Pirelli. He was also to be measured for a costume fitting at the same time. I sat and watched him being measured by the wardrobe person and he smiled back with a look of "I just HAD to get in this business, didn't I?" He then sang beautifully and perfectly the Pirelli material and went on his way. Cuuuuuute!!!!!! And tall!

And home we went.

Paul had been luring me in with stories that it looked good—especially after I had met Burton—that I might be flown over to London for six weeks to help prepare the rest of the cast for the recording sessions. Too good to be true! Paul went over to London for some meetings and called long distance. We were chatting away and then he dropped the bomb. He said, "You have your 'friend' Jonathan Tunick to thank for this. Tunick told the producers not to bother hiring you, and that he knew someone right around the corner in London who could play all of that stuff." Thanks, Jonathan! But I did receive payment for all duties and time up to that point. The movie was made. I thought it was a vast improvement over the show (simply because half the songs were cut), but Paul told me he rarely, if ever, saw Depp again. Ah well... everyday a little death (said with the appropriate sour grapes). Ah well, I never really liked the show anyway.

39. Good Thing Going... Going... Gone

PASSION 2009

Even though the original cast performance is available on DVD, the Ravinia concert version of *Passion* starring Patti LuPone, Michael Cerveris and Audra McDonald was deemed worthy of a live Broadcast from Lincoln Center. This was nothing but pure fun (as much as *Passion* can be fun). It was re-staged by Lonny Price for the new venue in the Time Warner complex at Columbus Circle. It really all went very well with only two standout remembrances for me.

A couple of years later I was at Patti's Connecticut home rehearsing the Patti/Mandy show and on her piano was a framed photo of Sondheim conferring with Patti (in her full Fosca costume) kneeling on the edge of the stage. I commented on the photo and she said that, yes, it had been a candid photo someone connected with the production had snapped and sent to her. What that person didn't know was what was transpiring in that moment. Patti said, "I had to frame it and keep it in a prominent place. That was the moment Sondheim told me I was giving a terrible performance and ruining the show!" Laugh Out Loud!

The other memory I have of this experience was of my family *all* choosing to tune in to this one particular television airing (of all my things over 30 years of performing in New York). The general consensus of opinion from Atlanta to Louisville to Cincinatti can be summed up in the words of *Saturday Night Live* veterans Steve Martin and Bill Murray: "WHAT THE HELL WAS THAT?" They never understood and never will.

ELAINE STRITCH 2010

My phone rang and I reluctantly picked it up just as my machine picked up, so we were being recorded. "Paul, I need you!" "Great, who is this?" "GUESS!" "Umm... talk more, please." "Well, I'm a VERY TALENTED person and I need your help..." "More, please..." "and I just LOVE you and I just LOVE MANDY and I need your help..." "Well, I'm glad but who *is* this?" (I was getting annoyed.) "Well, I have VERY STRONG feelings about the theatre. Some of the people are very talented but most of them are FULL OF SHIT!" "Oh... hey, Elaine..." (You better believe I saved this recording.)

She wanted me to come over to the Carlyle Hotel and help her learn her new material for her Sondheim show. Rob Bowman, her musical director, was off in Amsterdam doing *Chicago* for a few weeks so, of course, I said yes. I went over for three sessions and was invited to the first performance, which was fun and pretty together that night.

She left me with two stories—one of her own and one of my own, my very own. The first story concerned her time in London during the late '60s before returning to the States to star in *Company*. She was out drinkin' and smokin' with the gang, and who should also be hanging out (probably for one of the last times) but Judy Garland and her entourage. They were out tying it on and the subject of the Broadway show *Mame* came up. Garland had been approached to replace the current Mame to give the show a much-needed box office boost. As with *Valley of the Dolls*, it was a nice idea, met with enthusiasm and promises, that quickly died. That night, she and Elaine were discussing it and Elaine said, "Judy, let's DO IT! You play Mame and I'll play Vera! No, hold on! Wait a minute, wait a minute! Whad'dya think about this idea?" And Judy is listening intently. "How about this? On one night you play Mame and I'll play Vera, then after the performance you can go out and really tie one on, and the next night I'LL play Mame and YOU'LL play Vera! Then *I* can go out and tie one on!!" Garland looked at her, frowned, inhaled and sincerely inquired, "Wadda we do about the matinees?" You may have had to be there hearing this from Elaine's "horse's" mouth, but that was one of the funniest comebacks I've ever heard.

The other story happened when she asked me to play for her to sing a small memorial service at Sardi's for an old friend. Just one song, "Hey, Good Lookin'" by Hank Williams. I couldn't miss out on this. "But I need you to do me another favor," Elaine said. "I needja ta play COCCCKKKTAIL piano for an hour before." Grrrrrrrr... I told her I don't play cocktail piano, but "Anything for you, Elaine!" Her rendition of "Hey, Good Lookin'" was cute and funny and sweet, and I played my cocckkkktail piano while the guests moved as far away from the piano as they could get. At the end of the memorial, she came over and asked me, "Would you take me over to Orso? I'm going to the theatre tonight and I need you to keep me company while I eat a little something." No problem. It was pouring rain, so she called for her car service. We were picked up at Sardi's on West 44th Street between Eighth and Broadway to go to Orso, two blocks away. We had to drive east (one way only), make a right turn on Broadway, a right turn on 43rd Street, a right turn on Eighth Avenue going north, a left turn on 47th Street going west, a left turn on Ninth Avenue going south, a left turn on 46th Street, pulling up at Orso just west of Eighth Avenue. This took a half an hour. (See the map below.)

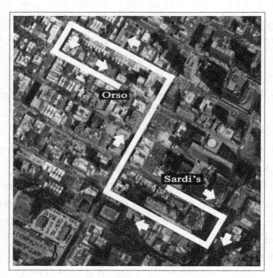

New York is a *mess* and this is all I have to say about New York traffic. The original idiots who laid out the city gave us disastrous crisscrossing avenues, and our previous idiot Mayor (Bloomberg) made it worse by turning Times Square into a *picnic ground*. In the hereafter, he should be forced to be a traffic cop 24/7/365.

We got out and ran into Orso. The place erupted with "Good evening, Miss Stritch! Usual table Miss Stritch? Stritch Stritch Stritch Strich." An echo of Stritches. A couple was forced to move from their table instantly and Elaine and I were seated. It was 7:30 and curtain was at 8 PM. She ordered soup. I didn't order. We waited and finally I said, "Elaine, it's 7:40. Maybe you better get it to go." She agreed. I asked, "What are you seeing tonight?" "That play on 45th Street. I'll just get the driver to pull around." (Good luck.) I said, "I assume you have your ticket..."

And she said...

"I just go to the box office and tell them, 'I'm Elaine Stritch. I want a single seat in the center orchestra, and I'm not paying.'" I laughed out loud but didn't start choking yet. Then I just had to ask, "Well, Elaine, has anyone ever said NO?" And without missing a beat she said, "Fucking *Mamma Mia!*" Then I started to choke. I was very grateful for that moment.

She also asked me a couple of weeks later to escort her to the Prince Rainier III Artistic Achievement Awards, a big fancy deal at Cipriani's. She was to present an award to Mandy Patinkin. Of course, I said yes, and I put on my tux and went. When we arrived, there were paparazzi and they were all over Elaine. Also in front of us was an actress I admired (briefly) and had just worked with in the dreadful Roundabout Theatre revival of *Pal Joey*. Martha Plimpton gave the best performance in *Pal Joey* playing Elaine's role from the 1952 production. They must not have met before because Martha sidled up to me all hugs and kisses and show business *urgency* to be introduced. I did, and they yakked and had photos taken. Funny, Martha rarely spoke to me or made eye contact during the whole *Pal Joey* debacle, but she was sure happy to see me that night! Ah, show business... everyday a little death...

HAPPY 80th BIRTHDAY STEPHEN SONDHEIM 2010

Lonny Price was set to direct an 80th birthday tribute to Stephen Sondheim at Avery Fisher Hall to be televised on PBS. Paul Gemignani was to conduct the New York Philharmonic and I was to play. To make a long and nostalgic story reasonably short, here are some rehearsal highlights. All of the rehearsals were videotaped from the beginning (and I have them!)

This was the first time since 1994 that I was in the same room with Mandy and Bernadette. It was a quiet, solemn event, almost as if we all should avert our eyes and not watch them. We rehearsed "Finishing the Hat" with Mandy, followed by "Move On." Bernadette was filming a movie, so her hair was "straightened." She said, "I feel like Ann-Margret!" and started to do the "Lot of Livin' to Do" choreography from the *Bye, Bye, Birdie* film! Funny! There was very little conversation after that, only complete focus.

Joanna Gleason and Chip Zien singing "It Takes Two" was enough to kill me with nostalgia. Enough said. It was an honor and a privilege to play my second favorite Sondheim song, "The Road You Didn't Take," for the original singer John McMartin. He was terrified but pulled it off. This would rank high in the greatest moments of my entire showbiz life. Jim Walton, my old neighbor, accompanied himself and sang "Growing Up" from *Merrily We Roll Along* beautifully and made the *cut* for the broadcast, as well he should have.

And here comes the Elaine Stritch story. She was to sing "I'm Still Here." Great! Perfect! And the story she regaled us with was the following:

I was in London and appearing on an awards telecast, and Eartha Kitt was scheduled to sing "I'm Still Here," but her plane was late. They kept moving the number to later. Finally, she arrived all glammed up in gold lamé and three-sheets-to-the-wind! She went onstage and planted herself. Paul, (Elaine speaking to me) *play the intro! And this is what happened.* (I played the intro and Elaine sang as Eartha Kitt.)

> *GOOD TIMES AND BUM TIMES,*
> *I'VE SEEN THEM ALL, AND MY DEAR,*
> *I'M STILL HERE.*
> *PLUSH VELVET SOMETIMES,*
> *SOMETIMES JUST PRETZELS AND BEER,*
> *BUT I'M HERE.*
>
> *STUFFED UKULELES*
> *IN MY SHOES...*

Eartha came to an abrupt halt... She broke up onstage. Me and my pal Brian Bedford were in the wings wetting our britches!

The lyric is supposed to be "I stuffed the dailies in my shoes, strummed ukuleles, sung the blues..."

So now I have my own video of Elaine and I doing her impersonation of Eartha Kitt, smashed, trying to get "I'm Still Here" off the ground. Happy ending, though. Eartha started it over and is completely brilliant! How do I know? It's on YouTube!

Elaine did a good job, as well, although the dress rehearsal and first of the two performances were disastrous in what she was singing and what the orchestra was playing. She'd stop singing and take a break whenever she felt like it, despite the fact that the orchestra had to keep going. Can someone say "train wreck?" The next night she was 90% on, and between the two takes another legendary theatre performance was patched together.

All through this performance, I thought to myself that this was the last time all these people will be together. One more thing about Elaine... the minute we started rehearsing, she stopped me and said, "We're gonna do this a little slooooower, please!" exactly as she had in 1985 on the *Follies in Concert* documentary.

So, on a tribute like this, with Elaine Stritch in the lineup, what of her signature tune, "The Ladies Who Lunch?" Patti LuPone did it, and did it great. She directed the classic line, "Does anyone still wear a hat?" to the audience, then glanced over to Elaine... who was wearing a hat. No one upstages Elaine Stritch! And they hugged each other on stage. A really fun moment!

George Hearn was present and I finally remembered to ask him if he remembered a 1973 matinee of *The Changing Room* when 80 high school kids freaked out at the nudity in the play. He said, "Oh, that happened all the time!" Audra McDonald and Nathan Gunn sang "Too Many Mornings," and Lonny Price focused the camera so I was right between their faces! He later asked me if I liked that, because he had intentionally used that angle. I said "Sure!" But I wasn't even playing on that song. I'm just glad I wasn't picking my nose! Jason Danieley and Marin Mazzie performed together on the "We're Gonna Be Alright" number from *Do I Hear a Waltz?* He is a great guy and one of the few leading men I like. We did the long, original version last heard on the 1973 Scrabble Tribute which was fully orchestrated. Paul Gemignani was not interested in looking for the chart, so it became a trio number (the only solo piano of mine I liked on the show). Other piano solos were an ineffectual "So Many People" for Laura Benanti, an "almost there" arrangement of "Don't Laugh" from *Hot Spot* for Victoria Clark (the most interesting song on the program), and "Beautiful Girls" for David Hyde-Pierce, a joy as always. In fact, his hosting of the evening was a lucky stroke.

I felt the song stack was somewhat uninspired, but where do you begin with Sondheim...?

But here's the inside story... and a sign that show business and I were on the decline...

The choreographer Josh Rhodes was to devise a *pas de deux* (yikes!) to the music from *Reds*, specifically the song "Goodbye for Now." He was working with the soundtrack album version and wanted to do that particular arrangement. Jonathan Tunick did the orchestrations for the movie. What was discovered was that Tunick had only orchestrated the *first half* of the three-minute track. The movie studio commissioned another orchestrator to add the big showy second half *strictly for the album*. The job here was to ask Jonathan to orchestrate the piano chart I had written out reflecting the recording. I asked Paul repeatedly if he wanted me to give Jonathan the recording to listen to, and Paul repeatedly said, "No, I'll do it." But Paul and Jonathan didn't always communicate, to put it lightly. At the orchestra rehearsal, a day away from the performances, the ballet dancers were *pas de deux*ing, the orchestra was playing the first part exactly as on the recording, and then we got to the second half. What was meant to be *tutti* orchestra, all lush and loud and dazzling, suddenly dipped to HARP AND FLUTE to the end! This had to be a joke. A bad one. Lonny, Josh, and the dancers were completely freaking out, as well they should have been. Right then and there I said to myself, "Paul Ford, you are going to have to improvise a big fat concerto-like piano solo (accompanied by harp and flute!) to save this *show business emergency*." The rehearsal stopped and was over for the day. Paul Gemignani left the hall and left the building, saying to me "You fix it." I was left with Jonathan and the fuming Lonny Price and Josh Rhodes. I was asked to retreat to the lobby with all of them, including everyone's assistant and masseur and valet... All eyes were on Tunick and me to fix it. He said he had no time to fix it overnight and that it would cost $5,000! So, I went home and practiced a piano part late into the night. Then a late email from Gemignani came saying, "You're going to have to play a piano solo on the second half (accompanied by harp and flute)." As if I didn't know. I've never been any kind of solo pianist and couldn't really do a Liberace job on it, but I did my best. What a disaster, one that did not have to happen, and all because male egos got in the way. Such nonsense! I had one foot out the door.

Both evenings went smoothly and most of the numbers made the cut for the telecast, but for me it was a somber melancholy evening.

I was to follow this event with the Encores! concert version of *Anyone Can Whistle*, and their own birthday salute. That evening was conducted by Rob Berman and had many people who didn't make it to Avery Fisher Hall. Angela Lansbury, in an unbelievably snazzy silver lamé gown, did "Liaisons" (great),

Mrs. Michael Douglas did "Send in the Clowns" (just as dramatically absurd as on the Tony broadcast), Maria Friedman did the insipid Julia McKenzie oh-so-British-version of "Broadway Baby," the entire original quartet from *Into the Woods* was wasted on "No One Is Alone," Joanna Gleason and Chip Zien repeated their "It Takes Two," and on and on... oh, and B.D. Wong led "Someone in a Tree" from *Pacific Overtures*. (Why does no one sing "Poems"?????) It was a nice concert, though not on the grand scale as the Avery Fisher Hall.

40. Anyone Can Whistle, Encores! 2010

When Rob Fisher stepped down as conductor of Encores!, Paul Gemignani was approached to take over. What a great gig! His first season choices were *Kismet* (good), *70, Girls, 70* (good), and he wanted to do *Funny Girl*, but Jack Viertel overrode him and chose *Of Thee I Sing*. *Kismet* was somewhat miscast, and due to Gemignani and director Lonny Price's penchant for cutting music and *revisal-ing* (which was not what Encores! was all about), the production faltered and was not a true Encores! example of allowing the work to stand on its own. *70, Girls, 70* was a miscast disaster, a horrible experience, but *Of Thee I Sing* was back to business. The next season was to be *Follies, No, No, Nanette*, and some kind of Ziegfeld revue mishmash. Gemignani was interrupted by the filming of *Sweeney Todd* and missed all three shows. The next year, Rob Fisher was back.

A consolation prize (for me) after the aborted Paul Gemignani takeover of the Encores! series, was my being allowed to play rehearsals for the concert version of *Anyone Can Whistle* in 2010. (I had to beg for the job.) This unloved but unique show will probably never get as much loving care as it did in this beautifully mounted presentation. Very well cast with Donna Murphy, Sutton Foster, and Raul Esparza, the only thing missing (as always) was the "Everybody Says Don't" ballet. I'll never understand why these ballets are tossed away as being extraneous, when in this case it is a central part of the show, the way "The Dance at the Gym" is to *West Side Story*. The music has only recently been recorded and it is a knockout piece in three parts devised by Betty Wahlberg, based on Sondheim's song. The Cookie Ballet however was beautifully choreographed by Casey Nicholaw, and it would seem that he could have easily turned out a decent representation of the other ballet, especially with still-living original cast members such as Harvey Evans to consult. Beggars can't be choosers.

Several people have expressed their apathy toward this performance (and the show itself) to me, and I guess I can understand why. Many people don't like a mirror held up to themselves. At the end of the show when the fickle townspeople run to the next town because of reports of a new "miracle," Donna Murphy as Mayoress Cora Hoover Hooper is left alone in the town square. Her political partner in crime comes to her and she asks, "Aren't you running, too?" To which actor Edward Hibbert replied, as only he can, "My dear. Running is for the herd." The night I sat out to watch, the audience gasped at this line. Why? There must have been a lot of future Trump voters in the house to cause a reaction like that. The whole show (for me) is about being true to oneself, against all odds. Hibbert's character got it right. And I don't think the audience liked the implication that one of the most corrupt characters of the play, would have the ultimate word about humanity. At least in my not so humble opinion, this is a show for everyone. The plot basically remains open-ended with nothing but possibilities. It also has a language of its own and one of the most enjoyable show-stopping scores of any show. What fantastic songs! It has become one of my desert-island favorites. Just playing rehearsals for the production was an honor. No funny stories, no drama, just slick professionalism putting forth the ultimate cult show with more substance than any other Broadway flop (and most of the hits on Broadway today). Of course, there was no recording, or transfer. Too bad. The following year, Sutton Foster opened in yet another revisal of the empty-headed *Anything Goes*, which ran for 15 months, raking in the bucks. Donna was wasted in a hopeless new musical (two chapters away) and Raul had to wait two years to lead yet another tiresome contemporary gospel-singin' attempt to turn Broadway into something it never was (Vegas) with *Leap of Faith*. What a waste.

41. The Beginning of the End

ANNIE GET YOUR GUN AT RAVINIA

I finally got to do a production of *Annie Get Your Gun* 32 years after playing auditions for it on my first day in New York. This would be a very different *Annie Get Your Gun*. A staged concert version at the Ravinia outdoor music festival in the suburbs of Chicago. In 1978, the Jones Beach outdoor production I played those auditions for, must have been a gigantic production—they always were—with circus acts, rodeo acts, Indian tribal dances and probably a company of 60. Most likely they used the 1966 revised version (script and music) with those great orchestrations, dance sequences, and Wild West Ballets. I did not see it, but at the time you could rest assured you would get your money's worth at a Jones Beach production. And the cost was probably only ten bucks a seat.

The production at Ravinia was to star Patti LuPone and Brian Stokes Mitchell, two great voices and great personalities. Ravinia is outdoors and usually limited to only three performances. But the show is backed by the Chicago Symphony, so all of those Robert Russell Bennett orchestrations would be done justice to. Even though the Ravinia productions were usually hybrid concert/fully staged and costumed deals, they usually gave a nice representation of an old show. I loved the 1966 Lincoln Center revival recording with Ethel Merman, and her version of "I Got the Sun in the Morning" is in the top 20 of all Broadway tracks for me. Give me Ethel Merman's joy any time. It also had a great Overture, dazzling, exciting, and to the point.

The trouble, and I do mean trouble (and I was growing weary of trouble), began with an angry phone call from conductor Paul Gemignani. "This music doesn't match the recording. Where's the rest of the Overture? Why don't they match?" "Well, Paul, what recording are you listening to?" "I'm listening to the Ethel Merman recording!" "Well, Paul, you know there have been 4,000 different recordings of *Annie Get Your Gun*, which one are you listening to?" "The one with Ethel Merman, the original cast recording." "Well, check it and see, because the original 1946 Decca original cast recording does not have the Overture on it." "It says... 'Stanley Black Conducts the London Sinfonia, *Annie Get Your Gun* starring Ethel Merman.'" Sighing, I said, "That's the rerecording that was done in the '70s with all new orchestrations. And the Overture is definitely *different* from the actual show score. You need to get the RCA 1966 Lincoln Center revival recording or the 2-CD complete recording with Judy Kaye. Those have the show orchestrations, and the Judy Kaye contains every single note of the score we are using." (I always knew, know now, and will always know *my stuff!*) "Send them to me," he ordered. (I sent him the links to Amazon.com, thank you very much.) A short time later I received an email. "I hate this Overture. I want to do the other one." "Well, call the Rodgers and Hammerstein office and ask Bruce Pomahac if it exists." (It didn't.) Sigh...

Soon, we would be meeting in my apartment—Paul Gemignani, director Lonny Price and choreographer Josh Rhodes.

Paul started the conversation. "Okay... All this dance music is cut from this 'Bad, Bad Man' number. All this 'Wild West Ballet' goes. What's this Entr'acte?"

206 | Paul Ford

I told him it was "There's No Business Like Show Business."

"No one wants to hear that again," Paul said. "Cut it! And we're not doing this Indian stuff. Cut all this tribal dance and that whole 'Indian' song. No curtain call and no exit music."

So, we have the Chicago Symphony Orchestra and they are going to play only the spare accompaniments to "Doin' What Comes Naturally" and the like, and have nothing symphonic to play except a two-minute Overture? Yes! Exactly. Granted this was a concert, but Encores! concerts in New York City generally played *all* of the wonderful music just to hear it, otherwise why are we doing it? And the "I'm an Indian Too" number is a celebration, not a put-down of a group of people. Annie Oakley is being made an honorary member of the tribe! What's offensive about that? Thank God, Paul didn't screw around with the arrangement of "I Got the Sun in the Morning!" I would have torn my last hair out.

All of this "fiddling" had become very frustrating for me as I cherished all of this music. I now refuse to see any revival of *any* show because of the "political correctness" nonsense and the denigration of the original arrangements.

News came that Brian Stokes Mitchell was out, and Patrick Cassidy was in. Fine. Patrick was fun and funny and, like his father Jack, could play a strutting, preening peacock. He was perfect for the role.

Our production ran for about 40 minutes an act. It was threadbare with all the cuts. But a special nod goes out to all the terrific Chicago singers/dancers/actors, every one of them better than we deserved.

A week before the *Annie* performances, we did an 80th Birthday Sondheim Concert thrown together by Lonny and Paul, for a special event at Ravinia. It would again feature the Chicago Symphony Orchestra and star Patti, George Hearn, Audra McDonald, and Michael Cerveris. All of these people knew multiple Sondheim songs, but for some reason the song list was short and, worst of all, extremely uninteresting. I truly believe that no one on a picnic at Ravinia or anywhere, ever needs to hear "Every Day a Little Death," "Send in the Clowns," "You Must Meet My Wife" or "A Little Priest" while they are eating, trying to enjoy themselves, or simply *again* for that matter. The piano/staging rehearsal was fun because Sondheim came to visit. (Thank God he didn't stay for the concert!) He was feeling good and was fun to be with. I kept playing some of his old favorites like Bernard Herrmann's *Psycho* theme. He would have a newspaper up in front of his face and would rattle it in response. A fun afternoon.

The actual concert the next night ran for *less than an hour* and was a show business scandal for the whole week in the local newspapers and on TV and on the radio. Boycott Ravinia! Is Ravinia only for the rich?! We got shafted! And so forth. Our quartet of performers could have very easily sung two more songs each, with a few days' notice.

Needless to say, after that *scandal* and the lackluster *Annie Get Your Gun*, there were no musicals at Ravinia the next summer... or the next... This was, as the title of a classic '50s science fiction movie says, "The Beginning of the End."

For me.

42. The End

THE PEOPLE IN THE PICTURE 2011

During the two years leading up to this production, I rehearsed two terrible Roundabout Theatre revivals, *110 in the Shade* and *Pal Joey*. The original material for both was raped and violated by a creative team that knew "better" and insisted they could fix what was never "broken." (I never even stayed around to see a performance of *Pal Joey*.) I played rehearsals for Kander and Ebb's *Curtains*. I was fired from subbing on *Curtains* because I couldn't handle the complicated technicalities of the hybrid keyboard in the pit, and couldn't wrap my brain around the atrocious orchestrations by Bill Brohn. It was my first firing, but a relief to be away from all these catastrophes. I was 57 years old and things started to crack (inside my body and inside my brain) especially after the *Annie Get Your Gun* production at Ravinia.

Paul Gemignani hired me to play a two-week staged workshop of a musical that had been around for a while called *Laughing Matters*. There existed a full demo recording with Randy Graff in the leading role, but Donna Murphy was slated for it now.

The plot of *Laughing Matters* was a jumble of contemporary scenes (1970s New York) and flashbacks (1930s Poland), and concerned a Holocaust survivor, her daughter, her granddaughter, family secrets, Yiddish Theatre, 1970s television comedy writing, betrayals, 1930s movie making, Alzheimer's, the Holocaust and so on and so forth... oy! The book and lyrics were by Iris Dart, author of *Beaches*, and the music was jointly "composed" by two Hollywood veterans, Mike Stoller ("Hound Dog") and Artie Butler (Peggy Lee's former musical director).

These two men were terrific guys, funny, generous, but had no real skills for delivering music and no experience in writing a Broadway show. These guys scribbled tunes on decades old manuscript paper, using chord symbols instead of composing. There existed some fairly solid arrangements from previous workshops of the show, courtesy of the previous musical director-arranger David Loud—all computerized—but these files were buried in a Los Angeles-based copyist's computer and to get to them would be murder. We did have a New York music copyist, Anne Kaye, but no one had taken the trouble to transfer the files or really update anything. No written record existed of what had been done in the last reading or for the demo recording, so there were many versions of the songs—all very confusing. No one knew what was what. I finally got some of the files in my computer from the Los Angeles guy, so I could get the score ready for the workshop.

Neither of the composers nor Paul Gemignani nor our associate conductor had any computer skills or quick arranging skills to deal with the daily work that goes into mounting a brand-new Broadway musical. No one else was paying any attention to or cared about this minor detail. Except, of course, me. It all fell into *my* lap.

The workshop went fine despite this. The cast was delightful—Donna was her usual meticulous, hardworking self. We had the wondrous Chip Zien (who should be in every musical just because of his beautiful voice), Heidi Blickenstaff, Jayne Houdyshell, Christopher Innvar, Emily Skinner, and Neal Benari. It went very smoothly and I was proud and happy with the run-throughs. A friend, who turned pages for me, had huge reservations about the structure of the show, as did Paul Gemignani. Paul also was not happy with most of the cast, except for Chip and Donna, and really campaigned to recast. There was no choreographer as of yet (did it need one?) and the director was opera and *Master Class* director, Leonard Foglia.

Foglia looked at me every day—no, every minute—as if he smelled limburger cheese. For an opera director, he was completely inarticulate about music, and got very frustrated when he wanted to hear something that simply wasn't there in the score. (As with *Rags*, there really wasn't any SCORE to begin with!) Paul was being a pretty good fencer at this point in dealing with the affable, but very long-in-the-tooth, composers and the people-challenged director, but they just basically sat there.

Mike Stoller (composer number one) was a good guy and gave me an autographed autobiography which was delightful and funny to read, and Artie Butler (composer number two) was nothing short of hysterical. Think of Morey Amsterdam/Buddy Sorrell on *The Dick Van Dyke Show*.

Two fabulous stories from Artie...

1. Artie was in London with Peggy Lee performing for Queen Elizabeth and staying at Buckingham Palace. "You know, Peggy and the Queen were tight." he informed me. After their work was done, he and Miss Lee were riding in a limo to the airport, and she asked the driver to roll the partition up to give them privacy. She whispered to Artie, "Did you take a souvenir?" "What?" Artie said, panic growing, sweat breaking out. "Did you take a souvenir from Buckingham Palace?" she again asked. "What?! No! Are you crazy?" "I DID," Peggy Lee said with a smile. "For God's sake, what?" "Toilet paper. Six-ply!" Artie, in disbelief, said "Toilet paper?" "Six-ply!" she emphasized. "Why toilet paper?" And she replied, "Oh, you men are all alike. *You* get to stand up! But we women have to *sit* and wipe and you don't know how *gooood* that six-ply feels down there!"

2. Artie was close to Milton Berle up to his death and literally took care of him, lifting him and bathing him at the end. Milton Berle was known for the size of his penis and publicly joked about it. Artie was with him in Las Vegas once at a benefit. They were looking out the window of their hotel across the skyline to another big hotel. Berle pointed to the hotel and said "Aimee Semple McPherson. (Pause.) 30 years ago. (Pause.) Shtupped her... from here!"

Artie and Mike were great, but in way over their heads on this show. We all were.

A few weeks later, we came back for a one-day reading with Leslie Kritzer in for Heidi Blickenstaff and Marilyn Sokol in for Jayne Houdyshell (Jayne had graciously bowed out, though both are hilarious, wonderful performers), and some major changes in the script. A third of the show had been cut, eliminating half of the daughter's role and focusing on Donna Murphy's character, which seemed to make sense at the time. It certainly got rid of a lot of extraneous loose ends and underdeveloped ideas. But with these cuts went most of the comedy and romance, and suddenly the title *Laughing Matters* didn't make much sense. I started to notice that instead of really working on the show, there was a lot of crying, weeping, nose-blowing, and *kvelling* over the tragic plot turns of the story. Tears every time right on cue from writers, actors, assistant stage managers, but how about what really needed to be worked on? This reading went smoothly, and Todd Haimes of the Roundabout Theatre was about to go for it. I did like some of the ballads in the show—the Jewish-flavored '30s ballads and the softly pop '70s ballads. All of the show business *fun* numbers were lost with the script cuts, and the remaining Yiddish theatre up-tempo comedy numbers, uninspired musically, were full of *tuchus* jokes. And the song about a "tap dancing dybbuk" was from hunger.

We were headed for Broadway but unfortunately not the great Studio 54 space, perfect for this intimate show, but the Roundabout's big barn on 42nd Street. Sanity and luck prevailed as the company's revival of *The Importance of Being Earnest* was such a success on 42nd Street, Todd Haimes decided to let our show go into Studio 54. Good news! The only good news!

We now had a choreographer. Choreographer? Andy Blankenbuehler, the Tony Award-winning choreographer of *In the Heights*, and later *Hamilton* and *Bandstand*, was the last person in the world to choreograph a simple nostalgic little show with older character people.

I was not sure I still had a job, since this development meant the need for a dance music arranger, which I am not and never was. I had a couple of meetings with Blankenbuehler where, admittedly, I was very nervous and played very badly. We went through the score and frankly I didn't see where dancing was necessary for this show. The most disturbing thing about these meetings was that I literally couldn't understand what he was saying to me. He spoke in such an impatient, rapid fire, fragmented way ("millennial speak!"), that I really couldn't follow what he was saying. (God, I'm getting old!) We did no more preproduction, but I wrote out a sketch of a prelude for the top of the show to his specifications and made notes of places dances were to be inserted.

Leslie Kritzer was passed over, and there were many, many auditions for the role of the daughter, Red, and some decent current musical theatre actresses learned two new songs written for the character. Finally, the role went to Nicole Parker of *Mad TV* fame. Great voice and interesting choice, but there was really no humor left in the role, and eventually one of her major songs would be rewritten and finally cut. It was a waste to hire her.

During these auditions there was a meeting where Paul Gemignani and director Lenny Foglia decided to tell the creative team to stay in California for two weeks to give the cast a chance to learn the material and get it on its feet. They agreed. After all, Stephen Sondheim does it. He shows up the first day, leaves and comes back later. He does not hover and make everyone nervous, but then comes back and gives terrific notes and suggestions. He also is producing material for the show while we're working. In this case, I was the only one who was really putting computer keys to paper, arranging, editing, and changing keys.

Our associate musical director barely helped, and having no computer skills, spent all the rehearsals putting colored "sticky notes" in his music, pretending to do something! He also refused to play if I was in the room. Mind you, I was not even going to play this show in the orchestra pit for the run.

I was slated to work on three other projects in the middle of this show AND do weekend gigs with Mandy Patinkin! I found myself writing half-baked dance arrangements (unpaid), underscoring (unpaid), updating the score every night, which took up to three or four hours a night, ALL UNPAID. There were no composers on hand with assistants to copy, distribute, or take care of all this. Our associate musical director wouldn't come near *any* of it. The composers simply *couldn't* do it.

Then another decision was made. Paul Gemignani wanted the music copying service of Emily Grishman to be the official music preparers on the show, taking the job away from Anne Kaye who had been the composers' choice. Fine. Some hurt feelings and pissed-off people, but when I asked Kathy Edmonds at the Emily Grishman office if she had received all of the computerized music files so we could start updating, she told me, "Oh, we have nothing. They're not getting the files from Anne Kaye." "What do you mean 'they're not getting the files from Anne Kaye???'" I called Paul Gemignani and he said, "Oh we don't have the heart to ask Anne Kaye for the music files after taking the job away from her."

Excuse me? A multimillion-dollar musical and you don't have "the heart" to get the music files for the entire show? All I had in my computer were hybrids of what I had been updating and not the complete score that I had given Anne Kaye from the last reading. We're talking about the entire score of this multimillion-dollar musical and it's stuck in a fired music copyist's computer? The composers didn't have files, and I didn't have *complete* files... what the fuck? So, I had to get in touch with the original copyist in Los Angeles, who sent me his original files, which had absolutely nothing to do with the current state of the score, and then, using my rehearsal copy, make a completely new score which only I had in my computer. All of this was happening while we were rehearsing and took hours and hours after rehearsal. All because we didn't have "the heart" to ask for the files from a fired copyist! Whose music was it? Who did it belong to? What the fuck? And what a fucking nightmare!

The title of the show was now *The People in the Picture*. There was no *Laughing Matters*, and certainly no laughter at this point.

Somewhere in this mess, one of our daffy producers came up to me in rehearsal and said, "We're trying to set a time for tonight for you and Julie to rehearse." Tonight? Rehearse what? Julie who? Andrews? London? Newmar? "Oh, we want you to play for Julie Budd who's singing a song from the show at a benefit tomorrow night. Didn't anyone tell you?" Thank God for Paul Gemignani at this point because he momentarily was not talking on his cell phone and overheard this exchange. "Not for under 500 bucks he doesn't!" he piped in. "Oh... okay..." she said. My question was, "Why couldn't our associate musical director go do this?" But he was scurrying out the door with his sticky notes. I wasted two nights dealing with the sweet (though typically obsessively neurotic) Julie Budd, playing a crappy synthesizer in an endlessly long, crowded benefit at some downtown museum. I'm getting paid, right? Right. Wish I was being paid for the four *extra* hours a night I was slaving at the computer!

After the first week of rehearsal, I was grateful to have two days off to do a spectacularly fun reading of the Cy Coleman, Comden and Green musical, *On the Twentieth Century*, starring Hugh Jackman, Kristin Chenoweth, Andrea Martin, and *White Collar*'s Matt Bomer. What fun, but exhausting. I was grateful to be playing a REAL score that was WRITTEN DOWN!! Then I had to fly somewhere and do a show with Mandy Patinkin on my day off. Then back to *The People in the Picture*. Then the Roundabout was in the midst of their spring gala and wanted to do a big tribute honoring Alec Baldwin (ALEC BALDWIN?), directed by Scott Ellis. What songs? Who's singing? Who's compiling music? Simple questions. "You'll know when I know," Paul Gemignani said. Oh, he knew alright but wouldn't tell me. As usual, no one would ever lift a finger and I would do ALL OF THIS WORK MYSELF! On top of this, I agreed (I know, I know, this really is ALL MY FAULT. I did not have to say "yes") to help with the New York City Ballet's new production of Kurt Weill's *The Seven Deadly Sins* starring Patti LuPone, so I was playing auditions for those singers in the wee hours of the morning or after rehearsal, and still trying to stay on top of the music for *The People in the Picture*.

I had to take a day off to go for a concert with Mandy and they insisted I bring in a sub, so I secured Grant Sturiale. But I was the only one who had played anything after three weeks, so why couldn't our associate conductor just play on that day instead of bringing in a whole new sub? Then the choreographer insisted on bringing in a drummer! Now we had a drummer! Why? What did this show have to do with drums, for God's sake? It was all ballads! And HE needed a copy of the score, too! Finally, the words "dance arranger" started floating around, and Andy Blankenbuehler's personal arranger, Alex Lacamoire (now a *three*-time Tony-winning orchestrator) was brought in during the third week. Well, it was about time someone came in to literally *compose* the show, so he started whipping up new wild arrangements for many of the songs, and dancers were flying around us, and Blankenbuehler was jabbering away, talking a mile a minute, always impatient and always unintelligible, shoving non-dancing character people around and taking poor

Donna Murphy by her fragile shoulders and yanking her this way and that. I was trying to sight-read all the new dance arrangements with "Snippy" Blankenbuehler clapping his hands at me and mumbling at supersonic 21st century hip-hop speed.

The composers and lyricist arrived back on the scene and were asked to write a new song, and—as in the manner of Charles Strouse on *Rags*–brought in an old piece of manuscript paper with pen scratches on it and everybody including the assistant stage manager's rabbi was allowed to pontificate on the new song. The composers were complaining, "What's with all the dancing and the dancers? Why are our characters offstage for so long?" I was still updating the score at night, but Alex Lacamoire was being paid and I wasn't.

And now, Patti LuPone (this was a *new* addition to the workload) was asking for *all* the ensemble numbers in the upcoming Avery Fisher Hall *Company* concert, starring Neil Patrick Harris, to be transposed down a third. (She was right, the keys were too high for that television cast of non-singers.) But Gemignani was not looking at *Company* and not making decisions. I was starting to have to rehearse with the *Company* cast members *after hours*, including Stephen Colbert (thank God, he was a professional and came prepared). And I was having to chase down paychecks from the New York City Ballet, as they had lost my first set of tax forms, then they lost my invoice. I was losing my mind.

And speaking of paychecks. Not including Mandy's generous and (yes, I believe) appropriate remuneration for my services, working this current schedule on five projects for three weeks, 12 hours a day, seven days a week, after taxes, I found I was taking home maybe $900.00 a week. On Broadway! I'm sorry. I took home *three times as much* with one two-hour Mandy concert.

BIG QUESTION: Did I want to endure the limburger cheese sneers of Leonard Foglia, the snip-snip-snipping of Andy Blankenbuehler, the 80-year-old composers, the chasing down of paychecks, the "can you work with the choreographer for free so that the ever-so-poor Roundabout Theatre doesn't have to pay for a dance arranger" implication, everybody sitting around texting texting texting and talking talking talking and me being the only one listening and paying attention to what was going on, the getting snapped at when I've heard something that has not been heard or observed by anyone else, the no *good mornings*, the no *thank you*s for providing the whole motor of the musical. My career had become nothing but trouble shooting, sweeping up shit at the circus, and getting snapped at for it. And certainly NOT about making music.

So, I lost my mind.

It was March 10, 2011, a Thursday, and we started rehearsal at 10 AM. At one point, Donna walked by the piano and made eye contact with me, communicating what I thought was "Are you okay, honey?" Needless to say, I wasn't. Soon it was 5 o'clock and Grant Sturiale was coming at 6 to pick up his score so he could sub for me the day I would be out. I got up from the piano, walked over to our associate conductor cowering behind his multicolored sticky-noted score and said, "You're playing the rest of the rehearsal." I sat down next to Paul Gemignani and took out the sub piano book and spent the last hour making notes and marking new cuts in the score. It was very quiet in the room and the associate conductor played absolutely beautifully, as we all knew he could. After a bit, Paul patted me on the shoulder and said, "You okay?" I said, "Just tired and I need to get this score ready for Grant." 6 o'clock came and Grant showed up. I wished him well and headed for the elevator.

I walked home (through the armpit of hell, Times Square), got inside of my apartment and sat down at my computer. I didn't open my music. I didn't start fixing the score. I addressed an email to Paul Gemignani. I thought for only a minute and wrote, "As of today, I am resigning from *The People in the Picture, Company* at Avery Fisher Hall, *The Seven Deadly Sins*, and the Alec Baldwin Tribute. Any files or materials I may have, I will gladly provide. I will not be coming in tomorrow morning. Paul Ford."

I didn't hit the send button. After 16 years of sobriety, I knew to pause and wait. I immediately called my therapist and (hallelujah!) he picked up the phone. Our conversation was short. "I'm quitting. I'm not going back there. Here is the email I am sending. What do you think?" He said, "Well, you know this will bring a big change... but I certainly have been hearing this coming for a long time." I said thank you and goodbye, then hung up and got very scared.

I breathed a few more times and hit the send button. I put my coat on and went to the 6:45 PM AA meeting around the corner. I walked in and, remarkably, sat down next to a cast member from the show! (Who of course shall remain nameless.) When the chairperson asked if there were any "burning desires," I took it for the first time in 16 years. I simply said, "Paul. Alcoholic. I just quit my job and left a 30-year working relationship." Period. My friend grabbed my arm and said "What?! We're having dinner after!" We did, and I told him what I felt and pretty much everything you've just read. He said, "Well, Paul, they were treating you horribly!"

I came home and there were five emails from Paul Gemignani with a variety of questions. Then I received an email from him that said, "Are you kidding?" I wrote back, "No." Then the phone calls started. I let the machine take them. "This is really terrible, this is not good. What's going on? Okay, you're not talking. Well, call me." Then another call. "Okay, what if you take the weekend off and come back on Tuesday and we'll forget it ever happened. I'll just tell them you're sick. Okay, you're not talking." Then another. "Listen, you can talk to me. If you want to talk, please call me... as a friend. You're one of my only friends. You and Lonny. Call me." Then more emails asking for an explanation. Finally, I wrote an email. "I don't want to do this anymore. I'm going to spend time with my family and do other projects." He wrote back, "I know, sometimes I feel like quitting too. But call me if you want to talk."

I didn't want to talk, and I didn't go into work the next day.

The truth is, I now finally know that I am just an afterthought and just a piano player, and my time and effort and convenience and sanity are the last to be considered. I never saw *The People in the Picture*. I never saw *The Seven Deadly Sins*. I never got paid for *On the 20th Century* by the Roundabout Theatre.

A few weeks later, I was answering phones and scrubbing floors at AA intergroup the night *Company* had its first performance at Avery Fisher Hall. It gave me great satisfaction when I looked up and saw 7:59 on the clock and went back to scrubbing the floors. The show was *starting*, and I was exactly where I wanted to be.

43. The Nail in the Coffin

Two months later, I was settling in on merely being Mandy Patinkin's pianist. The phone rang and, frankly, I was flattered to receive a phone call from musical director David Loud (who had always been kind to me, and could read music) asking if I was available for a four-hour production meeting for an upcoming revival (a show I had loved and practiced the score of for decades). I had just turned 58 years old. I had turned down a few things to avoid any more of what I had been through in the winter, but I thought "Oh, why not?" I was told I would be provided with a score. What could it hurt? Just a four-hour production meeting.

I showed up early (a lifetime habit and the real reason I had a career) and waited. Finally, several people arrived. I approached a stage manager and said, "I'm Paul Ford and I'm here to stand in today for (musical director) David Loud." "Hi," he said. "Here's the music." I sat down at the piano and in the remaining time flipped through the score to see if there was anything unfamiliar. It bore little resemblance to the score I knew and loved.

A skinny, listless, bedraggled "hippie" woman came in. When she was settled, I introduced myself. "I'm Paul Ford and I'm here to play for David Loud." "Huh," she said. The door opened and a sloppy, dreadlocked "thing" walked in. When she was settled, I said, "I'm Paul Ford and I'm here to play for David Loud." "Huh," she said as she hiked up her jeans over her dirty thong. Finally, the door opened and a grotesque creature walked in. When *IT* was settled, I introduced myself. "I'm Paul Ford and I'm here to play for David Loud." "Huh," *IT* grunted.

The "creative" meeting (of a show that I presumed had already been created) began. I had to play three or four selections and was finally let go after a four-hour "listen-a-thon." I raced home to go online and type into Google, "revival of *Porgy and Bess*." Immediately a trio of pictures came up of the bedraggled, listless "hippie woman," the sloppy, "dreadlocked thing," and the grotesque "*IT* creature." They were the director of *Porgy and Bess*, the "book writer" of *Porgy and Bess*, and the "musical arranger" of *Porgy and Bess*. At last, I knew who I had been sitting in the room with, as I was never given a name or introduced, not even by stage management. I read who they were: "Tony nominated," "Pulitzer Prize-winning," "Musical Scholar," and yet not one had the manners or decency or respect to let me in on who I was in the room with.

My mind flashed back to the meeting. When I had first looked through the score, I found much unfamiliar music. The famous Overture was cut to what looked like 24 measures, several songs were missing, there were odd "arrangements" of some of the more famous songs, and one song, "It Ain't Necessarily So," was just a fraction of the length of the original.

There was talk of finding other things to give the character of Sportin' Life to do, as said classic song was deemed "too minstrelly." The "Oh, I Can't Sit Down" number was turned into a jungle dance (so much for political correction!) and the lyrics were being altered to the likes of "with Mater and Pater standing by" in "Summertime."

Everyone was looking at scripts. I had a great big score I was following, very nicely printed out, with very clear instructions on underscoring and where dialogue fit in. "Why am I the only one looking at a score?" I thought. "This is a musical." At one point, in a panic, the "hippie woman" said, "How do we figure out if the music and dialogue work together?" After a long waffling period during which *IT*, the musical arranger, never said a word (nor did stage management), I raised my hand and said, "Perhaps I could play the music and someone could read the dialogue to see if it fits together." "Okay, let's try what HE said," the "hippie woman" grumbled. I wanted to cry. I started playing and, according to the music, where it was clearly marked the dialogue should begin, I nodded for the "hippie woman" to start the dialogue. Typically of a director, she raced through the dialogue as one long run-on sentence. Despite that, the scene timed out with the music and I said reassuringly "Perfect." The "hippie woman" snapped back at me, "Whad'dya mean perfect?" I clarified that according to the *music* I was looking at, the dialogue all followed correctly in the music and clearly made sense and timed out. I received back a suspicious look. IT still had not said a word. (Even if you are not a musician, it would seem logical and an easy learning experience to follow the musical score, not the script, during rehearsals. After all, IT IS A MUSICAL!)

Once again, a renowned piece of musical literature had been put in the hands of three illiterates with little to no experience in working on a musical, and with absolutely no knowledge or respect for the original writers' work. So much for the Gershwin estate. There was talk from "Dreadlocks" about motives for Bess's behavior. Why would she go back to Crown when she has Porgy waiting at home? Well, "Dreadlocks," obviously Bess is a drug addict and addicted to Crown, and since he weighs 300 pounds and he has her by the neck, she goes with him... Motive? How about the motive that Dubose Heyward, the original writer, said so! It's the story as he wrote it! PERIOD! I knew that! Anyone who ever saw it or read the script would know that. More talk about "such-and-such character would never say this line or that line," and "how to make it palatable to today's audience." Folks, it may be today's audience but the characters in the story are living in the 1920s. It was written in the period by a person who did his research thoroughly. As an audience, we have the right to the truth of the times. And who's to say that what we think we know today is *right* and *correct* will always remain so? Just look at history.

I had not heard yet about the "creators" rewriting the character of Porgy as no longer being a cripple (AND the "improvers" wanting to add a "back story" as to why Porgy was NOT a cripple!) and I was unaware of the happier, more hopeful ending planned. (Fortunately, someone put their foot down and the ending was changed back.)

At the end of my session, I was asked to play the new "arrangement" of "It Ain't Necessarily So" with its one verse, one chorus and off, plus new "soul train" dance music. Still, IT did not look at me or speak, but when I started playing, IT was sputtering and waving IT's arms madly over my tempo. However, no eye contact was made, nor a word said.

As I left, I couldn't wait to find out who those people were! And there was no "Thank you" from anyone. Not even the stage management. Ah, well...

Every day a whole buncha death... Once again, I was a sucker. It was not worth the $200 I received to sit and watch a piece of theatre I cherished denigrated in this manner. No more.

So, what does all this have to do with Stephen Sondheim?

A few weeks later, a friend called and said, "Guess you pegged that one right." He pointed me toward a letter published in *The New York Times* in response to an interview given by the three Macbeth witches, written by Stephen Sondheim. Over the years he has been quoted as saying that *Porgy and Bess* is one of if not his favorite piece of musical theatre. His letter should be read in classrooms. It exposes the ego, misguidedness and illiteracy behind most theatre people and says, quite clearly (as only my one true hero, Judge Judy, would say), "Get an education, get a job, learn something, THEN get married and have children." In other words, don't do *Porgy and Bess* if you don't know anything about the history of the musical theatre, history in general, literature, reality and, especially, music. Sondheim took the interview line by line and challenged the reasoning behind every quote. Finally, it came down to, in *his* and *my own* words, "don't write someone else's work, write your own." Write your own original musical!

The Gershwin's Porgy and Bess opened in Boston with rave reviews for the star and mediocre ones for the production. Ditto for Broadway. But ultimately... who cares? Nobody. It's the 21st Century.

And I was now through, finished, and done with musical theatre.

During this period, I received an email from Stephen Sondheim addressed to both me and Paul Gemignani in which he included a link. The link was to a video of a dog playing the piano. Sondheim's caption for the video? "Who needs Paul Ford?" (Meaning a dog can play better than Paul Ford.) I found it utterly demoralizing AND very funny at the same time. Sort of, you might say, "Sorry/Grateful."

Where did I stand now? Why did I do it? What did it get me? What was music all about for me all along? What do I think of music now? Today, I don't want to use the dreaded H words (HORRIBLE or HATE, take your pick), but it's hard to describe how I feel about the world of music today without them. I feel assaulted by music today. I feel intruded upon. I don't like music in public areas, in restaurants, in airplanes, airports, offices, taxis, stores, even music stores. I don't understand the extreme loudness of it and the harshness of it. When sitting next to someone on an airplane and they are listening with headphones, I marvel at the relentlessness of the cymbals and the drums I hear seeping through. It begins to sound like a fly buzzing around my head and we all know how annoying that is. Remember how we used to make fun of "elevator music," partly because it was so saccharine, but also because it was just so inescapably *there*? (I'll take good old elevator music any day!) Now you can't escape loud blasts of noise in every public place you go.

The most alarming moment I experienced was in Tower Records 30 some years ago. I was in the Broadway section, which just happened to be where they hung their in-store speakers. The music was some heavy metal junk with some guy screeching his head off and the cacophony rising to such a fever pitch that I had to cover my ears. Then it stopped. And there was silence in the store. And being in the hung-over state common to me in those days, I threw my head back and screamed, "THANK YOU!! JESUS CHRIST, THAT WAS TOO LOUD!" Of course, only a couple of people looked up. No one noticed or reacted or cared.

I simply find it unbearable to walk in any store today. It is an assault on all of my senses. I will never understand the appeal of ugly people wearing ugly clothes standing on a stage playing electric guitars and drums and yelling repetitive gibberish into microphones at piercing volumes. Men, women, teenage boy groups, teenage girls dressed as sluts, country music geared to the lowest common denominator, ugly toneless violent rap, and never a moment of relief—no harmony change or change of tempo or moment of subtlety or grace. Or sophistication. God, how I miss sophistication. I want women to be adults and stop mewling like kittens. I want to see men stand up straight, dress cleanly and behave modestly. I don't enjoy a guy pounding on the piano or on the drums or two guys aiming their guitars like machine guns at the ground and jumping up in midair. I want grace. I want soft-shoe. I want tap dancing. *Happy* tap dancing. I don't enjoy the guitar or the drums. We have thrown the baby out with the bathwater. Between opera/classical music and rock/pop/country/rap there is no middle ground. Music has become atonal, formless, dull, humorless, cold, and stale on the classical front, and angry, hostile, mechanical, grotesque, and yes, *extremely* stale on the popular front.

So where did I get my musical tastes, and will they survive this Armageddon? They started with the 1958 film *South Pacific*, specifically, the song "Bali Ha'i." The musical direction of Alfred Newman and the choral work of the Ken Darby Singers made such an impression on this 5-year-old, I couldn't shake it. The Technicolor photography and location work added to it, of course, but I kept hearing that sound in my sleep and my daydreams. The promise of getting away from everything and living in a fantasy world had begun.

My brother was playing typical '50s rock 'n' roll at home and I tried to connect to it but found it so aggressive and angry and rude that it just made me sick. Others may have found it joyful, outgoing, free, but I was afraid of it. "Bali Ha'i" gave me chills and goose bumps and I had those glorious images in my head—that visual connection. Which is why I obsess over film music to this day. It has been difficult for me to enjoy music without a visual or theatrical connection attached to it.

In a nutshell, over the years I have come to love music that is exciting, evocative of time and place, story, and character. I love *pastiche*, which is now a dirty word. Music can be dark and mournful, dramatic, definitely melodramatic, epic and grand, and even funny. Orchestral music minus any vocal is my favorite. There are very few voices I appreciate. Most of them are long dead. I like music that changes mood, feeling, tempo, and style in rapid succession. That is why I like overtures and show music so much. The variety! Film music with its combination of source music and dramatic scoring is equally satisfying. Dance music in films and Broadway shows used to be done with great, if not inspired, imagination. Give some expert arranger a little song and let him go to town on it. I love big band and swing music because of the inventiveness and pure joy and humor in the arrangements. I even love jazz because of its harmonic intricacies (something non-existent in pop music). There is simply no joy, surprise or humor in music today. Just the deadly relentless beat, harsh and overbearing from first sound to last.

Which brings me to my second great influence—the original cast recording of *Flower Drum Song*, specifically the song "Grant Avenue" and its reprise at the end of the first act. I was 9 years old and we listened to the record for weeks in my fourth-grade class. That same year, I listened to the Beatles' first album and rejected it like a bad liver transplant. *Flower Drum Song* said "Be happy and joyful" to me. The Beatles said "Fuck you! I'm who I am and fuck you if you don't like it!" This is the message I get from all music today.

And now I want to just walk away from all of it. I am burned to a crisp. Lost and alone.

44. An Evening with Patti LuPone and Mandy Patinkin

A year later and I'm on a plane flying from Kansas City, Missouri, to my hometown of Atlanta, Georgia. I had completed a ten week/eight show-a-week Broadway run of a concert called *An Evening with Patti LuPone and Mandy Patinkin*, and we are on tour with three weeks off before traveling again. I plan to sleep in Atlanta on my 94-year-old mother's couch for a week. Then it is back to New York City for two weeks where I hope to reconnect with friends and perhaps finally have a life.

Ever since I went into show business at age 17, I've always believed that the *show* was top priority and all my energy and thoughts had to be preserved in order to do the best possible job (hangover or no hangover). To me, this meant putting my life perpetually on hold. Granted, I drank and partied a great deal of the time, but I still kept a laser-sharp focus on showing up for the *show* at all costs. Working at night for over 40 years has, for my money, forbidden me from having a real life. Others have done it, had it all. I couldn't. Even though I had lost my stage fright years ago (in 2005), there still existed an anxiety that began when I open my eyes on the morning of a "show day," and the clock all too quickly counted down the hours before I had to walk on a stage or into a pit and be *perfect*, whether my body and my brain were feeling it or not. Being a follower now of 12-step programs, I have come to believe that every day is "progress, not perfection." (Which helps. But only a little.)

Progress, not perfection. Well, progress does not, nor has it ever applied to show business! Perfection is expected *at all times*. My last actual *run* of a show was the *Pacific Overtures* revival in 2005. In 2012, I was no longer doing the standard Broadway theatre schedule of eight shows a week, and I certainly didn't miss it, but the *Patti/Mandy Show* was an exception. Somehow my yearly financial *nut* was being met, and I had become a freer human being. That ten-week engagement at the Ethel Barrymore Theatre with Patti and Mandy, as lucrative and sometimes enjoyable as it was, certainly was a reminder of the eight show a week grind. "Sleep, eat, sleep, AA meeting, rush to the theatre, warm Patti up, sleep, half hour, PERFORM TO PERFECTION! YESSIR!" Then "home, eat, sleep." Day after day. A year had passed since I made the decision to forego any more Broadway musicals. I would just play concerts until my retirement (in which I was a total believer). No more playing auditions for Broadway musicals, no more production meetings for Broadway musicals, no more writing a Broadway musical composer's score for him (or her or them), no more rooms full of Broadway musical actors who don't know my name, no more need to be perfect from the first millisecond of rehearsal, while everyone else is allowed room for "growing pains," no more suffering in silence, no more saving people's asses—the list of *no mores* goes on. Most often, the very last thing on my mind in all of this was "making music." That tour with Mandy and Patti had been a revelation in regard to being allowed to play the piano in front of an audience, without that exhausting stage fright, and to actually *make music*. In Kansas City, I had a bright, delicate-to-the-touch Yamaha grand piano that responded to my needs beautifully. I was actually so comfortable, I was able to daydream during the show. I could play and express myself while thinking, "How lucky am I now... and how lucky I have been." I was playing "Some Enchanted Evening" for Mandy Patinkin to sing. I had first heard the song 53 years before and I've never tired of it. How did I get there? To be playing a program of songs on a nightly basis, that go directly to the heart of my 5-year-old self and my 58-year-old self. Luck, I guess. People asked, aren't you tired of playing the same old songs? No, these are "my songs" I have collected in my heart since I was aware I was alive. And now I was fortunate enough to be playing them with "feeling" while accompanying two legendary performers. I was only just beginning to feel free.

Our repertoire for those concerts consisted only of Broadway show tunes ranging from the years 1928 to 1995. No pop songs, no rock songs, no country songs, no rap, no jazz tunes, no heavy metal, no bluegrass, no fusion, no blues, no rhythm 'n' blues. Nothing but sophisticated, intelligent, and enduring American theatre music, unfortunately and officially a dead art form. I didn't get tired because I never felt compelled to "riff", or showoff, or compete, or *American Idol*-ize, or top the next guy, but to express myself with what I am feeling at the moment in conjunction with supporting and providing service to Mandy Patinkin and Patti LuPone. Mandy and Patti are very much purists and have great respect for the composers and lyricists who came before us. Few people today have a clue. When I hear someone spout a list of scores from a decades old baseball season, who was at bat, who won this or that (yaddayaddayadda), I remember that there is nothing wrong with my cherishing a hundred years of music that has, for the most part, been hung out to dry, dismissed, and forgotten. I have every right to this cherishment and I feel no shame and yet lots of shame, because I feel so alone with it.

With this isolation also comes bitterness and resentment. Every time I see another revival of *Guys and Dolls* looming, or worse, *Grease*, I think about 1997 when London was treated to a rare "full out" production of a true masterpiece of the American musical theatre art, Kurt Weill, Ira Gershwin, and Moss Hart's *Lady in the Dark*. London got *Lady in the Dark*. What did we Yanks get? Revivals of *Godspell* and *Hair* and my least favorite golden era musical, *Guys and Dolls*. There is so much more in our grand glorious musical theatre history. So, I take great pride in my tiny contribution to the preservation of this vast collection of theatre music by supporting singers who appreciate and love this music as I do.

So what exactly is it that I have been doing all these years since accepting my first paycheck as a working musician?

The concert that played the Ethel Barrymore on Broadway for ten weeks with Patti, Mandy, John Beal on bass and me on piano, had been gestating since 2000. We played to 80% capacity, but I felt a lack of support from the theatre community. Patti kept asking, "Where are my *gays*?" and I said they were home taking care of their twins. She laughed, but it's true. Different times. And the cell phones in the audience and the talking and the coughing and the sneezing and the eating and the texting and the late-coming and the sleeping and the videoing and the depositing of their *Playbills* on the stage and putting their feet up!... It's a different world. Patti devised a "spit take" early in the show where she literally spit water on the front row to wake them up or interrupt the texting or to get them to take their fucking feet off the stage! I wholeheartedly endorsed it.

The response to our show was at least consistent, the laughs and applause were where they were hoped for. And we did our job with pride. I felt so lucky to be playing the opening scene from *South Pacific*, one of my favorite Broadway comedy songs, "April in Fairbanks" (remember when Broadway was funny and fun?), "Everything's Coming Up Roses" from my all-time favorite show, *Gypsy*, with la LuPone belting the shit out of it, several songs from my second favorite show, *Follies*, and another favorite, "If I Loved You," with my piano arrangement based on the orchestration from the ballet in the film version of *Carousel*. Another song on the list, "I Want a Man," is an old song I have just begun to know. As a teenager I thumbed through my "bible," *The World of Musical Comedy* by Stanley Green, and came across a startling picture of singer Libby Holman in 1928, standing in a doorway in an incredible satin gown, holding a cigarette. The caption read "Libby Holman sings 'I Want a Man' from the Youmans/Hammerstein musical play, *Rainbow*." It took 40 years for me to finally arrange and play that song. It was worth the wait.

The Patti/Mandy show began in 2000 when Mandy received an offer to perform at the opening of a new performing arts center in Richardson, Texas, outside of Dallas. He was told that Patti LuPone would be sharing the bill, and would he like to do a concert with her. He said yes. Patti LuPone received an offer, as well, and was told that Mandy would be sharing the bill, so she said yes. This would be a reunion of the two original stars of the Broadway show *Evita* 21 years later. Of course, they discovered that they both had been hoodwinked, but what the heck. Mandy, never one to take the easy road, felt that instead of a Mandy solo act, followed by a Patti solo act, followed by a gratuitous chorus of, say, "Getting to Know You," perhaps a whole show especially arranged for the two of them was in order. Mandy brainstormed, and I went to work gathering songs and imagining ideas. Right away he insisted on starting the concert with the opening scene from *South Pacific* and ending the concert with the "Bench Scene" from *Carousel*. Everything in between was up for grabs. Patti was up for it. Starting with those two pieces it was very quickly decided to fill out the *Carousel* sequence by adding "What's the Use of Wond'rin'" for Patti, Julie Jordan's speech over Billy Bigelow's dead body, the Graduation speech for Mandy, and what else would you end an over-the-top Patti and Mandy show with but... "You'll Never Walk Alone!"

To facilitate matters, I suggested that Patti would be comfortable with her favorite pianist, the late Dick Gallagher, so we had two grand pianos for the performance. Arrangements would have to be figured out.

The most interesting part of any show is how to start. At first we were contemplating "Lights up! Patti and Mandy! Dialogue from *South Pacific*." But... both parties felt a musical duet opening was the ticket. Lifting from Mandy's *Celebrating Sondheim* show, we thought the "Another Hundred People"/"When" pairing of songs might make for a nice prelude before the *South Pacific* sequence. The first song, "Another Hundred People" was originally intended (by us) to be much slower, with a sparser accompaniment from the original Sondheim (this did not last), followed by the original duet version of Sondheim's "When" from the truly frightening and gorgeous made-for-television horror musical, *Evening Primrose*. This and our *South Pacific*/"Getting Married Today" sequence all fell into place in Mandy's head and was set early on.

From there we wanted a big, beautiful Patti solo. I knew she had done the only faithful, "real" version (using the original orchestrations and arrangements) of *Pal Joey* since 1940, the Encores! concert version, and one of Patti's signature songs had become "Bewitched, Bothered and Bewildered." Good choice. Mandy always loved *Guys and Dolls*, so as a follower, I thought "My Time of Day" would be nice. Mandy also liked "Baby, It's Cold Outside." Fun! These songs were setting up a playful cat-and-mouse routine between the two stars. Asking Patti what other songs (new or old) she might like to sing, her suggestion of "A Quiet Thing" seemed up next. But not before Mandy had a big solo, "Everybody Says Don't."

At the end of "Everybody Says Don't," we considered having Patti put her hand over his mouth before his last "...afraid," shushing him, and then she, gently soothing him with "A Quiet Thing." (We finally let him finish the song, but I still like the original idea, which was Patti's.)

What to follow that? Mandy suggested perhaps segueing to our arrangement of Sondheim's "It Takes Two," which starts romantically before picking up steam. Mandy then wanted his "character" to again shy away from Patti's, so I suggested "I Won't Dance," followed by some *dancin'* courtesy of Ann Reinking! Mandy also was dying to throw in the *King and I*'s "Shall We Dance" polka, just for fun. After this he would flee the stage, leaving Patti's character alone again in frustration.

"April in Paris" was a nice rueful song for Patti here, mainly because I wanted them to do the "send-up" version, "April in Fairbanks" (already a Mandy solo concert staple). This would become our big "I love you" reconciliation duet. Out of Mandy's head popped the idea of Reinking choreographing some sort of goofy ice-skating ballet... on rolling secretary chairs, ending in a comic crash in the wings.

What to follow that? Well... give 'em something they really expect to hear—*Evita*! We now had a chunk of *South Pacific*, a medley of solos and duets, a chunk of *Evita*, and a chunk of *Carousel* for Act Two with the *Evita* a logical first act ender.

On to Act Two. Of course, we had to do some more Sondheim, somewhere. A chunk of it, for sure, but first, how about something funny for Patti? Since we were pairing "April in Paris" with "April in Fairbanks," perhaps another juxtaposition. Sondheim's "The Boy From..." with music by Mary Rodgers (which Patti didn't know) seemed a fun thought. But how to open Act Two with this? I played "The Girl from Ipanema" for Mandy (since it was the inspiration for Sondheim's parody "The Boy From...") and he sang it seriously and longingly (and beautifully) before we slipped into the comedy of Patti's song. This was going swimmingly. But Mandy wanted to mix it up even more. He thought that he should *become* the "Boy from..." In other words, the "super gay" character that Patti was singing about. This would require him to exit and re-enter as a flamboyantly mincing character and perhaps sing a bit of yet another song. My suggestion was "On This Night of a Thousand Stars," complete with a "Cathtilian Lithp!" Patti would then finish big with the final half of "The Boy From..."

Okay! Let's give it a go. Now, I loathe and abhor political correctness, but I must say, in my humble opinion, Mandy's gay act was disastrously offensive, even to me! But we gave it a go.

Patti believed we should do more contemporary *non-theatre* songs (yikes, ohmigod, not that!) and brought in a Linda Ronstadt song called "Adios." She worked on it with Dick Gallagher and we tried to find a place for it after "The

Boy From..." We started a new sequence with "Adios" and then Mandy thought up something very special for Patti to do. He would sing "Somewhere That's Green" from *Little Shop of Horrors* while Patti mimed a housewife solemnly puttering around the house. He sang it, she did it, and it was set. Bullseye! In our Sondheim show, Mandy and I had done a variation of "In Buddy's Eyes" which I had found in a box of music brought up from Sondheim's basement (with his permission, of course). The song was called "In Someone's Eyes" and was in pencil. There was a second melody that fit on top of the chorus, obviously for a male singer. In Mandy's solo show, we sang "In Someone's Eyes" from the chorus, then I played the tune over again while he sang the alternate melody ending with the lyrics "Who remembers, who remembers, who remembers?"

I had never heard this piece of Sondheim esoterica before (or since). It seems to have been our discovery, a real "find." Now that we had Patti, we could do the entire "In Buddy's Eyes" song, verse, chorus, and duet extension. To continue this Sondheim sequence was my favorite ballad, "Losing My Mind," but sung by Mandy. Then it seemed logical to slide right into the dialogue, "Are you working on something new...?" which led into *Sunday in the Park with George*'s "Move On." Another sequence finished!

To keep up with the "sequence" idea, Mandy wanted to pay a quick tribute to *Fiddler on the Roof*, starting with a bit of "Sunrise Sunset," followed by the duet "Do You Love Me?" As this song ended, Mandy sneaked in the first line of the *Carousel* scene, "Have you had your dinner yet...?" And off we went into the *Carousel* sequence, ending the show. Our only encore was "Ya Got Trouble (in River City)" which they both knew, but Mandy took the lead while Patti acted as a Groucho-like assistant, cheering the audience on to participate. It was one performance only in Richardson, Texas, but it went extremely well.

In 2007, we decided to resurrect the show and play the Prince Music Theatre in Philadelphia (which would ignite a three-year tour, ending in Australia and New Zealand). The first thing to think about was the sad fact that the wonderful composer, arranger, pianist, and human being, Dick Gallagher, had passed away. Since he was irreplaceable, I suggested a solo piano job with help from a bass player. Putting the show back together with more time available, prompted us to come up with new ideas. We were happy with Act One, but Mandy was dissatisfied with "My Time of Day," and wanted a stronger number. I thought of the Jerome Kern-Oscar Hammerstein song, "I Have the Room Above Her" from our *Oscar and Steve* CD. Problem solved. Act Two was a different matter. Patti and I approached Mandy with the notion that the "gay" act was not going to fly. We let go of all the "Ipanema/The Boy From..." medley. Too bad, because the first half was beautiful and funny. That left the opening of Act Two up in the air.

The whole second act was rather somber, so I thought we needed two solo showstoppers of the "upbeat" kind. I also had just done *70, Girls, 70* at Encores! and had loved the score. So I pictured Patti and Mandy as Carol Burnett and Harvey Korman playing "old folks" on their TV show... that's it! The song "Old Folks" from *70, Girls, 70*! The last lyric of the song is "If you want to see old folks, you're in the wrong hall tonight!" (Ah, good ol' musical comedy!) Then in my head I pictured Patti standing up and blasting out, "Anybody who stays home is dead! If I die it won't be from sittin', it'll be from fightin' to GET UP AND GET OUT!" and launching into her *Gypsy* song, "Some People!" After that, a no brainer—"Buddy's Blues" from *Follies* for Mandy! Patti approved, and the Act Two opening was solved!

Mandy was having cold feet about our Sondheim choices. ("Adios" bit the dust even before the Richardson, Texas show.) I suggested he and I play through Sondheim's *Merrily We Roll Along* and see what we could find. I had wanted him to try the complete version of "The Hills of Tomorrow" in earlier shows. What if... Patti and Mandy "graduate," a little "Pomp and Circumstance," and an edited *a capella* version of "The Hills of Tomorrow?" I thought Patti would love the song "Like It Was;" which is preceded by a refrain of "Old Friends." But what to do between "The Hills of Tomorrow" and "Old Friends?" A quick glance at the title song, "Merrily We Roll Along," with the lyrics leading into... "1975" (the year Mandy and Patti were just emerging in New York) was the trick. Then came the icing... how about the showstopper "Franklin Shepard, Inc." for Mandy? We worked and worked and worked and got it down and started to try it out in our solo shows. (We tried "Not a Day Goes By" for Patti after "Franklin Shepard, Inc." but she conceded that it was a little too much *Merrily We Roll Along*.)

Rescuing the best from the old Act Two sequence, Alan Menken's "Somewhere That's Green" with Patti's mime, coupled with "In Buddy's Eyes" was solid. Mandy let go of "Losing My Mind" and felt that "Move On" was too closely associated with *Sunday in the Park with George*. When he sang the end of "In Buddy's Eyes" (the "Who remembers..."), he naturally slipped into the *Carousel* dialogue. So out went *Fiddler on the Roof*, as well! Yes!! (I hate that show anyway!) Editing with big scissors here!

We needed something more interesting for the encores. I went on a silly fantasy head trip and said to Mandy, "Picture this: 'You'll Never Walk Alone' ends, blackout, bows, the two of you leave the stage, then Mandy, you come back on again looking curiously in the wings. Where's Patti? I'm playing trilly, angelic music, we hear Patti doing a light vocal 'cool down' offstage. Mandy, you start singing 'I hear singing and there's no one there...' and from offstage we hear Patti vocalizing more operatically, with big whooping sounds. Mandy, you continue with 'I smell blossoms and the trees are bare...' and we hear a toilet flush! As if Patti's microphone is accidentally left on."

Mandy and I laughed for five minutes over this. Patti laughed too, but only the Irving Berlin song, "You're Just in Love," remained. Lastly, I thought a longer version of Mandy's concert staple, "Coffee in a Cardboard Cup," with the original Broadway arrangement's "doo-wahs," "wah-wahs," and the insertion of "Nobody Knows the Trouble I've Seen" might be good. The vocal harmony that Mandy improvised on top of Patti singing the melody fell into place, and frankly they sound absolutely terrific on this song. It was always tricky matching their voices in the few places where we included harmony. Sometimes Mandy would sing above Patti's melody, but other times it seemed necessary to give Patti a harmony. My favorite moment in all of this was Patti repeatedly announcing, "I DON'T DO HARMONY!" Oh, yes you do, Patti, yes you do!

Mandy's friend and teacher Gerald Freedman (co-director of the original *West Side Story*) stopped by one day and Mandy asked if he and I could run through the show for him. (I sang Patti's part.) He said sure, and we "stumbled" through the new order. Freedman had one sticking point—Patti's first song, "Bewitched." He felt that what followed didn't match the tone the song set, "seductive and sexy." He left, and we thought about it. Something more innocent, less knowing. I was already playing "I'm Old-Fashioned" from our *Experiment* album as a quiet prelude to the show, so why not Jerome Kern and Johnny Mercer's "I'm Old-Fashioned" as a running theme through the show? Problem solved. So off to Philadelphia we went. And off on tour.

I found myself having to change all of Patti's keys to make it comfortable to do several times a week, but the first two big topics of discussion were "Some People" and the *Evita* songs. Patti wanted something more high-powered than "Some People"—"Everything's Coming Up Roses?" "If you want to see old folks, you're in the wrong hall tonight!" (bass note tremolo) "I had a dream..." Problem solved. *Evita* was not so easy. To make a long story short, Mandy bowed out, letting go of "Oh What a Circus" and Patti did "Don't Cry for Me Argentina" alone at the end of the act. This stayed for a while. Patti was never happy with the "I Won't Dance (Dance)," the song yes, the dance no, but it stayed for a long, long time. This is how we toured for almost two years.

Towards the end of the second year, Patti decided to let go of her *Evita* number, too, and we ended the first act with the "ice skating ballet."

On the very last performance of our second year of touring, we were *Evita*-less. At intermission, Mandy called Patti and me to his dressing room. He suggested (and we bought it) that after the song "Like It Was" in Act Two, where the lyrics end with "How did we get here from there? Which was the moment and where?" we would cut "Franklin Shepard, Inc." Instead, Mandy would say something short and sweet about their early days working together, and we would do "Oh What a Circus" and "Don't Cry for Me Argentina" (in that order). The big difference being that Patti would casually stay on stage rooting him on, then Mandy would escort her center stage for her number, looking on affectionately and then leading the applause. WOW! What a difference, and it only took us nine years from Richardson, Texas to figure that out!

Year three of touring was bump-free except for a growing dissatisfaction with the "I Won't Dance (Dance)." "It's just not good enough," Patti would protest.

When the Broadway run actually started to become a reality, we put our heads together one more time. Patti believed we absolutely had to cut the dance and the *King and I* polka. And she was hoping for a better song to replace "April in Paris." She asked me to look at "I Want a Man." I actually had heard Patti sing it years earlier at a benefit. On that night, she asked the audience if they knew what show the song came from. I knew it, of course. "Rainbow," I shouted. "Oh... (gasp)... Yooooouuu!" she called back. I thought this song was a great idea, a real old-fashioned torch song. She sent me the music and I played it for Mandy (after all, he was our director), and I started arranging. We had a wonderful weekend at Patti's South Carolina beach house, and the three of us collaborated on the song. I'm very proud of the arrangement and it made for a lovely gift to open on Broadway with.

This is a detailed example of what my job has been since putting together high school revues, the many Atlanta cabaret revues, all of Mandy's various concerts, participating in all of the PBS tributes and evenings and birthday celebrations, and exactly *how* I've contributed beyond the mere putting notes on the page and playing them. Not just playing the piano, but arranging, suggesting and coming up with ideas, sometimes actually "directing," editing and researching material. This, plus rehearsing and performing many traditional Broadway musicals from 1979 to 2005, all of which required much more from me than just playing the piano. The Sondheim shows were always easier and required less of me because of the professionalism of the "master." He certainly didn't need my help. And what a pleasure!

Sondheim came to see the Patti/Mandy show at the Ethel Barrymore Theatre and came backstage. I dropped by Mandy's dressing room to say hello. Steve said "You look good. You've kept the weight off." (I hadn't.) I said, "Thank you." "Who did the arrangements?" he asked. Jokingly, I said, "Well, YOU did some of them!" He waved that aside and said, "No, really, who did the arranging, the bass arranging and all?" I said that I was "guilty," hoping for a compliment. "Well... you look good," he said. And that... was it.

Those were the last words Stephen Sondheim would say to me... ever. Well, that's not completely true. At my publisher's suggestion, I sent an email to Steve letting him know about my proposed book:

His response was:

All fine with me. I'm flattered. Nice to hear from you.
Glad you're okay and, apparently, thriving. Steve.

45. In the Remainder Bin

My last performance in public and for a paycheck was on May 31, 2015. For three years, Mandy Patinkin, award-winning performance artist Taylor Mack, Susan Stroman, and I, fashioned a show called *The Last Two People on Earth: An Apocalyptic Vaudeville* out of existing music from various genres. There was nary a note of Sondheim music in sight. We performed the show at the Henry Street Settlement in New York for two weeks, in Richardson, Texas for one week, and at ART in Cambridge, Massachusetts for three weeks. This was my swansong. My last two years of performing amounted to barely enough to live on, as Mandy was busy with his series *Homeland*. I worked five weeks my last year, living on my savings. I gave Mandy a year's notice and May 31 was the final day. The show itself might continue without me, but it has not resurfaced. It also contained music by people I have absolutely no respect for, therefore I myself could not continue. But that is another story entirely.

The final performance of a Broadway musical attended by me as an audience member was in 2014. I sat through a revival of one of my top five favorite musicals, *On the Town*. The good news was the material was honored, the orchestra was large, and very little was edited or rewritten. The bad news was the ticket price (a major reason I refuse to ever see another Broadway show again) and that there was not one performer on stage who deserved to be there. The physical production was okay. I'm grateful my last show was *On the Town*, but I will not subject myself to the mediocre, over-priced fare of the modern theatre ever again, one day at a time. I've seen the best of the best, the last of the best, and much of the tail-end of what once was a lavish, varied, sometimes artistic, unique American form of show business, now corrupted by the British drabness, Walt Disney multi-gazillion dollar children's theatre, and corporate lack of know-how. Everything is diminished to what I always called "dinner theatre" level. But you don't get dinner, just a diminished show.

Slides have replaced sets, gym clothes have replaced costumes, synthesizers and drums have replaced orchestras, the casts are whittled down to a handful of people, and American Idol losers have replaced stars.

The last Sondheim show I enjoyed was an expanded version of his 1974 Yale show, *The Frogs*. In 2004, Susan Stroman directed a big Broadway version with many new (terrific) songs. Sondheim was back in gear. The spark was there after the 14 wasted years on *Wise Guys/Bounce/Road Show*. *The Frogs* is barely mentioned today. It's a lost show. But it was a great reminder of the old Steve. Not well cast or directed, but a real musical *comedy* with a joyously entertaining original cast recording. All other recent Sondheim productions have been revivals in heavily edited, once again "diminished," gimmicked-up versions more suitable to community theatre than Broadway. I unfortunately witnessed a few of these and refuse to even acknowledge they existed. Yet the "herd" (see *Anyone Can Whistle*) keeps going and spending gobs of money to see a bare skeleton of what these shows used to be. My memories will remain intact. No more corruption for this once true believer in the great Broadway Musical.

Because of our sparse schedule during my last two years performing with Mandy, I began practicing the piano for two hours a day just to keep up my "chops." And I discovered the magic of music again...

Six years into retirement, my aim has been to play the piano for three hours a day, for no audience, no money, and no more corruption. Not a note will I play that I don't consider quality music. I have 12 large notebooks of film scores, Broadway music, piano solos, jazz charts, and my own transcriptions from recordings and films where no music exists. I am back to my early years of musical discovery, practice, and last of all, pleasure. I am 10 years old again.

46. The Little Things We Do Together

Even though I spent 25 years off and on working for and with Stephen Sondheim, our private moments together were few. Here are a few more glimpses into our exchanges, stories he told me, opinions shared, and gifts tossed my way.

Starting with *Gypsy*, when I asked what he thought of the 1962 film version (one of my favorite movies of all time), he described the moment Natalie Wood as Louise watches the three strippers do their thing in "You Gotta Get a Gimmick" as a magical moment. I, of course, couldn't agree more. He also admired Cynthia Gibb in the Bette Midler TV version. In a phone exchange, I mentioned to him that *Gypsy* would always be my favorite musical. His response? "Watch it!" —meaning that I should be careful what I'm saying. I laughed and bravely countered with, "But my second favorite show is *Follies* and, besides, what greater set of lyrics are there than the ones you wrote for *Gypsy*?"

At the Sondheim birthday concert at Ravinia, as we waited at the hotel for our car to take us to the rehearsal, Steve told me a "top secret" story about the original tryout for *Forum*. The cast included a favorite actress of mine who played Philia. She was always a daffy dame, showing up at the orchestra rehearsals barefoot, and locking herself out of the theatre on the roof of the marquee and having to call for help. She was let go because, though vocally able, she often got slightly off-pitch and would remain so throughout an entire song. She went on to a very successful career in films! He asked me "not to tell anyone," but by now I believe it is common knowledge!

The song "There's Always a Woman" was cut from *Anyone Can Whistle*, but after hearing Marin Mazzie and Donna McKechnie perform it in our *Beautiful Girls* concert, Steve told me that the accompaniment was a "great vamp" even if the song didn't work in the original show.

Steve has always been very generous in giving out copies of private audio recordings or videos of his work. I was lucky to receive from him two video tapes. One was the TV version of *Evening Primrose*, a truly sad and frightening mini-horror musical which I love dearly, and the other was a copy of the Japanese broadcast of the final performance of *Pacific Overtures*, since I had missed the original production. The final gift he bestowed on me was the sheet music for the entire film score of the movie *Stavisky*, which I have been wanting to play on the piano for 40 years! I'm very grateful.

When the first London production of *Follies* opened in 1987, I asked him how he felt about the drastic revisions. Steve usually answered questions such as this with one or two very specific items. In this case, he enthusiastically singled out Linda Baron, who sang "Who's That Woman." On the recording she is definitely a standout, but in a terrific excerpt from the Olivier Awards that year, the entire number is preserved and she is, indeed, hilarious.

Steve attended the concert version of *A Little Night Music* I played with the Philadelphia Orchestra, and afterwards I mentioned that Irene Worth (who had played Madame Armfeldt) was giving me a lift back to the city. He took me aside and said that I absolutely had to ask her about a production of a classic play (the name escapes me) where she gave a very scandalous, erotic performance. I wasn't sure I wanted to do this. He had a twinkle in his eye, leading me to think he might be setting me up for a joke. Sure enough, I mentioned the show to Ms Worth and if looks could kill, I would certainly be dead. She did *not* expound on the subject and we had quite a cold ride back to New York City! Oh, that Steve!

During the early rehearsals of *Passion*, Steve chose to give me a "piano lesson" in front of the company, the only time he ever did this! He was trying to teach me about "rubato," something this ill-trained piano thumper knew nothing about. I wasn't completely mortified, but I've since tried to be aware of it in my playing. Fortunately, he never publicly lectured me again. In fact, he rarely commented on my playing, unlike other composers who hovered and were ready to pounce if you made one tiny little mistake.

We had a great conversation about the peerless film score composer Bernard Herrmann composed for the 1940s thriller, *Hangover Square*, specifically about the "Concerto Macabre." The first chords heard in this concert piece are scattered throughout the *Passion* score. He said it was totally intentional. My theme song for Stephen Sondheim whenever he entered the room became the opening chords from the *Hangover Square* concerto (or just to mix it up, the opening chords from *Psycho*).

The evening we spent together making the *Wise Guys* demo recording (a long session), he asked me to stay and have dinner. It was the only time we ever sat across a table from each other. We discussed the musicals *Allegro* and *Pal Joey*, and he told his famous stories about the first out-of-town preview of *Allegro* where he was an assistant, including the dreadful technical problems and the backstage fire. I expounded on *Pal Joey* (I would end up doing a flop revival a few years later) and why there were so many jinxed productions over the years. Everyone always claims to LOVE the score of *Pal Joey*, but they are judging it from the movie version. I admitted that I really didn't like the stage score, as fun as it is, because most of Joey's songs were dumb little ditties that set up pages and pages and pages of dance music. Unlike the movie where Joey was a singer only and other Rodgers and Hart songs were thrown in, I waxed on with my belief that Joey's persona and charm were all told through his feet and his dancing, and without all the dancing there was not much in the original material. Steve thought that this was horseshit and told me so! I wanted to crawl and hide under the table. Ha!

Although he wasn't present, I had a very interesting afternoon in his townhouse going through boxes of cut songs, early versions of songs, and fragments looking for choice bits for Mandy Patinkin's *Celebrating Sondheim* recording. I found the early version of "In Buddy's Eyes," a funny birthday song for the baby emperor in *Pacific Overtures*, several complete alternate versions of well-known *Night Music* songs, and a piece of manuscript with a recognizable tune but unknown lyrics. The tune was the dance music for the Vincent and Vanessa dance number in the original *Follies*. This number is invariably cut in most productions, but here was evidence that it was originally going to be a song!

Before the Roundabout's production of *Sondheim on Sondheim*, I had the opportunity to record 30 or 40 songs, including a lot of rare material not previously published, for a comprehensive work demo for director James Lapine. This is not a perfect recording by any means, but the singers were terrific and it's my favorite "private" recording. Steve was not present, but I hope he enjoyed hearing the recording as much as I enjoyed making it.

I *just recently* discovered that in the original published vocal scores of *Sunday in the Park with George*, *Into the Woods*, *Assassins*, and *Passion*, the four Sondheim shows on which I worked, I am thanked in the title page credits for my help! Who knew! On those four shows, Sondheim never played the entire scores on the first day of rehearsals, but one song he demonstrated to everyone's delight was "Hello, Little Girl" from *Into the Woods*... as only *he* could do it.

Here is the list of Sondheim-related material from his shows in my current workbooks:

Silly People (*A Little Night Music*)
Suite of Waltzes (*A Little Night Music*)
Cookie Chase Ballet (*Anyone Can Whistle*)
Everybody Says Don't Ballet (*Anyone Can Whistle*)
Overture and Exit Music (*Anyone Can Whistle*)
Tick Tock (*Company*)
Overture and Title Song (*Do I Hear a Waltz?*) Music by Richard Rodgers
Who's That Woman (*Follies*)
Entire film score (*Stavisky*)

Organ Prelude (*Sweeney Todd*)
Overture, Prologue, Dance at the Gym, End Titles (*West Side Story* film
    version) Music by Leonard Bernstein
There are so many more titles to include, but these are the *crème de la crème*.
Gypsy will always be my favorite show, *Follies* my second favorite and the
greatest live performance I have ever witnessed. *Anyone Can Whistle* is my
ultimate guilty pleasure and playing for *Sunday in the Park with George* on
Broadway was the best time of my life.

47. Epilogue

MARY PAUL PARSONS FORD

I was born into a large family from Kentucky and Tennessee. My father
had three brothers and a sister, all centered around Owensboro, Kentucky.
They were mostly farm people. This part of my life feels long, long ago, as
most of these relatives have passed including my dad. My mother had one
brother now deceased. Her mother was a musician (where I got it from) and
her father worked for the railroad and was a tennis pro, all from Nashville.
My dad and his first wife had my half-brother and half-sister. His first wife
died of cancer and he remarried (the "two-week one," as she was described).
He then met my mother, who was just out of a bad marriage herself and they
married. She became the stepmother to my dad's preteen kids before 'birthing'
my older brother and then eight years later—that "wonderful surprise"—me!

My parents, Ken and Mary Paul Ford, were the two nicest, funniest, most
lovable and loving people on the planet. Since my two half-siblings were much
older than I was and already married when I was born, for the next seven years
there appeared a new niece or nephew from one or both couples, pushing me
further from the "spotlight." And I knew it. Seven nieces and nephews!!! I felt
like Maria von Trapp with her seven "fucking Trapp kids" (quote from Googie
Gomez). By the time I was 10, I had an insatiable lust for attention, and that
has remained to this day.

I was born eight years after my youngest sibling and 22 years after my
oldest. My mother had me when she was 36 and started to go through
menopause at an early age. She always apologized for her behavior during this
time. She used to yell at my brother and me a lot. I can visualize her in bed with
a terrible expression on her face, screaming at us to stop fighting or making noise
or whatever we were doing. This is all I remember of her "bad behavior."

What I remember most about her is a woman fascinated with everything, eager to get up, get out and experience life. Her interests included world events, art, movies, music, theatre, history and travel. Whatever happened with that menopause thing, she got over it and was up and running. If she went to a movie, she took me. She had ultra-sophisticated tastes and loved to preview for me what we would be seeing—its background and history—without judgment or prejudice, just excitement. She was fascinated with everything. She started me on Disney movies. Not the computerized dreck, but the shimmering original hand-painted animation. We hit *Peter Pan, Fantasia, Song of the South, Dumbo, Bambi, Cinderella, Sleeping Beauty,* and *Snow White and the Seven Dwarfs*—all of which she considered great works of art, not children's fodder. She was right. I learned about colors and fabrics and details of historical eras from those films and, for a few years, feverishly tried to match with crayons the images I remembered. In kindergarten, I could draw a reasonable facsimile of Prince Charming kissing Sleeping Beauty. I guess it was graphic enough because Miss Frost (yes, Frost), my kindergarten teacher, ripped it from under my pencil, tore it to shreds and coldly snapped, "Draw something else!" I was really into Prince Charming rescuing *me,* and that *South Pacific* film made me yearn for an exotic escape.

"Mary Paul" took me on long drives through the beautiful Buckhead area in north Atlanta, with its Italian Palazzo-style mansions from the 1920s. We made regular rounds to two streets, Habersham Road and West Paces Ferry Road. These streets are still as beautiful today as in the 1950s and are full of the beautifully maintained designs of Philip Shutze and Neel Reid.

This was what filled my consciousness in the first five years of my life, big Disney Technicolor animated fantasies with music, and beautiful stately mansions with rolling lawns, gardens and fountains. She loved them... and I was hooked. Nothing against my dad. He did everything he could to be a good father, but he had his interests, too. Nine holes of golf before the sun set, seven days a week and all day every weekend.

Mom loved to sit me down and share an old movie that she liked on TV. Many times, these were dark, odd, or scary movies. And she loved to narrate and comment to make certain I knew exactly what was going on. She made sure I knew who Dracula was, who the Mummy was, who the Wolfman was, who Frankenstein was, and, especially, who Lon Chaney, Sr. (her favorite) was, with his famous unmasking scene from *Phantom of the Opera*, which had affected her greatly when she first saw it. We also enjoyed high-quality thrillers such as *The Bad Seed, The Spiral Staircase* and *The Secret Garden*. I saw all of these at home on late-night television (or when I learned how to "act" sick and stay home from school). It was always, "We're going to stay up and watch this great old movie. I can't wait for you to see it."

We went to the lovely little Capri Cinema in Buckhead, our suburb of Atlanta, constantly, and saw *Breakfast at Tiffany's*, which I cried over, and the coming attraction for *Midnight Lace* with Doris Day, which looked like a neat little thriller. When mother and I rushed there on opening day, they wouldn't let me in! I had to be 13 years old! I saw it finally on TV and can act out Doris Day's breakdown scene and play the fabulous main title theme on the piano — one of the greatest credit sequences ever filmed! One film that would become a part of my soul for the rest of my life, even though for some reason we missed it the first time around, is William Castle's *House on Haunted Hill*. The trailer was my first real haunted house visual image—it's three minutes of heaven. Just that alone was enough to daydream on all day long and take my mind off those idiots I was forced to play with on the playground. I could now mentally check out quite effectively anywhere, anytime.

Mom and I took art lessons for a couple of years until I was 10 from an old childhood friend of hers in an adjacent neighborhood. The teacher's maiden name was Adair Loving. "Isn't that a wuuunderful name!" mother would say. Her married name was Adair Williams. We would work with other mothers and children in her basement or, weather permitting, in her garden. It was all pastel work, which I was neither here nor there about. They were drawing fruit. I was drawing haunted houses. I lost interest in art once the music and piano lessons started.

We took our first trip to New York City when I was 8. All of this was masterminded by my mother. Without her, we would have gone absolutely nowhere. We saw the Radio City Music Hall Rockettes show and the movie, a boring Disney thing called *Bon Voyage*. (I was more discerning at 8 and had moved on to more sophisticated things than family comedies.) We stayed at the Holiday Inn on West 57th Street and because my brother was a natural blond, my mother decided we should all go blond. She poured peroxide on our heads in the Holiday Inn sink. Out we went—my dad, my naturally-blond brother, and two flaming "orange heads" heading for the Empire State Building. When the elevator doors opened on the 86th floor and we were to step out into the observation area, I froze and clung to the wall with my eyes shut the whole time. My brother, of course, spat off the balcony and poof! we were back in the elevator. On the way down we stopped on a floor and two Japanese men got on with cameras, jabbering away. My mother started to giggle. Again the elevator door opened and this very tall bald man and his wife got on. The man had such big bug eyes and big ears and such a big shit-eating grin on his face, that my mother burst out laughing hysterically, looking back and forth between the Japanese tourists and the goofy-looking man. My brother said, "What's wrong with you?" Laughing uncontrollably, she tried to say, "Your dad... your dad told me something hysterically funny." My dad stepped away from her and said, "I didn't tell you anything!" We just looked at her. On the street, she explained what she was laughing at. My mother had a low tolerance for funny-looking people and got the "uncontrollable giggles."

Another world my mother took me to, was the strange, scabrous, southern gothic world of Tennessee Williams plays, novellas, and films. She started with the lush 1958 film version of *Cat on a Hot Tin Roof*. What registered with me at the age of 5 were those wonderful "no-neck monsters" and how they terrorized the household, especially Elizabeth Taylor, and their den mother, the perfectly cast Madeline Sherwood (*Do I Hear a Waltz?*) with her flat, dreadful southern drawl.

But the real stunner came a little later when my mother searched the *TV Guide* to find something "juicy" for us to watch. This was probably 1964 and I was 11 and knew a few things by now. "AHA!" (She found something!) "Tennessee Williams! Great! *Suddenly Last Summer*! With Monty Clift and Liz Taylor and Katharine Hepburn. Oh, this is a good one! Do you know what this is about, Paul? I'll tell you what it's about, it's about this man who is called a homosexshul and homosexshuls love other men and this homosexshul makes a bunch of boys mad at him and they jump on him and cut him up and eat him. I think Van Johnson is a homosexshul, but he's a nice man. Let's watch this tonight!" And we did, and I was horrified and terrified and titillated and fascinated and I luuuved it!

Where was Little League? Where was swiping from the five-and-dime? Where was playing cowboys and Indians? Where was summer camp or Boy Scouts? I'll tell you where—RIGHT WHERE THEY BELONGED. And far away from me! I was loving everything my mother showed me. So onward to *Streetcar Named Desire*, *Night of the Iguana*, *The Roman Spring of Mrs. Stone*, Gertrude Lawrence in *The Glass Menagerie* (I liked her!), *Baby Doll*, *Sweet Bird of Youth*... and on and on. All of this "mellerdrammer" injected into my blood for eternity. Throw in a little bit of Lillian Hellman's *The Children's Hour* and I was ready to face the world as a healthy, carefully groomed, well-informed, well-adjusted, self-respecting, upstanding, confident, and thoroughly self-destructive "homosexshul."

Around the same time of the mind-blowing of *Suddenly Last Summer*, mom dropped me off—yes, dropped me off—at the Cherokee movie theatre to see Disney's *Emil and the Detectives* starring 12-year-old Roger Mobley. I made her take me back the next day and told her not to pick me up until I had sat through three showings. I was in love with child-star Roger Mobley. I just recently Facebook friended him, and he wrote me a nice note. But the real wallop over the head was just around the corner. We went to see a movie at the Lenox Square Cinema that really didn't look interesting to me, but mother said, "Oh this is the third one they've made. The first two were wuuuunderful, especially the one about Russia!" We were sitting there, and I was sort of intrigued by the credits with this woman singing REALLY LOUDLY! and the movie started. There was a lot of intrigue around a Miami hotel swimming pool, and the next scene shifted to one of the hotel rooms. The camera panned over trays of room service food, champagne, and then quickly up two pairs of legs intertwined, landing on Sean Connery and Shirley Eaton sucking each other's faces off. The phone rang and Connery rolled over and displayed his hairy chest and pits. Both my mother and I gasped. Loudly! She said, "Oh maybe we shouldn't have come to this..."

This was it. I was officially homosexshul! That minute, that second. I was now obsessed for years with hairy chests and would feel faint when one of my brother's friends would come over and the little curls would peep out over their collars. What did I think I wanted to do with them? Rub my face in them? Pull them with my teeth? Lick them into swirly little designs? Yes! And that hasn't changed. I... was... obsessed with Sean Connery. I was obsessed with "naked." I'm obsessed with "naked" now. I was 11. Thanks, ma! No! Really! Thanks! Forget little boys—I wanted me a "ma-yun," as Olive Oyl would say. Oh, and the movie was *Goldfinger*.

Where was touch football? Where were BB guns? Where was the ole swimmin' hole? Fuck that shit! *Vertigo* was on tonight and mother said "WAIT...till you see this one! Let me tell you about Alfred Hitchcock!" Instead of telling you what my impressions of that movie were that night, let me just tell you the 45-year aftermath of that night. I've worked in San Francisco many times over the years and cannot resist visiting one of the locations from that wondrous film, whether it's the Mission Dolores graveyard, Ernie's Restaurant, Scotty's apartment on Lombard Street, Madeline's pink stucco apartment building, Judy's hotel, the sight of the McKittrick Hotel, the Palace of the Fine Arts, or Fort Point under the Golden Gate Bridge. I have multiple recordings of the score. I have seen it in movie theatres multiple times, including the last restoration at the Ziegfeld with my "virgin" friend Tony Geralis who reacted to it so satisfyingly. He jumped out of his seat on the first low chord of Bernard Herrmann's opening credit music and was just as wasted and devastated by the ending as I was in the early '60s. Thanks to the Internet, I have found, deep in some California photo archives, a dozen color photos of the demolished Victorian house on the corner of Eddy and Gough used as the creepy McKittrick Hotel. I am severely, compulsively obsessed. And thanks to Mandy Patinkin, I got to spend Christmas Eve of 1996 in the Hollywood Hills home of Jim Katz, talking to him about his painstaking restoration of *My Fair Lady* and... *Vertigo*! *Vertigo* is in the top two (yes, top two) of my favorite films. Why at age 11 was I so into Jimmy Stewart's obsession with Kim Novak? Why did I love this strange, tragic, sad storytelling? What was I relating to? Where was fishin' and caddyin' for daddy? What was the matter with me?

Mom and I were downtown at Davison's department store getting ready to drive home, and she began to tell me "Well... there *is* another Alfred Hitchcock movie that hasn't come on TV yet and it's somethin' else!" "What? What is it?" "Well... I saw it at the movie theatre. This woman steals some money and runs away and checks into a motel. There's this big, scary old house on the hill behind the motel where the owner lives. She checks in and chats with the owner and then she goes to her room. She gets in the shower and ALL OF A SUDDEN THIS CRAZY OLD LADY RIPS THE SHOWER CURTAIN OPEN AND STABS HER TO DEATH WITH A GREAT BIG BUTCHER KNIFE!!!"

"Oh... when is that gonna be on?" I asked.

"Oh, some time. We'll have to keep our eye out for it. You just gotta see it." (Oh, I saw it... and saw it... and saw it... and studied it...and studied it...) When it was finally going to be broadcast, mom and I were so excited. "*Psycho* is gonna be on! *Psycho* is gonna be on! Isn't it wuuuuunderful!?" Alas, some politician's daughter in Alabama was murdered that week and the station decided maybe now wasn't the best time and pulled it. I was livid.

Ah well, there was a consolation prize—and what a consolation prize! A double-feature at the Capri. A return showing of Hitchcock's *The Birds* and... *Marnie*? (whatever that was). So, Mom took me and my boy scout, softball playin', jock, sneaker-wearin', spittin', cussin' best pal and we sat down for a long afternoon. *The Birds* was everything it should have been and, yes, I've been to the schoolhouse location in Bodega Bay. But this *Marnie* thing... it looks boring... oh!... Sean Connery is in it?... Oooooh! Sean Connery in a bathrobe?... Oooooh! Sean Connery rips Tippi Hedren's bathrobe off!... Ooooooooooh! Sean Connery is laying Tippi Hedren down on the bed!...

Ooooooooooooooooooh! Sean Connery is slobbering his tongue all over Tippi Hedren!!!... Okay!... *Marnie*! Still one of my favorites. Great, great, GREAT music. One of the strangest movies. Nothing else like it. Bizarre, over-the-top performances, and I think Tippi Hedren was great, but her career went nowhere. I liked her much better than that one-note, non-wonder Grace Kelly.

So, the fourth grade "Oriental" pageant came and went, and I was hooked on *Flower Drum Song* and musicals and buying records and taking piano lessons and my mom took me regularly to my two favorite stores, Symmes sheet music store and Jim Salle's record store in Buckhead, right next door to the Capri movie theatre. Mr. Salle and I became fast friends and he gave me special rates for my manic enthusiasm. I was off and running.

In 1964, my mother took my dad and me to see Walt Disney's *Mary Poppins*, and the following year *The Sound of Music*. In 1968, the three of us took a trip to New York and saw *Mame* and the Lincoln Center revival of *West Side Story*. Back home, Mom and I sat up one night to watch the woman my mother referred to as "the one who yells." It was a spectacular color TV special with a new singer. The next day we were at Jim Salle's record store buying the LP. My mother was capable of being proven different (never wrong) and we started our love affair with Barbra Streisand and *Color Me Barbra*. We were at the first showing of *Funny Girl* in 1968 at the newly-redecorated Capri Theatre, with its sleek new black-and-white paint job and show curtain of sparkling prisms. But as incredible as *Funny Girl* was to this 15-year-old, Julie Andrews's biopic about Gertrude Lawrence, simply titled *Star!*, proved to be the fatal dose of the next batch of "Kool-Aid" I swallowed. I had never heard the music in that film and became obsessed with Kurt Weill, Cole Porter, George Gershwin, and Noel Coward. With all of these incredibly sleek, beautiful examples of Broadway and film musicals being lavished on me, those four arrogant gee-tar plunkin', toy drum poundin' nitwits, the Bee-ulls, never stood a chance with me. How could four guys with bowl-cut haircuts compete with Streisand in *Funny Girl* showing up for a romantic dinner in a Vincent Minnelli-red dining room wearing a gown of lavender and purple flowers and sparklies, or Julie Andrews in *Star!* entering a 1920s art nouveau supper club in a floor length maroon satin evening coat with giant blooms on the shoulders, only to reveal a sequined black and orange gown underneath. The '60s had a lot to answer for with its ugly hippie takeover and toneless Bob Dylan atrocities. For me the die was cast, and it was indelible. I wanted to see and hear beautiful things and would accept no grunge. I still cringe at dirty, ripped blue jeans on women. And women with tattoos! Just shoot me!

Mother was a history nut, and as with the movies, loved to give me all the gory details about man's inhumanity to man from the Inquisition to the Civil War, up through the Nazis' treatment of the Jews in World War II and the Japanese pushing bamboo shoots under prisoners' fingernails. She didn't pull any punches in describing the evils that men can do and how we must "live and let live" and stick together as a "human" race. My mother was a Methodist, but her opinion of the Bible? Good stories with good lessons, but none of that nonsense ever happened. Her spirituality boiled down to the Golden Rule.

She died in October of 2013 and I played "Stardust" on the piano for her. She was my light, a light that is now much dimmer. She gave me everything.

Special thanks to:

My Mother and Father
Christine Andreas
Julie Andrews
The Andrews Sisters
Robert Armin
Lucie Arnaz
Boris Aronson & Florence Klotz
Fred Astaire
The City of Atlanta
Burt Bacharach
Lauren Bacall
Michael Bennett
George Balanchine
L. Frank Baum
Busby Berkeley
Leonard Bernstein
Jay Blackton
Carol Burnett
Mario Cantone
The Capri Theatre
Patrick Cassidy
Michael Cerveris
Stockard Channing
Martin Charnin
Petula Clark
Cy Coleman
Dorothy Collins
Betty Comden & Adolph Green
Barbara Cook
Patrick Dennis
Billy G. Densmore
Gregg Edelman
Scott Ellis
Peter Filichia
Bob Fosse
Philip Fradkin

Scott Frankel
Victor Garber
Judy Garland
David Garrison
Mitzi Gaynor
Paul Gemignani
George Gershwin
Joanna Gleason
Robert Goulet
Dolores Gray
Nathan Gunn
Lillian Hellman
Jerry Herman
Dana Ivey
Shirley Jones
Madeline Kahn
Lisa Kirk
David Krane
Robert LaFosse
Margaret Landon
Nathan Lane
Angela Lansbury
James Lapine
Arthur Laurents
Gertrude Lawrence
Gypsy Rose Lee
Staci Levine
Marcia Lewis
William Ivey Long
Robert Lopez
Dorothy Loudon
Patti LuPone
Taylor Mack
Gordon MacRae
Mary Martin
Donna McKechnie

Johnny Mercer & Gene DePaul
Ethel Merman
Ann Miller & Mickey Rooney
John Monaco
Debra Monk
James Morgan
Donna Murphy
Northside High School of the
    Performing Arts
Mandy Patinkin
Bernadette Peters
Donald Pippin
Hal Prince
Linda Purl
John Reardon
Ann Reinking
Lee Remick
Jerome Robbins
Richard Rodgers &
    Oscar Hammerstein II
Herbert Ross
Rosalind Russell
Jim Salle's Record Store
John Schneider
Jeanette Loflin Lang Shackleford

Thomas Z. Shepard
Stephen Sondheim
Michael Starobin
Charlie Stramiello
Elaine Stritch
Susan Stroman
Charles Strouse and Lee Adams
Jule Styne
Symmes Music Company
Theatre Under the Stars
David Thompson
Tommy Tune
Jonathan Tunick
Twiggy
Gwen Verdon
Maria Von Trapp
Janet Hayes Walker
Nancy Walker
Tony Walton
John Weidman
Kurt Weill and Ira Gershwin
Natalie Wood
Maury Yeston
York Theatre Company

and the 100-year history of the Broadway musical.

Also Recommended

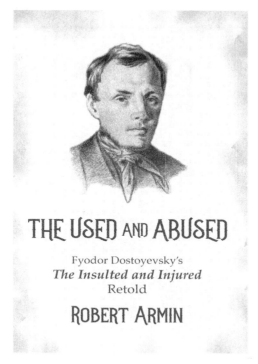

In Nineteenth Century Russia, a young novelist looks back on a dramatic year in his life in *The Used and Abused*, a fresh retelling of Fyodor Dostoyevsky's 1861 novel, *The Insulted and Injured*, which drew heavily upon the writings of Charles Dickens for its inspiration. An orphan girl in distress, an unrequited love affair, a scheming and manipulative aristocrat, and an angry father who casts his daughter out of his life, are just a few of the ingredients that make this lesser-known Russian novel a delight to read. More than simply a new translation, novelist Robert Armin has expanded upon and enhanced the characters and dialogue of Dostoyevsky's surprisingly witty and poignant early novel to give modem readers a full and engaging reading experience from beginning to end. (An unabridged audiobook read by actor Philip Hoffman is also available.)

Trade Paperback ISBN-13: 978-0-9960169-7-1 Paperback $19.95
Also Available in **Kindle eBook** and **Audiobook**

MORECLACKE PUBLISHING

Also Recommended

SPOTLESS
Memories of a New York Childhood

Sherman Yellen

In *Spotless*, two time Emmy Award-winning writer Sherman Yellen lovingly recreates the world of his impoverished forebears before World War I; his troubled, prosperous, mendacious father; his beautiful, willful fashion-model mother, and especially his own New York childhood in the 1930s and 40s. Yellen witnessed both great events and the everyday life of a city boy in an embattled family, viewed through the eyes of an observant little boy waiting impatiently for his body to catch up to his all-seeing consciousness. Yellen summons up this lost world of a New York Jewish-American family with candor and love.

Trade Paperback ISBN-13: 978-0996016926 Paperback $19.95
Also Available in **Kindle eBook** and **Audiobook**

MORECLACKE PUBLISHING

Also Recommended

MORECLACKE PUBLISHING

Also Recommended

Three new plays by two-time Emmy Award® winning (*The Adams Chronicles* and *An Early Frost*) and Tony Award® nominated (*The Rothschilds*) writer Sherman Yellen, with a Foreward by Pulitzer Prize winning lyricist Sheldon Harnick. Featuring both comic and dramatic female roles from 40 to 80 and male roles from 20 to 60.

Trade Paperback ISBN-13: 978-0996016902 Paperback $16.95

MORECLACKE PUBLISHING

Also Recommended

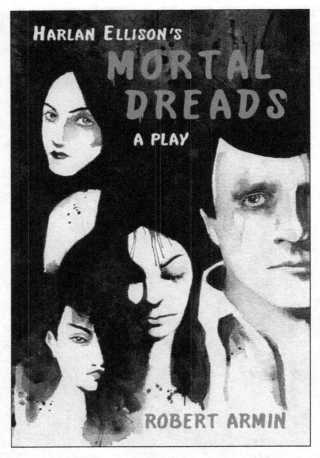

Welcome to *Harlan Ellison's MORTAL DREADS*, an anthology play by Robert Armin, featuring dramatic adaptations of six short stories (including *Shatterday* and *Paladin of the Lost Hour*) by acclaimed fantasist Harlan Ellison. Six extraordinary tales that tear through the fabric of space and time and reveal the gaping hole which opens onto Some Other Place. If you find these dark dreams troubling, maybe it's because they're your dreams!

Trade Paperback ISBN-13: 978-1478310884 Paperback $11.95

MORECLACKE **PUBLISHING**

Also Recommended

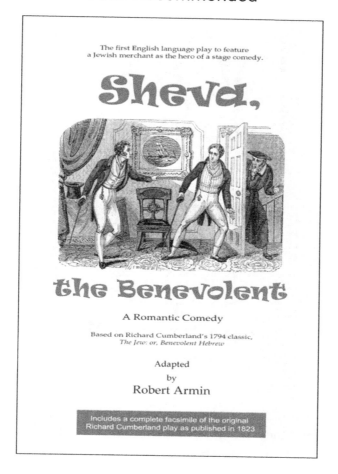

Sheva, the Benevolent is a faithful adaptation of Richard Cumberland's 1794 comedy, *The Jew: or, Benevolent Hebrew*, featuring Sheva, the first Jewish moneylender to be portrayed as the hero of a stage comedy. Includes a Preface by playwright Robert Armin, an introduction by 18th Century theater scholar Jean Marsden, and a high quality facsimile of the original play as published in 1823.

Trade Paperback ISBN-13: 978-0615663166 Paperback **$11.95**
Also Available in **Kindle eBook** (without facsimile)

MORECLACKE PUBLISHING

Also Recommended

From the pen of one of America's finest painters and illustrators, James Montgomery Flagg, best remembered today for his iconic recruiting poster of Uncle Sam ("I Want YOU for U.S. Army"), this delightful collection of comic poems and cartoons takes a tongue-in-cheek look at the many justifications people come up with to wed. First published in 1906, this Moreclacke Rediscovery Series volume features newly reset and more legible text, and crisp, detailed illustrations reproduced directly from a rare first edition copy of the original.

Trade Paperback ISBN-13: 978-0996016933 Paperback $6.95

MORECLACKE **PUBLISHING**

Coming Soon

Mabel Wynne and Other Tales of the Romantic Age is a selection of short romantic fiction and poems by Nineteenth Century American writer, editor, journalist and international travel correspondent, Nathaniel Parker Willis (1806-1867), newly edited and introduced by novelist Robert Armin. Beautifully illustrated with rare etchings and decorative drop cap lettering all reproduced from vintage books of the period. Also included are five essays by Willis on the American Woman, as originally published in the *New York Mirror* and *The Home Journal*.

Trade Paperback ISBN-13: 978-1499187229 Paperback $9.95
Also Available in **Kindle eBook** and **Audiobook**

MORECLACKE PUBLISHING

Made in the USA
Las Vegas, NV
15 May 2024

89959742R00148